Row 1
1. Jim Powell
2. Mack Bennett
3. Zack Campbell
4. Elbert Campbell
5.
6. Jack Fitzgerald
7. _____ Sloan
8. Walter Dunlap
9. Frank Woods

Row 2
10. _____ Sloan
11. Fannie Price
12. Sula Dunlap
13. Lillian Campbell
14. Rebecca Bennett
15. Emma Sloan
16.
17. Alice Woods
18. Lillie Breeden
19. Teelie Chaphan
20. Sudie Coleman

Row 3
21. Anna Bell Harper
22. Sally Beth Harper
23.
24. Minnie Sloan
25. Gay Campbell
26. Kittie Dunlap
27. Mattie Fitzgerald
28. Marian Campbell
29. Chessie Dunlap
30. Dee Mayfield
31. Anna Bennett
32. Anna Dunlap
33. Miss Effie Gillespie
     (*music teacher*)
34. Miss Pearl Mayfield

Row 4
35. Will Fitzgerald
36. Harry Bennett
37. Charlie Bennett
38. Clayton Powell
39. Nell Coleman
40. Cary Hardison
41. Hessie Senter (*teacher*)
42. Walter Hess (*teacher*)
43. Bob Fitzgerald
44. Dan O'Conner
45. Ira Fitzgerald
46. Bob Powell

Row 5
47. Tom Dunlap
48. Ross Campbell
49. Clarance Fitzgerald
50. Charlie Dunlap
51. Hamlet Powell
52. Ralph Powell
53. Eugene Mayfield
54. Sam Bennett
55. Curry Bennett
56. Zack Coleman
57. Dorsie Bledsoe
58. John Woods
59. Hugh Bennett

High Hill School
About 1890
North of Humboldt, Tennessee

THE DAVEISS-HESS FAMILY

FROM POWHATAN TO THE PRESENT

OUR INDIAN ANCESTRY

◆DAVIS◆HESS◆BURKS◆ CAMPBELL◆DUNLAP

AND ASSOCIATED LINES

COMPILED BY
LILLIAN JOHNSON GARDINER &
MARIAN KNOWLES ALBRIGHT

TURNER PUBLISHING COMPANY

TURNER PUBLISHING COMPANY
Publishers of America's History

Copyright © 2002 Lillian Johnson Gardiner
& Marian Knowles Albright
Publishing Rights: Turner Publishing Company
All rights reserved.

Turner Publishing Company Staff
Editor: Tammy Ervin
Designer: M. Frene Walker

Library of Congress Control No. 2002116697

ISBN: 978-1-63036-899-2

Additional copies may be purchased from
Turner Publishing Company. Limited Edition.

Table of Contents

About the Authors

Lillian Johnson Gardiner

Lillian became interested in genealogy through her husband, Laurence Gardiner. After marriage in 1944, they traveled all over the United States in the course of Laurence's business, spending many hours pouring over documents in court houses, libraries and private collections. For over 40 years they compiled reams of information on their family lines, and also helped friends with research.

Both were active in many genealogical organizations. Lillian and Laurence helped organize the Memphis Genealogical Society. Lillian originated "Ansearchin' News," the magazine of the Tennessee Genealogical Society, which is still in publication today. She has co-authored several genealogical research books and has written articles for various research magazines. Her list of accomplishments is quite lengthy.

Now in her 92nd year, after helping so many people with their family trees, she is finally finding time to publish part of her own.

Marian Knowles Albright

Marian's interest in family research was due, in part, to the many tales of our earlier generations told when any two or more family members were gathered. Some of her most pleasant memories were of visits with the Gardiners, Lillian's sisters, Marian's mother and lots of cousins, all reminiscing.

Given this background it was only natural that Marian should join "Lil" in compiling this family history. They have been in the process of organizing material, which Lil already had, gathering more, and writing the actual manuscript for at least four years.

Marian is a wife, mother, grandmother and retired nurse who started writing the book and learning to use the Family Tree Maker computer program all the same day. As she said, "It was not smart. I needed lots of help. This has been a real challenge on one hand, but a great joy on the other. We have met so many cousins in the course of this writing and have enjoyed learning of their immediate families and how they connect with ours. I'm truly thankful that Lil talked me into this project."

(Authors are pictured on page 82.)

Introduction

Without the extensive research done by Lillian Gardiner and her late husband, Laurence, this book could never have been started much less completed to this point.

During their years of travel throughout the United States (for Laurence's work) they spent many hours in cemeteries, courthouses and going through private papers shared by relatives.

Laurence had always been interested in genealogy and in order to occupy herself while he read "dusty old tomes," Lil started helping him, and caught the "bug" herself. The two put together exhaustive research on both families and we are so fortunate to be recipients of their tireless efforts.

Lil also spent time looking up ancestors in England, Scotland and Germany. On one of her "ansearching" trips her luggage was stolen and although she didn't care about her clothes, she gladly paid the hefty ransom to have her genealogy notes returned.

Another relative to whom we owe much is the late Colonel M.J. Kelley of Owensboro, Kentucky and Pittstown, New Jersey. Colonel Kelley had done a great deal of research on our mutual Davis line in Virginia, Kentucky and Tennessee and was very generous with his information.

To you family members who have graciously shared your knowledge of our history and ancestry we extend our sincere appreciation. You have greatly added to the interest of this book.

If any errors are noted, please forgive us and send corrections to Marian.

Descendants of Chief Powhatan

Generation No. 1

1. Chief¹ Powhatan was born abt. 1550 in Virginia, and died April 1618 in Richmond, Virginia. He married **Queen Winganuska**.

Notes for Chief Powhatan:

Powhatan! The very name evokes a sense of mystery and awe, coming from the dim mists of our nation's infancy. As young people, we thought of this man only in the background of stories of early settlers, of Pocahontas, of John Smith—but there was so much more to this great leader who was the only "Emperor" this country ever had—and was our family's earliest native ancestor.

Unfortunately, much of the information regarding the earlier inhabitants of this land is no longer emphasized and the authors feel it important to Powhatan and his descendents to tell his story the best we can from the sketchy facts available. Several accounts of Powhatan's life and family come from various early settlers and historians, similar but not exactly alike. Somewhere therein lies the truth.

Powhatan inherited, from his mother, the title of Chief of eight small Indian tribes [1], and by shrewd cunning and superior talents established his authority over at least thirty tribes, eventually commanding over eight thousand warriors. His confederacy controlled Chesapeake Bay and its tributary rivers. This corresponds to Eastern Virginia, most of Maryland and Delaware. [2] Each tribe had its own village with houses built of bark over wooden frames. Along with other crops they planted corn, and tobacco; they hunted and fished. Every few years as the land became depleted, they would abandon the old village and build a few miles away.

Early historian, William Strachey, said Powhatan was referred to as Emperor—or King [English translation of the Indian term]. He took the name Powhatan in his youth from the area then called by that name, where he was born about 1550 near Balcony Falls on the James River in Virginia. The inhabitants, especially his neighboring chiefs, still called him Powhatan as an adult. His own people called him Ottaniack, and sometimes Mamanatowick [which means "great King"] [3]; but his proper name with which he was saluted personally was Wahunsenacawh.

Powhatan was not a young man when the English came. "I am very old, and I have seen many generations of my people," he told Captain John Smith. Yet he was still an impressive figure. Captain Smith described him thus: a tall well proportioned man with a "sour" look. Later, on better acquaintance, Smith changed "sour" to "grave, majestic countenance," and said he looked almost like a god. "His head somewhat gray, his beard so thin it seemed not at all, his age near sixty, of a very able and hardy body." [4] Early historians such as Strachey, Beverly, Kegley and others all commented that Powhatan, Opechancanough, Pocahontas and Cleopatra looked "different" from the other Indians. It was said that his father had come from the West Indies, run out by the Spanish. [5] This West Indian heritage could account for the different appearance. Our cousin, the late M.J. Kelley, managed to obtain copies of paintings of Powhatan, Opechancanough; the wedding of Pocahontas to John Rolfe and the "Coronation" of Powhatan, showing his wife, Queen Winganuska, daughter Pocahontas, daughter Cleopatra, etc. and commented that it was plain to see the difference, especially in the women. The Indians, themselves, said that Opechancanough was not "one of them," but had come a long way from the south. [6]

Captain Christopher Newport served the London directors of the New Colony as Admiral in charge of transporting men and women to Virginia, and bringing back valuable cargo, and was commander of the Original fleet in 1607. On the occasion of the Second Supply, he sailed from England with, not only fresh commodities for the New Colony, but with presents from King James to Powhatan. He carried orders to crown Powhatan "Emperor" of all the Indians [thereby making him subject to England and thus validating ownership of the land for England]. [7]

Captain John Smith delivered the invitation to Powhatan to come be crowned, and receive presents. Powhatan's reply: "If your King have sent me presents, I also am a King and this is my land. Eight daies will I stay to receave. Your Father [Capt. Newport] is to come to me, not I to him, nor yet to your fort neither will I bite at such baite." There were many instances of trickery and crafty deceit between Powhatan and the newcomers, especially Capt. Smith. It seemed that he and Powhatan were in a constant battle of the wills, so it is no wonder that Powhatan was reluctant to place himself in the power of the Whites at their fort. Powhatan won this round; the English delivered to him at his Capital, Werowocomoco, a tin pitcher and basin, a bed complete with mattress, and a copper crown, which he refused to kneel to receive. "He neither knowing the majestie nor meaning of a crowne, nor bending of the knee, indured so many perswasions, examples and instructions, as tired them all. At last, by leaning hard on his [Powhatan's] stooped shoulders, Captain Newport put the crowne on his head. Then remembering himself to congratulate their kindnesse, Powhatan gave Captain Newport his mantle and his old shoes." [8]

Powhatan maintained a treasure house watched over by guards at each of the four corners: one dressed to represent a giant, one dressed as a bear, one as a wolf and the fourth like a leopard. [You can't help wondering where they had ever seen a leopard in Virginia.] The building was sixty feet long and one can indulge in flights of fancy as to what "treasures" were kept there. Perhaps ceremonial pipes, his wonderful war bonnet of eagles feathers, bows, arrows, shell and bone jewelry—and one writer suggests it probably housed some of the very finest scalps. [9]

Wahunsenacawh, "the mighty Werowance" who ruled over Attanoughkomouck of Virginia was a great man in his time and place. He might sometimes appear naive in the eyes of the English, but his was not the simplicity of a child or of low mentality. Remember the English colonists almost starved to death in a land of plenty, something Powhatan would never have done. He was merely a man confronted with the unfamiliar, the-to him-inexplicable. Indeed, he was a man of the highest intelligence. He had to be. The historian, Meade, said of him, "the noblest and most powerful of the native chiefs of North America who by his superior wisdom and aptitude had established his authority over all the tribes from the James River to the Potomac, from Kicquotan at Hampton, to the Falls at James River, with the exception of the Chickahominy," who were ruled by priests and their assistants called "cawcawwassoughes" - [this from Capt. Smith]. Captain Newport wrote, "Keeping peace among his Algonquins, fighting the Sioux and the Iroquois, reading the minds -- and forestalling the actions of any among his chiefs [capable of treachery to further their own secret ambitions] was no job for a weakling or a fool." His territory was vast and required someone very shrewd and intelligent to maintain it as a cohesive confederacy. "I too am a King!" he said, and indeed his "royal" blood figures prominently in the genealogy of many of this nation's outstanding citizens, both male and female. The "Emperor" Powhatan died in 1618 near Richmond, Virginia.

[1] Colonel M.J. Kelley, family historian

Thomas Nimo, "Virginia Notes," p. 162, entry of April 1614

[2] William Strachey, "Historical Jamestown Narratives, Eyewitness Accounts of the Virginia Colony, the First Decade"

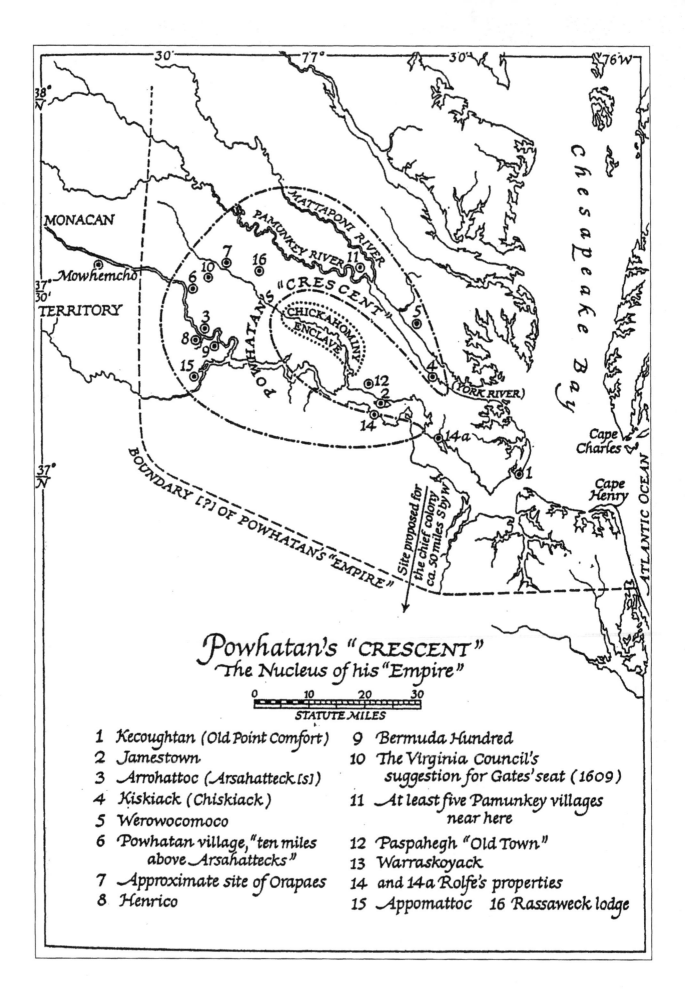

Powhatan's "CRESCENT"
The Nucleus of his "Empire"

0   10   20   30
STATUTE MILES

1 Kecoughtan (Old Point Comfort)
2 Jamestown
3 Arrohattoc (Arsahatteck [s])
4 Kiskiack (Chiskiack)
5 Werowocomoco
6 Powhatan village, "ten miles above Arsahattecks"
7 Approximate site of Orapaes
8 Henrico
9 Bermuda Hundred
10 The Virginia Council's suggestion for Gates' seat (1609)
11 At least five Pamunkey villages near here
12 Paspahegh "Old Town"
13 Warraskoyack
14 and 14a Rolfe's properties
15 Appomattoc
16 Rassaweck lodge

[3] Hugh Watson, "Climbing Your Family Tree," article - Historical Rarities, Sunday, July 27, 1958

"Captain John Smith's America," edited by John Lankford Harper and Row

[4] Ibid

[5] Thomas Nimo, "Virginia Notes," p. 162, entry of 1614

[6] William Stith, "History of Virginia," republished 1865, p. 133-135

[7] Captain John Smith's America

[8] "Narratives of Early Virginia, 1606—1625," edited by L.G. Tyler, Pres. of Wm. and Mary College, p. 154, 155

[9] Rose Chambers Goode McCullough, "Yesterday When It Is Past," p. 327

Although no relation of ours, mention should be made of Captain John Smith who played such a vital role in the establishment of Virginia and the Colonies.

The epitaph over his grave in St Sepulchre's Church, London, begins:
"Here lies one conquer'd that hath conquer'd Kings,
Subdu'd large Territories, and done things
Which to the world impossible would seeme,
But the truth is held in more esteeme." [1]

Smith was one of the first Englishmen to see the new land as more than a get-rich-quick scheme; to fall in love with it and to see its potential. Beyond the forests and Indian fields he envisioned growing towns and cities; thriving trade and commerce. To him America was the setting for a new civilization.

He busied himself collecting information on the several Indian tribes, their languages, customs and fighting strength. He noted topography of the land and coastline, later publishing his observations and a map, which remained useful throughout the Colonial period. [2] It was he who gave New England its name.

Through his map [the best made to that date] and his writings of the region he indirectly assisted both Pilgrims and Puritans. [3] Much of our information of that time comes from these writings.

Captain Smith was personally acquainted with Chief Powhatan, Pocahontas [as you know], John Rolfe, Cleopatra, Opechancanough and all our Indian predecessors of that era. He lived among them and knew their ways. He, Powhatan and Opechancanough were constantly trying to outwit each other. It took cunning on both sides to stay afloat in this on-going battle of wills.

Left: Through trade and by stealth Powhatan acquired several hundred swords. Found by a Civil War relic collector in Henrico County, where Powhatan and his immediate followers lived during the latter years of his life, this broadsword may have been one such Indian trophy. Surviving length 19 $^1/_4$ inches. **Right***: John Smith trading with Indians in New England; detail from a de Bry engraving. The proffered knife is drawn with sufficient accuracy to show what appears to be the mark of the London Cutter's Company on its blade.*

[1] True Travels and Works of Captain John Smith, edited by Arber, Edinburg 1910, Vol. 11, p. 971

[2] Ibid. p. 384

Children of Chief Powhatan and Queen Winganuska are:

+   2   i.   Pocahontas[2], born abt. 1595; died in Gravesend, England.
+   3   ii. Cleopatra, born in Virginia; died abt. 1644.

Left: *Captain John Smith.* **Right**: *This print of Pocahontas in European attire, worn while she visited England with her husband John Rolfe in 1616, is but one of many unusual contemporary drawings in the publication, "Virginia 1584-1607," edited by Alan Smith.*

Generation No. 2

2. Pocahontas[2] (Chief[1] Powhatan) was born abt. 1595, and died in Gravesend, England. She married **John Rolfe** 1614 in Jamestown, Virginia. He was born 1585 in England, and died in Virginia.

Notes for Pocahontas:

Powhatan had 10 wives, 20 sons and 11 daughters. His last and most favorite wife, Queen Winganuska, a noted beauty, was the mother of the famous Pocahontas and OUR ancestress, Cleopatra. Let us emphasize that we are NOT direct descendents of Pocahontas, but of her younger sister, Cleopatra. [It is believed that the Indians would never have heard of the name Cleopatra and that it was suggested by the English, perhaps even by John Rolfe as a fitting "English" name for his wife's little sister.]

We are quite happy, however, to claim Pocahontas as "Aunt" and her descendents as distinguished cousins. Let us make a few remarks regarding Pocahontas, as her son, Thomas, figures prominently in our verification of Cleopatra. We quote from an article from the Cobb County, Georgia Genealogical Society, Inc. by Geraldine Hartshorn Wheeler:

"Is There a Princess in Your Past?"

"Although the recent Disney movie portrays Pocahontas as a seductive 18 year old maiden fascinated with John Smith, the truth is that she was an 11 or 12 year old girl when she met the English Captain. It was only when she turned 18 that she became involved with a white man, marrying John Rolfe, an Englishman and a Virginia colonist, in April 1614.

After their marriage, Pocahontas and her new husband traveled to England where the Powhatan Princess was entertained by nobles and royalty. In 1615, she gave birth to a son, Thomas. Two years later, she died at Gravesend, England.

The simple fact is that if people cannot trace their ancestry to Thomas Rolfe of Virginia, they are not her descendents.

We know that Thomas Rolfe of Virginia inherited his father's Virginia holdings and that he fathered only one child himself, a daughter, Jane Rolfe.

In 1675 that daughter married Col. Robert Bolling of Cobbs Plantation, again the marriage produced only one child, this time a son - John Bolling of Cobbs Plantation.

John Bolling married Mary Kennon and their issue was one son and five daughters.

This fourth generation is what genealogists call the "gateway key" to descent from Pocahontas. If you cannot prove your descent from one of these children, you aren't related. The children were: Major John who married Elizabeth Blair, niece of James Blair, founder of William and Mary College; Jane Bolling who married Col. Richard Randolph of Curles [one of their descendents was Thomas Mann Randolph of Edge Hill, Governor of Virginia and husband of Thomas Jefferson's daughter, Martha]; Elizabeth Bolling who married Dr. William Gay; Martha Bolling who married Thomas Eldridge; and Anne Bolling who married James Murray of the ancient clan of that name.

Legitimate descendents of Pocahontas include Harry Flood Byrd - a U.S. Senator and Governor of Virginia - and his brother Richard Evelyn Byrd, discoverer of the South Pole.

Mary Ann Harrison, wife of former New York City Mayor, John Lindsey, is a descendent as is Anne Cary Randolph, who married diplomat and U.S. Senator, Governor Morris. Robert E. Lee's wife, Mary Ann Custis, also could claim Pocahontas as a forbear.

The only descendent of Pocahontas to occupy the White House was Edith Bolling Gait Wilson, the second wife of Woodrow Wilson. She descended from the marriage of John Bolling III and Mary Jefferson, sister of President Thomas Jefferson."

Ralph Hamor, early colonist [Secretary of the Colony 1613—1614, preceding John Rolfe], tells of the wedding of Pocahontas. She and John Rolfe were married in church by the Rev. Richard Buck. Powhatan had sent his old uncle, Opachisco, and two of Pocahontas' brothers to Jamestown to bear his formal consent and to be present at the wedding. Opachisco, representing her father, gave the bride away, and her two brothers stood beside her. [1]

[1] Thomas Nimo, "Virginia Notes," April 1614, p. 162

Rose C.G. McCullough, "Yesterday When It Is Past," p. 329

Notes for John Rolfe:

The Rolfe family has been in England since Saxon times. "Rolf" mentioned in Doomsday Book owning 28 caracutes of land at Horsea near Yarmouth. He was one of the many small land owners of Danish or Norwegian extraction left undisturbed by William the Conqueror.

Marguerite Quarles gives the following table of immediate ancestors of John Rolfe of Virginia:

Robert Rolfe———mentioned in the Herald's Visitation, 1534, had son

Eustace—————1516-1593—married Joanna Jenner in 1560, had son:

John————————1562-1594—married Dorothy [Dorothea] Mason-1565-1645, had son:

John—————1585——————came to Virginia, married Princess Pocahontas in 1614.
[After the death of his father, John's mother, Dorothy Mason Rolfe, married Robert Redmayne.
They had three sons: Eustace, Edward and Henry.]

Thomas Rolfe-1615—only child of Princess Pocahontas and John Rolfe. [1]

John's family lived at Heacham Hall, which had been in the Rolfe family a long time - and is still standing. It was home for the family when John introduced his bride, Pocahontas, to English society. More than likely his Mother was still living there, though his father had died and she had married Mr. Redmayne. She must certainly have known Pocahontas and little Thomas for she lived years after John and Pocahontas were gone.

John was a widower of 26 when he met the 18-year-old Pocahontas and fell in love. They were married by the Rev. Richard Buck in the presence of certain members of her family. Two of her brothers attended, as did Opechancanough, and according to a painting, her Mother and sister, Cleopatra, were also witnesses. Her Father, Chief Powhatan did not attend. [2] That same year John was appointed Secretary of the Colony to succeed Mr. Ralph Hamor. The couple's brief life together seems to have been very happy. Their home in Virginia was in Chesterfield County where Rolfe had gone with Sir Thomas Dale in 1611. He took up land there and named his place "Varina" after the best Spanish tobacco. He was very interested in tobacco culture and after much experimenting produced a product which competed successfully with tobacco from the West Indies.

After the death of Pocahontas in England, John had returned to Virginia, in 1616, but his young son, Thomas was too ill to make the journey and was left behind in the care of John's half brother Henry Redmayne. Whatever plans he had to bring Thomas to England came to an end with the death of John. The circumstances of his death are not clear, but it is believed he was killed, ironically, in the Indian massacre of 1622. One writer carefully states, he was never seen after this. The little boy whose mother was an Indian probably never saw an Indian until he came to Virginia in 1635, when he was 20.

He took over Smith's Fort, land specifically willed to him by his father [who had had the foresight to have title to the land, given him by Powhatan, confirmed under English law]. This tract was enlarged by still further gifts from his mother's people. In 1641, Thomas asked permission of Gov, Berkeley to visit his aunt - his Mother's sister, Cleopatra, and his kinsman, Opechancanough, who had given him a tract of land near Smith's Fort—in the vicinity of lands received from his Father's estate. [3]

[1] Quoted by Margaret Stewart Quarles in "Pocahontas" published by the Asso. For Preservation of Virginia Antiquities

[2] Virginia Notes by Thomas Nimo

[3] "Footnote to The Will of John Rolfe" by Jane Carson—Va. Hist. Mag., Jan. 1950—p. 62
    Maryland Historical Society Documents—Jamestown Records 1630 to 1641

Child of Pocahontas and John Rolfe is:
+   4   i.   Thomas[3] Rolfe, born 1615.

3. Cleopatra[2] (Chief[1] Powhatan) was born in Virginia, and died abt. 1644. She married **Chief Opechancanough**. He died abt. 1644 in Jamestown, Virginia.

Notes for Cleopatra:

Our line descends from this youngest daughter of Chief Powhatan. Although very little is known about her, we can verify her existence with several sources, the most important being her nephew, Thomas, son of Pocahontas and John Rolfe. Matters became so bad between Indians and Whites that a "no man's land" was established between their lines which no one could cross [except truce-bearers] under penalty of being shot. To insure strict obedience to this pact a law was passed at Jamestown imposing a "Special Permit" from the Governor's Council - and the General Court to anyone wishing to cross this line. In 1641 Thomas Rolfe requested permission to visit his aunt - his mother's sister, Cleopatra, and his kinsman, Opechancanough who had given him a tract of land near Smith's Fort, in the vicinity of the lands received from his father's estate.

The Council record reads: "December 17, 1641 Thomas Rolfe petitions the Governor to let him go see Opechancanough to whom he is allied, and Cleopatra his mother's sister."

The Record of the General Court reads: "December 17, 1641 Thomas Rolfe petitions Governor to let him go see Opechanko, to whom he is allied, and Cleopatre, his mother's sister." [1]

Cleopatra was still living in 1641 and was with Opechancanough at his capital [near what is now West Point]. Not long after Thomas Rolfe visited his Aunt Cleopatra, Opechancanough sent his warriors against the settlers in the terrible attack of 1644. The English retaliated, killing and dispersing the tribes and driving them from their towns. Cleopatra was surely part of this dispersal - she was never seen again - we have no record of her after this. [2]

From the union of Cleopatra and Opechancanough descend some of the most prominent people of Virginia and Kentucky—people who helped shape the destiny of our country through the first 150 years. Many were political leaders, some outstanding educators and physicians. Jefferson Davis, President of the Confederate States of America, and John Cabell Breckenridge, Vice President of the United States were their descendants [though Jeff Davis did his best to deny his Indian connection]. Other notables from this line were John Floyd - two times Governor of Virginia and the only Kentucky born to be so honored, his son, Gov. John Buchannan Floyd, Gov. Issac Shelby and Gov. William Cabell. Their progeny also included the Davises, Burks, Randolphs, Venables, Henrys and many others. [3]

[1] Maryland Historical Society Documents—Jamestown Records 1630-1641

Colonial Virginia by William Brodus Cridlin, Secretary of Virginia Historical Pageant Asso. 1923—p.123

Footnote to "The will of John Rolfe" by Jane Carson—Virginia Historical Magazine Jan. 1950—p. 62

[2] Irish Burks of Colonial Virginia and New River by Patricia G. Johnson—p. 12

The Conquest of Virginia, The Forest Primeval by C.W. Sams—New York Putnam and sons 1916

[3] Col. M.J. Kelley, family historian

Floyd Biographical Genealogies by N.J. Floyd—Baltimore 1912

Notes for Chief Opechancanough:

Was thought by some to have been Powhatan's brother, but reliable information suggests he was Chief of a Southwestern tribe defeated by the Spaniards, and that he led his people Northeast where he was adopted into the tribe of Powhatan.

Chief Opechancanough was a brilliant warrior who lived to a very old age and died of a gunshot wound in the back inflicted by a British soldier.

When Opechancanough called his warriors together on the banks of the Pamunkey in April 1644, his physical fires were burning low. He could no longer stand in the Council house and drive a tomahawk into a post as a signal for war. He reclined on a couch unable to hold open his eyelids, as he told of his plans to exterminate the hated Englishmen crowding upon his lands from the Atlantic Seacoast. He did not want to die until he had delivered his country from the menace of the White men who had begun coming with Captain John Smith in 1607. Powhatan, before his death had temporized with the newcomers from across the sea, and had even allowed his favorite daughter, Pocahontas, to marry one.

Succeeding Powhatan as Chieftain, after the death of Powhatan and his invalid brother, Opechancanough had been tolerant and friendly toward the newcomers [except for one violent revolt in 1622]. He had furnished them corn when they were starving, had called them brothers, had attended the marriage of Pocahontas to the white John Rolfe and had permitted them to build shelters in the forest. But in late years he was disturbed by the ever-increasing stream of people who came from across the water. As they grew in number and demanded more and more territory, he realized they would never be satisfied until they had driven the Indian from his own land.

So in 1644, his decision made, Opechancanough summoned the tribal leaders, made a desperate appeal and outlined his strategy: sweep down on the white settlements: Kill-All. Although worn by his years, his will to fight was strong.

Carried on a litter into battle, Opechancanough led his warriors against settlements between the York and Pumunkey Rivers and swept them clean. In two days time more than 300 white men, women and children were massacred. Sir William Berkeley, Governor of the little colony at that time, hastily assembled an armed force, met the Indians close to Jamestown and defeated them soundly. Unable to flee, the aged Chieftain was captured and taken to a Jamestown jail where a young guard maddened over the loss of loved ones shot the "helpless" old man. As life ebbed away he asked that his eyelids be raised that he might see his enemy. A light of hatred gleamed from his dull old eyes as he said to Gov. Berkeley, "Had it been my fortune to to take Sir William Berkeley prisoner, I would not have so meanly exposed him as a show to my people." Chief Opechancanough's eyelids closed, he stretched out on the ground and died October 5, 1644. [1]

Although he was known for his brutality, we have to remember he was fighting for a cause that was, to him, as justified as the white man and maybe even more so—the preservation of his people, his land and his culture.

He is of particular interest to this family as he was married to our ancestress, Princess Cleopatra, and was the father of Nicketti.

[1] The Wilderness Road - Chapter 1 "Discovery of the Trail" by Robert L. Kincaid Harrogate, Tn. 1955, p. 21, 22

Historical Recollections of Virginia by Henry Howe—Charleston, S.C., 1845 p. 61

The History of Virginia by Robert Beverly—London 1722—2nd Edition. p. 50, 51

Smith avoids Opechancanough's trap and instead takes the king prisoner. It is likely that Smith had some say in the rendering of this illustration for his Generall Historie. *If so, the treatment of his falchion sword and pistol may be relatively correct.*

Children of Cleopatra and Chief Opechancanough are:

+   5   i.   Nicketti[3] Powhatan.
+   6   ii.   Cornstalk Powhatan, born in Augusta County, Virginia; died November 11, 1777 in Point Pleasant, Virginia.

Notes for Cornstalk Powhatan:

The Shawnees, called the "Arabs of the New World," were a small but valiant tribe dwelling on the lower Scioto. In mental power they stood much above the average level of the "Red race," and it was not unusual for one to be able to converse in 5 or 6 languages, including English and French. They were generous, and their women were superior housekeepers. So conscious of their prowess were the men that they held in contempt the battle ability of other tribes.

During the time of which we write, the most eminent war leader among these people was Cornstalk, who according to early historians was the grandson of Powhatan, son of Cleopatra, brother of Nicketti. He was the most distinguished among a number of contemporary chiefs who ruled over the Shawnee and other northwestern tribes in the latter 18th Century—a band of native heroes who made the most generous struggle of which human nature is capable—fighting to the last for the deliverance of their country, without hope of victory or thought of renown. They have scarcely left any authentic traces on the pages of history, so we are truly indebted to the historians of that time who recorded what little information we have, describing these people and the events of the time.

Although his name once struck terror throughout Virginia and the "West," in Cornstalk, we are told, was the excellence of the whole race, and the very image of savage greatness. He was gifted with eloquence, statesmanship, heroism, beauty of person and strength of frame. In his movements he was majestic, in manner easy and winning. Of his oratory, Col. Wilson, an officer in Dunmore's Army says, "I have heard the first orators in Virginia, Patrick Henry and Richard Henry Lee, but never have I heard one whose power of delivery surpasses that of Cornstalk."

Keep in mind, the whole savage race was alarmed by the attempts of Whites to occupy Kentucky. A tribal confederacy was formed with Cornstalk at the head. Plundering and reprisals by Indian and White alike followed mutual aggravations on the frontier. This culminated in the Point Pleasant battle of 1774, which was disastrous to the Indians. The Shawnee were the backbone of this assault and Cornstalk was General-in-Chief. Even though he was not in favor of war, [he had been overruled by his tribe at council] he disagreed with the Peace Treaty previously concluded with the Indians by The Earl of Dunmore, Governor of Virginia. In his speech, proving himself an orator as well as soldier, he sketched his remarks in lively color: the once prosperous and happy condition of his people assailed by the deceit of the Whites and the dishonesty of the traders. He proposed that no one should be permitted to trade with the Indians on private account—that fair wages should be agreed upon and the traffic of commerce be committed to honest men. Finally, he requested that no "fire-water," which brought evil to the Indians, should be sent among them.

During the short peace which followed, Cornstalk from time to time returned to Ft. Randolph at Point Pleasant horses and cattle, which had been lost by the Whites [or stolen from them].

By 1777 the Shawnee were again restless. They had been worked on by the British and by White renegades. Cornstalk came, with a Delaware and one other Indian, to Ft. Randolph under what was virtually a flag of truce to warn Captain Arbuckle, the Commandant, of the feeling of his tribesmen. His mission was an effort to avert open hostilities. According to Indian standard, Cornstalk was an honorable foe, but he knew he ran a risk by putting himself in the power of the Whites. Arbuckle thought it proper to detain the Indians as hostages while matters were being discussed. One day while Cornstalk was drawing a map on the floor of the blockhouse room where he was being detained, his son, Ellinipsico, came to check on him. It so happened that while he was visiting, two men of Captain McKee's Company, a Gilmore, and a Hamilton went out hunting turkeys. Gilmore was killed by some lurking Indian and his body taken back to the Fort. Enraged comrades raised the cry, "Let's kill the Indians in the Fort." They refused to listen to the remonstrances of Arbuckle and in fact threatened his life. The mob rushed the blockhouse forcing open the door. Cornstalk, hearing the commotion and realizing what was about to happen, stood erect, facing his murderers. He fell dead, pierced by 7 or 8 balls. His son and other companions were also slain.

Patrick Henry, who was then Governor of Virginia, denounced the deed in scathing words. He regarded it as a blot on the fair name of Virginia. Years later Colonel Theodore Roosevelt called the killing of Cornstalk, "one of the darkest stains on the checkered pages of frontier history." Through the efforts of their friends, the perpetrators were never punished.

Cornstalk was remarkable for many great and good qualities. He was disposed to be a friend of the White man and an advocate of honorable peace. Indeed, he had warned his people that peace with the Whites was the only hope of survival. Yet when war was forced upon him, he fought with all the cunning, valor and savagery inherent in his race. It is unfortunate that it is this savage side most commonly recalled by historians. How sad that descendents have denied their Indian ancestry and blurred the records—even denying relationship to Pocahontas—because they refused to be linked to Cornstalk.

Cornstalk, Chief of the Shawnees in the Scioto Valley of Ohio.

History of Augusta County, Virginia by Peyton, p. 161-165

History of Rockbridge County, Virginia by Morton, p. 78-81

Historical Recollections of Virginia by Henry Howe

Journal of the House of Burgesses of Virginia, 1773-1776, p. 278, 282

Generation No. 3

4.   Thomas³ Rolfe (Pocahontas², Chief¹ Powhatan) was born 1615.

Child of Thomas Rolfe is:

    7   i. Jane⁴ Rolfe.

5.   Nicketti³ Powhatan (Cleopatra², Chief¹ Powhatan) She married **? Hughes** in Virginia.

Notes for Nicketti Powhatan:

Princess Nicketti was noted for her outstanding beauty. Her name meant "Beautiful Flower" and it was said of her that her beauty "swept the dew from the flowers." She married a noted Scotch hunter and fur-trader by the name of Hughes [first name unknown, could be Rice or Rees]. [1]

Generations later, truth regarding the ancestry of Princess Necketti was denied in Kentucky. The cause originated at the battle of Point Pleasant in 1774, when the Virginia and Kentucky Pioneers under General Andrew Lewis defeated the allied tribes - Shawnees, Cuyandottes and Delewares under the great war-chief, Cornstalk.

Cornstalk was regarded as a ferocious and vindictive tool of the Lt. Governor of Canada - and no Indian could have been more detested. Prisoners taken in that battle stated that he was a descendent of Powhatan through his youngest daughter, [this would have been Cleopatra, Pocahontas's sister - LJG/ MKA]. The Virginians and Kentuckians who had admired the gentle Pocahontas despised Cornstalk and indignantly denied any blood connection.

When the Floyds and Davises [direct descendents] living in Kentucky by this time heard the denial, they, being no longer in touch with those who knew the facts in Virginia, ignored the matter and "let it go at that."

Descendents of Charles Floyd, in whose home his mother, Abadiah Davis Floyd [great grandaughter of Nicketti] resided never doubted the accuracy of this tradition. [2]

The authors bring this out merely to acknowledge the disagreement and to affirm our belief in the authenticity of Nicketti as we have presented her in our family tree. Cornstalk was probably her brother.

[1] Floyd Biographical Genealogies by N.J. Floyd, printed in Baltimore in 1912, p. 12-14

[2] Memoirs of Letitia Preston Floyd, [Library] University of North Carolina Southern Collection 1970, p. 24, 25

Cabells and Their Kin by Alexander Brown, p. 46, 47

Kegley's Virginia Frontier, p. 23, 24

Brown/Holmes Letter   [Lillian Gardiner and Marian Albright have copy]

Notes for ? Hughes:
A Scotchman, hunter and fur-trader with headquarters near Balcony Falls on the James River.

Child of Nicketti Powhatan and ? Hughes is:
+   8   i.   Elizabeth[4] Hughes.

Generation No. 4

8. Elizabeth[4] Hughes (Nicketti[3] Powhatan, Cleopatra[2], Chief[1] Powhatan) She married **Nathaniel Davis (1)** 1680. He was born in Tregarron Cardiganshire, Wales.

In his history, N. J. Floyd writes, "In a region that was little more than primeval forest, now known as Amherst County, Virginia, William Floyd patented land on which he made a home for himself. A dozen miles distant was the commodious bungalow of Nathaniel Davis, one of the earliest settlers in that region. This Welshman had made a large fortune trading with the Catawba and other Indians, and by locating choice river bottom land for sale from what is now Lynchburg up to Balcony Falls on the James River. Mr. Davis had several children of excellent Welch blood on his side and Indian from their Mother, derived from the most distinguished Indian ancestry. His wife's Mother, Necketti, Indian equivalent for 'beautiful flower' was granddaughter of the noted

Powhatan (daughter of his youngest daughter), while the father of Necketti was chief of the small Cayauga tribe."

In the words of Col. M.J. Kelley, "Nathaniel and Elizabeth Davis left much to posterity. Their sons and grandsons helped write the first hundred years of our nation's history. Also the Davis women played a major role in the bringing forth and moulding of these wonderful men into whatever profession they chose, such as Governors, Doctors, Lawyers, Educators, Senators, Judges. We had more than our fair share, especially the politians who played such an important part in the building of this young nation.

After the Floyds went to Kentucky, several of the Davises moved there from Georgia and settled in what is now Todd County. One of the descendents born in Todd County, but carried to Mississippi as a weanling grew up to become President of the Confederate States of America." [Col. M.J.K.]

Nathaniel Davis's will may be found in Will Book #2, p. 83, Amherst County, Virginia.

Children of Elizabeth Hughes and Nathaniel Davis (1) are:
+   9   i.   Mary[5] Davis.
+ 10 ii. Martha Davis, born July 14, 1702; died February 18, 1765.
+ 11 iii. Robert Davis (1), died 1771 in Georgia.
   12 iv. Phillip Davis.
   13   v. Samuel Davis.

Generation No. 5

9. Mary[5] Davis (Elizabeth[4] Hughes, Nicketti[3] Powhatan, Cleopatra[2], Chief[1] Powhatan) She married **Samuel Burks** 1705. He was born in Hanover County, Virginia.

Notes for Samuel Burks:
The Hanover County records burned during the War Between the States and most were lost.

Children of Mary Davis and Samuel Burks are:
+ 14   i. Elizabeth[6] Burks, born abt. 1685; died September 21, 1756.
+ 15 ii. James Burks.
+ 16 iii. Samuel Burks, Jr..
+ 17 iv. Mary Burks.

10. Martha[5] Davis (Elizabeth[4] Hughes, Nicketti[3] Powhatan, Cleopatra[2], Chief[1] Powhatan) was born July 14, 1702, and died February 18, 1765. She married **Captain Abraham Venable II**, 1723. He was born March 22, 1699/00 in Louisa County, Virginia.

Child of Martha Davis and Captain Venable is:
+ 18   i. Colonel Nathaniel[6] Venable, born November 01, 1733; died December 07, 1804.

11. Robert[5] Davis (1) (Elizabeth[4] Hughes, Nicketti[3] Powhatan, Cleopatra[2], Chief[1] Powhatan) died 1771 in Georgia. He married **(1) Mary Lipscomb**. He married **(2) Abadiah Lewis**, daughter of Hugh Lewis and Elizabeth. He married **(3) Grace**.

Notes for Robert Davis (1):

Became his father's business agent at an early age.

His will appears in D.A.R. Library, Natchez, Mississippi Court Record #237, Book E, p. 238; also appears in Natchez Court Record, 1767—1805 Vol. 2, Book E, p. 182. [May W. McBee]

Children of Robert Davis (1) and Abadiah Lewis are:

+ 19   i.   Nathaniel[6] Davis (2), born abt. 1705; died abt. 1770. (our ancestor - MKA/LJG)
   20   ii.   Isham Davis.
   21   iii.   Robert Davis (2) died 1780 in Cumberland Gap, Tennessee. He married Elizabeth.

Notes for Robert Davis (2):

Wilderness Road by Robert Kincaid page 156 tells, "In the neighborhood of Cumberland Ford, Fleming and his fellow travelers met three white men and a Negro—the survivors of a party of 12 men from Lexington ambushed five miles ahead. In silent marching order, Fleming and his men rode on to the scene. They found the bodies of John and Robert Davis of Amherst lying scalped and mangled on the road. Two war clubs lay by the bodies, and on one of them was the figure of a lizard, which they believed belonged to Chief Spring Lizard of the Chickamauga. (May 1780)

In June of that year, John Floyd wrote to Col. Preston, "My Uncle Davis and his son were killed near Cumberland Mountain about five weeks ago as they were going to the settlement. There were four brothers of them who have all been murdered in the course of seven or eight weeks." This from the Draper Manuscripts, Wisconsin Historical Society 33s318 and 17cc182.

   22   iv.   Abadiah or Abigail Davis married William Floyd.

Abadiah or Abigail Davis lived to be over 90, died at the home of her son, Charles Floyd in Kentucky. Even at that age she was erect and handsome—with all the countenance, high bearing, courage and composure, which characterized the noble forest ancestry, inherited from Powhatan, which she never doubted.

Excerpts from a letter from Letitia Preston Floyd [daughter of Col. William Preston and wife of John Floyd, Governor of Virginia, 1830-1834], to her son, Rush, February 22, 1845. From "Memoirs of Letitia Preston Floyd," p. 24, 25 [published in the Richmond Standard June 26, 1880].

"I will now give you an account of your father Floyd's family.

Early in last century his ancestors came from Wales and settled on Eastern Shore of Virginia. Mr. William Floyd the Father of Col. John Floyd had 2 brothers, one named John who went north and whose family [if he ever had one] is lost sight of.

Charles - the youngest son went to Ga., and is ancestor of Gen. John Floyd of that state.

William Floyd left the Eastern Shore went up country as far as Amherst Co., Va. then a wild re-

The Warrior's Path of Kentucky, and the Great Indian Warpath in Virginia (later to be the route of the Wilderness Road). This is where the bodies of John and Robert Davis were found. (From map by W.E. Myers, p. 748, 42nd Annual Report of the Bureau of American Ethnology, 1928).

gion; he met with a family by the name of Davis whose ancestors had come from Wales. They had traded with the Catawba Indians and got much property that way. The father of Robert Davis had married a half-breed Indian girl, Nicketti. This Robert Davis was the father of Miss Abadiah Davis whom Mr. William Floyd married. Davis owned many of the rich lands of Amherst. His other daughter married a Mr. Venable.

John Floyd the oldest son of William and Abadiah Davis, was born in 1750 in Amherst County, Va. At the age of 18 he married a Miss Burnell Barfoot———." LPF

23   v.   Sara Davis married Samuel Burks.
24   vi. Elizabeth Davis married George W. Sexton.

Children of Robert Davis (1) and Grace are:
25   i.   Lewis[6] Davis.
26   ii. Landon Davis.
27   iii. Hugh Davis.

Generation No. 6

14. Elizabeth[6] Burks (Mary[5] Davis, Elizabeth[4] Hughes, Nicketti[3] Powhatan, Cleopatra[2], Chief[1] Powhatan) was born abt. 1685, and died September 21, 1756. She married **Captain William Cabell** abt. 1700.

Child of Elizabeth Burks and William Cabell is:
28   i.   George[7] Cabell.

Notes for George Cabell:
    Predeceased his parents. Nothing more known of him.

15. James[6] Burks (Mary[5] Davis, Elizabeth[4] Hughes, Nicketti[3] Powhatan, Cleopatra[2], Chief[1] Powhatan) He married **Lucretia**.

James had been on the Roanoke since 1742 and had a claim to Burk's Garden. The Indians ran him out and he went to Cumberland County, North Carolina. In 1760 he and second wife, Lucretia, sold land. They had two daughters and a son.

Child of James Burks and Lucretia is:
29 i.   Thomas[7] Burks.

16. Samuel[6] Burks, Jr. (Mary[5] Davis, Elizabeth[4] Hughes, Nicketti[3] Powhatan, Cleopatra[2], Chief[1] Powhatan) He married **Elizabeth**.
    Samuel Burks, Jr. had 800 acres on Pedlar River.

Children of Samuel Burks and Elizabeth are:
30   i.   David[7] Burks.

31	ii.	Richard Burks.
32	iii.	John Burks.
33	iv.	Charles Burks.
34	v.	George Burks.
+ 35	vi.	Samuel Burks.
36	vii.	Elizabeth Burks.
37	viii.	Mary Partree Burks.

17. Mary[6] Burks (Mary[5] Davis, Elizabeth[4] Hughes, Nicketti[3] Powhatan, Cleopatra[2], Chief[1] Powhatan) She married **Obadiah Smith**. He died February 18, 1777 in Chesterfield County, Virginia.

Children of Mary Burks and Obadiah Smith are:
    38   i. Peartree[7] Smith.

Notes for Peartree Smith:
   Descendants went to Kentucky.

    39 ii. William Smith married Elizabeth Mayo.
    40 iii. Lucy Smith married James Powell Cocke.
    41 iv. Elizabeth Smith married Issac Winton.

18. Colonel Nathaniel[6] Venable (Martha[5] Davis, Elizabeth[4] Hughes, Nicketti[3] Powhatan, Cleopatra[2], Chief[1] Powhatan) was born November 01, 1733, and died December 07, 1804. He married **Elizabeth Woodson** March 29, 1755, daughter of "Baron" Woodson and Anne Michaux. She was born June 1740 in Virginia, and died September 29, 1791.

Notes for Colonel Nathaniel Venable:
   Resided: "State Hill," Prince Edward County, Virginia.
   For those interested in tracing a Huguenot line, his wife's Michaux ancestry is a good source.

Child of Nathaniel Venable and Elizabeth Woodson is:
  + 42 i. Samuel Woodson[7] Venable, born September 19, 1758; died September 07, 1821.

22. Nathaniel[6] Davis (2) (Robert[5] Davis (1), Elizabeth[4] Hughes, Nicketti[3] Powhatan, Cleopatra[2], Chief[1] Powhatan) was born abt. 1705, and died abt. 1770. He married **Elizabeth** abt. 1725.

   Nathaniel Davis' (2) will was offered for proof in Amherst County, Virginia May 10, 1778; proved October 7, 1782.

Children of Nathaniel Davis (2) and Elizabeth are:
    43 i. Elizabeth[7] Davis married John Burks.
    44 ii. Nancy Davis married John P. Lewis.
    45 iii. Sally Davis married Stephen P. Lewis.
    46 iv. Matilda Davis married John Bagby.

47   v.   Isham Davis.
48 vi. Charles Davis.
49 vii. Theodocia Davis.
50 viii. Nathaniel Davis (3).
+ 51 ix. James Davis. (our ancestor - MKA/LJG)

Generation No. 7

35. Samuel⁷ Burks (Samuel⁶, Mary⁵ Davis, Elizabeth⁴ Hughes, Nicketti³ Powhatan, Cleopatra², Chief¹ Powhatan) He married **Elizabeth**.

Child of Samuel Burks and Elizabeth is:
+ 52   i. Richard⁸ Burks.

42. Samuel Woodson⁷ Venable (Nathaniel⁶, Martha⁵ Davis, Elizabeth⁴ Hughes, Nicketti³ Powhatan, Cleopatra², Chief¹ Powhatan) was born September 19, 1758, and died September 07, 1821. He married **Mary Scott Carrington** August 15, 1781, daughter of Judge Carrington and Margaret Reade. She was born November 14, 1758, and died March 21, 1837.

Notes for Samuel Woodson Venable:
Residence: "Springfield," Prince Edward County, Virginia

Notes for Mary Scott Carrington:
Her paternal grandparents were Col. George Carrington, born July 1, 1711— died February 7, 1785, and Annie Mayo born 1712 in Barbados and died February 15, 1785 in Virginia. They were married June 26, 1732.
Maternal grandparents were Clement Reade born 1707—died January 2, 1763, and Mary Hill born 1711—died November 11, 1780.

Child of Samuel Venable and Mary Carrington is:
+ 53   i. Nathaniel E.⁸ Venable, born December 05, 1791; died September 21, 1846.

51. James⁷ Davis (Nathaniel⁶ Davis (2), Robert⁵ Davis (1), Elizabeth⁴ Hughes, Nicketti³ Powhatan, Cleopatra², Chief¹ Powhatan) He married **Jane Black**.

Children of James Davis and Jane Black are:
+ 54   i. Joseph⁸ Davis, born August 04, 1745 in Bedford County, Virginia; died September 06, 1795 in Mercer County, Kentucky. (our ancestor - MKA/LJG)
   55 ii. John Davis.
   56 iii. Samuel Davis. He married Jane Marshall.

Generation No. 8

52. Richard[8] Burks (Samuel[7], Samuel[6], Mary[5] Davis, Elizabeth[4] Hughes, Nicketti[3] Powhatan, Cleopatra[2], Chief[1] Powhatan) He married **Mary Polly Harris** 1795 in Amherst County, Virginia.

He moved to Madison County, Alabama before the 1830 census. The household included Richard and Polly Burks, son, John F., son, Matthew and brother John Burks.

Children of Richard Burks and Mary Harris are:

      57   i.   John F.[9] Burks.
      58   ii. Matthew Burks.
+ 59   iii. William Pinkney Burks, born 1810; died 1866 in Drew, Arkansas.

53. Nathaniel E.[8] Venable (Samuel Woodson[7], Nathaniel[6], Martha[5] Davis, Elizabeth[4] Hughes, Nicketti[3] Powhatan, Cleopatra[2], Chief[1] Powhatan) was born December 05, 1791, and died September 21, 1846. He married **Mary Embry Scott** 1813, daughter of Charles Scott and Pricilla Reade. She was born 1793, and died March 19, 1866.

Notes for Nathaniel E. Venable:
Residence: "Longwood," Prince Edward County, Virginia.

Child of Nathaniel Venable and Mary Scott is:

      60   i.   Mary Pricilla[9] Venable, born October 08, 1815 in Prince Edward County, Virginia.

54. Joseph[8] Davis (James[7], Nathaniel[6] Davis (2), Robert[5] Davis (1), Elizabeth[4] Hughes, Nicketti[3] Powhatan, Cleopatra[2], Chief[1] Powhatan) was born August 04, 1745 in Bedford County, Virginia, and died September 06, 1795 in Mercer County, Kentucky. He married **Jean Hamilton** April 07, 1767 in Peaks of Otter, Augusta Co., Virginia, daughter of Robert Hamilton and Margaret McKee. She was born March 07, 1745/46 in Virginia, and died November 1806.

Joseph and his brother, Samuel, were very close. They and their families moved from Rockbridge, Virginia to Bedford County, Virginia ca. 1776. A few years later, ca. 1779, they again moved their families to Dougherty's Station near Danville, Kentucky on Clark's Run—to land they received for their Revolutionary War service. Their Revolutionary War Record may be found in Volume 1, page 186 of "Virginia Militia in the Revolution" by McAlister.

Paraphrased from Joseph's daughter Margaret's account to her children:

"In 1782 when the Commissioners were sent out by the Government to determine those entitled to draw lands, the 76'ers drew 1400 acres. Then there was a grant of 400 acres to all who had raised one crop of corn in Kentucky. Papa Daveiss held the corn right - and in addition, possessed himself of 600 acres of fine land adjoining his corn grant. Squire Daveiss now had succeeded in obtaining a hand mill. This was a thing notorious enough for people to come from other settlements to see it, and to get a little corn ground on it." More regarding Joseph Davis may be found in "Historic Families of Kentucky" by Green.

His will was probated October of 1795, executed by his son, Joseph Hamilton Daveiss.

Notes for Jean Hamilton:

In her father's [Robert Hamilton] will, he leaves to Jean [Jenn-Jennet] "that 50 acres of land in Caintuck'y."

The Hamilton family was for 400 years an important factor in the political, military and religious history of Scotland.

Early in the sixteenth century, Patrick Hamilton, a Catholic priest, left that church to embrace the doctrine of Martin Luther. He was charged with being a heretic and was burned at the stake. Historians agree that his martyrdom sealed the fate of the Catholic Church in Scotland. Within 50 years of his death the Presbyterian faith was that country's established religion.

Our line is proved back to Robert who was born ca. 1710 in Scotland, and died in 1778 in Kerr's Creek, Rockbridge County, Virginia, where his will is recorded. His parents came to America from Ireland after fleeing Scotland to escape religious and political persecution. One source names Robert's father as Ninian and his grandfather as John, and gives this account from the "History of Scotland" by Andrew Lang, Chapter XI, page 340 and following: "In 1745 the Hamilton Clan sided with Prince Charles of Scotland in his attempt to throw off English rule, and when this failed the Clan was all but destroyed by the forces of the Duke of Cumberland. Some 300 of the most prominent rebels were executed, two of whom were George and John Hamilton. They were hanged and their arms and legs chopped off before they were dead." We can't be positive this John was Robert's grandfather, but in his 1909 article Seldon Nelson says "This probably had more to do with the Hamilton's coming to America than religious persecution—the popular reason advanced for emigration at that time." Seldon Nelson was the great grandson of Robert and Margaret McKee Hamilton. This article was published in the Knoxville, Tennessee Sentinel in November or December of 1909.

It is hard for us to conceive of the hardships our forebears endured—run out of Scotland, then out of Ireland for their beliefs, then coming to America. Robert handed down a family Bible bound in deer hide still showing the imprints and scars of rocks and leaves from being hidden in the crags of Scotland. The Bible is owned by the family of one of our kinsmen, the late Mrs. Lucien Beckner of Louisville, Kentucky. She was a descendent of Samuel Daveiss, brother of our Margaret.

Robert was educated at the University of Edinburgh where he received his Degree in Medicine in 1738. The subject of his thesis was "The Effect of Freezing on the Human Body"—"DeFrigoris Effectibus in Corpus Humanum." Our cousin, Virginia Brooks had in her possession a copy of this thesis.

Robert married Margaret McKee ca. 1740 probably in Ireland. She also was a Scottish/Irish Presbyterian by birth. These protestant refugees settled first in Pennsylvania, and then moved to what is now Rockbridge County, Virginia. Margaret's 13 or 15 brothers came to America about the same time as the Hamilton's, also for religious and political reasons. Margaret was born about 1724 in Ireland, and descends on her mother's side from the illustrious Wallace tribe of Scotland. Her father, Robert James McKee married Marian Brown, daughter of Jeanette Peebles whose Mother was Margaret Wallace, a lineal descendent of Sir William Wallace, the great Scottish Chieftain, "Protector of Scotland" during the bloody battles for Scottish independence against King Edward I of England.

Once in America, Robert and his family took an active part in colonizing and settling the land of their adoption. He was one of the few learned men in the southwest, and Margaret McKee's Scottish family became prominent pioneers in Kentucky. Many fascinating tales can be told of the Hamilton's frontier experiences. One such incident bears recording:

The Kerr's Creek Massacre

In an interview with Alexander Hamilton (by Draper) in Franklin County, Kentucky, he tells of his Grandfather Robert Hamilton's Indian encounter in his own words: "Carr's Creek, Virginia Indian Irruption."

"My grandfather, Robert Hamilton, came from Ireland. Lived a while in Pennsylvania and then moved down into Virginia. Half of his family (just half were missing next morning), my father, Archibald Hamilton then 7 years of age, and 2 sisters were taken prisoner of Carr's Creek by a party of Indians. One of my uncles, a little boy, was leaning on his elbows in the cabin window (a side window, such as cabins have) and pointing out to an Indian running along said, 'See there Father, there's an Indian,' says he. Grandfather James McKee was along and saw no Indian.

Robert Hamilton and some women who had left their home, got into a cabin. An Indian put in his gun and shot him. The ball went in on his left breast and came out near the backbone. The house had not been closed when he was shot. He told those within to clear out and himself followed them, presenting his gun on the advancing Indians and keeping them at bay; and in that way he took three or four women up the lane, till he made his escape by concealing himself and party in some glady land. The Indians in their persuit took Alexander Hamilton and two of his sisters,who had been separated in some way from the rest of the party, and had not gotten to the cabin. (Old Mr. McGill says this was on Sunday and part of the family was at church: the way they came to be separated. He sung about thirty verses on it).

After leaving some distance, they (the Indians and captives) stopped in Walker's Meadows, which were four miles, and sent back two Indians to a still house to get some whiskey to have a frolic on. They were met by a party of one hundred men under Col. James McDowell, who when they saw the two Indians turned and precipitately fled, the advanced party saying they were coming in the thousands. The prisoners were carried along through mountain passes, where the whole party could have been readily cut off; crossing the Ohio, perhaps at the mouth of the Kenawha. The children were taken in custody and the council (Shawnees, Pickaway Plains, I expect) determined they would sell them. The squaws made motion to them when they were taken, not to be afraid, they wouldn't kill them. My grandfather spent three days at the Towns to get the children. Two others, I think there were that went with him at that time. It was winter and they suffered a great deal coming back. The snow was 2 feet deep in Ohio. One woman ran the gauntlet with her child in her arms. She bent over to shield it. She naked.

When my father (Archibald) went to come home, his mother squaw took him and dressed his hair in Indian fashion, with bear's oil, and told him to go home and tell his people she had treated him well. While with her he had had to carry about her papoose in a blanket tied about his neck. The boys would sometimes throw corncobs at him as he went about. If he didn't want to carry it, he would pinch it's legs and make it cry more and she would call and take it. His Indian father told him one morning to get up and make a fire. He was sleepy. The Indian drew out his tomahawk from under his head flung it and cut a gash. She scolded and raved about it so much that the Indian went off.

My grandfather paid for all three (children to be ransomed) but my father was supposed to be at a camp on the Scioto, and didn't get in till three or four months after my aunts, to Pittsburg, where he was to be delivered. When he got to Pittsburg, they gave him clothes from the King's store; I suppose a store from which prisoners were intended to be supplied with clothes. He threw them all off but enough to make a breechcloth. He had been an Indian so long, he had forgotten English and they were scarce able to identify him.

A grown man that was taken a year after my father while digging ginseng in the mountains, near Carr's Creek, knew my father when he got out there, and was brought into Pittsburg at the same time. The only one he (father) knew by name was Aunt Daveiss, said her name was Jinny. (This would have been Jean Hamilton Daveiss—LJG) She was the only one he recognized at first. There was a man at Pittsburg that made it his business to buy up prisoners. My father was nine years old when he got back."

Authors' note: Though this account is difficult to read, we thought it much more interesting in Alexander's own words than if we edited. If you are interested in more of his colorful interview, you will find it in Draper's Manuscript Vol. 11, The Kentucky Papers.

There were two Carr's Creek raids by the Indians: 10 October 1759 and June of 1763 (the date of the above account). The leader of this terrible raid was our kinsman, the Shawnee war-chief, Cornstalk, descendant of Powhatan.

Col. Joseph Hamilton Daviess

Children of Joseph Davis and Jean Hamilton are:

+ 61   i.   Margaret[9] Daveiss, born February 02, 1769 in Peaks of Otter, Augusta County, Virginia; died 1861 in Trenton, Tennessee.

+ 62   ii.   James Harvey Davis, born August 28, 1770.

   63   iii.   Robert Davis, born March 18, 1772. He married Ann Troy.

   64   iv.   Joseph Hamilton Davis, born March 04, 1774 in Bedford County, Virginia; died November 07, 1811 in Tippecanoe Creek, Wabash Valley, Indiana. He married Nancy Marshall.

Col. Joseph Hamilton Daveiss [known as Jo Daveiss] was educated in English, Latin and Greek, and was always at the head of his class.

At age 18, he entered the military. After completion of his assignment, he read Law in the office of Col. George Nicholas and was admitted to the Kentucky Bar in June of 1795. The following August he was qualified as an attorney in the Court of Appeals. He distinguished himself in his chosen field and was appointed Attorney General for the State of Kentucky. In 1801 or 1802 he visited Washington, being the first 'Western" lawyer to appear in the Supreme Court of the United States. In 1803 he married Miss Marshall [Nancy or Anne or perhaps Nancy Anne], sister of John Marshall, Chief Justice of the Supreme Court at that time.

While U.S. attorney, he acted as prosecutor of Aaron Burr in his famous trial for treason. Daveiss was defeated and as a result drew fire from many of his colleagues over this action, but history later proved him right and he was exonerated. Burr's scheme was to revolutionize the Western country, Louisiana and Mexico, establish an empire, with New Orleans the capital and himself as chief. Although he was acquitted, his political career was ended and he died in poverty and obscurity years later.

In 1811, Col. Daveiss once more entered the military, joining the Army of General William Henry Harrison in the campaign against the Indians on the Wabash. The "American Cyclopedia" tells of the Battle of Tippecanoe on the 7th of November 1811: "Seeing that the Indians were about to break through and effect the probable defeat of Harrison's army, Jo Daveiss led a cavalry charge against the Indians that was successful and turned the day in favor of the American troops. In that brave charge, Daveiss fell, shot through the breast. He survived from 5 AM until midnight, fully conscious all the time. His last words were 'Boys, they've killed me but don't give up the fight.'"

Joseph Daveiss was one of the most remarkable men of his day. Standing nearly 6 feet, his bearing was grave and dignified. He was courteous to those he admired and haughty to those he disliked. He was eccentric in his habits. At the trial of Aaron Burr he appeared wearing buckskins, and earlier while arguing a land suit before the Supreme Court he was dressed in buckskin, with a squirrel hat. Nevertheless, he was declared to be the most impressive orator of his time. Several states have honored him by naming counties for him [even though they misspelled his name].

Article in Louisville Paper, August 1949:

"I was greatly interested to read in the Magazine Section an article on Owensboro by Joe Creason; but Daviess—[should be spelled Daveiss - Col. Daveiss changed the spelling of his name, Davis, to Daveiss because there were so many settlers by that name in Kentucky and there was great confusion. He encouraged his whole family to do likewise—MKA]—County was named for Col. Joseph Hamilton Daviess, not Col. James Daviess.

Being a great-great niece of Joseph Hamilton Daviess, I was anxious to get it straight. Joseph Daviess, Sr. his father was with George Rogers Clark in the conquest of the Northwest Territory. It was to Ft. Harrod Jean Hamilton Daviess accompanied her husband on horseback from Rockbridge County, Virginia, with Joseph Hamilton on the saddle in front of her, and Samuel, my ancestor, on his father's saddle in front.

It was through this ancestress, [Jean], that Presbyterianism in Kentucky got its start. She wrote her pastor, Father Rice, [the Rev. David Rice] in Virginia, that she could withstand the perils and hardships of the wilderness if she had her Bible and her pastor. Her letter brought Father Rice to Kentucky where he founded Transylvania Seminary, later College. Counties in four states are named for Col. Joseph Hamilton Daviess: Kentucky, Indiana, Illinois and Missouri. He is buried at Tippecanoe where he fell at the age of 33. Many thought him the peer of Henry Clay in brilliance. Clay defended Aaron Burr at Frankfort when Daviess discovered Burr's treason and prosecuted him. (Marie Daviess Warren Beckner - Louisville, Ky.)

Suggested reading:

Marshall, "History of Kentucky II"

National Cyclopedia of American Biography

Thomas Marshall Green, "Historic Families of Kentucky"

Bernard Mayo, "Henry Clay," 1937, Riverside Press Cambridge, p. 395, 396

65   v.   Samuel Davis, born November 22, 1776; died 1856. He married Hannah McAfee 1810.

Notes for Samuel Davis:

Was a prominent figure in Central Kentucky. A Legislator, State Senator and Justice, member of Board of Internal Improvements and Grand Master Mason of Kentucky.

+   66   vi.   Jane Davis, born August 08, 1777.
+   67   vii.   John Davis, born January 01, 1779 in Danville, Kentucky; died November 17, 1852 in Daveiss County, Kentucky.
    68   viii.   Josiah Davis, born February 04, 1781; died June 24, 1784.
+   69   ix.   William Davis, born November 24, 1782.
    70   x.   Mary Davis, born November 10, 1784. She married Abraham Voris.
    71   xi.   Thomas Davis, born December 30, 1786. He married Hannah.

Generation No. 9

59. William Pinkney[9] Burks (Richard[8], Samuel[7], Samuel[6], Mary[5] Davis, Elizabeth[4] Hughes, Nicketti[3] Powhatan, Cleopatra[2], Chief[1] Powhatan) was born 1810, and died 1866 in Drew, Arkansas. He married **Anna Moriah Jones**. She was born in Giles Co., Texas.

Notes for William Pinkney Burks:
   Lived a while in Madison County, Alabama—and in Shelby County, Tennessee [1840 census; 1850 census].

Child of William Burks and Anna Jones is:
+   72   i.   Charles Martin[10] Burks, born in Shelby County, Tennessee.

61. Margaret[9] Daveiss (Joseph[8] Davis, James[7], Nathaniel[6] Davis (2), Robert[5] Davis (1), Elizabeth[4] Hughes, Nicketti[3] Powhatan, Cleopatra[2], Chief[1] Powhatan) was born February 02, 1769 in Peaks of Otter, Augusta County, Virginia, and died 1861 in Trenton, Tennessee. She married **William Hess** April 08, 1790 in Mercer County, Kentucky, son of Henry Hess and Margarethe. He was born February 22, 1767 in Easton, Pennsylvania, and died July 30, 1815 in Wilkerson County, Mississippi.

   On the 22nd of February 1769, at the foot of the Blue Ridge Mountains in the shadow of the giant Peaks of Otter in Rockbridge County, Virginia, Margaret was born to Joseph and Jean Hamilton Davis. She was of Welsh and Scottish and Indian lineage.
   As a young child Margaret had an encounter with none other than General George Washington, who stopped his company of soldiers to come to her rescue. Having heard that the General and his men were going to ride by her Virginia home, Margaret ran to the front yard and climbed the tall picket fence for a good view. In her excitement, she forgot to hold on and fell just as Washington was even with her perch. Her voluminous skirt caught in a paling of the fence and as she later put it, "skinned me just like a rabbit." Seeing her embarrassing predicament, the General stopped his troops, got off his horse and freed little Margaret. "My daughter, next time go round to the gate," he admonished her.
   When Margaret was 10 her parents decided to brave the perils of the wilderness and settle on land in Kentucky granted to her father for his Revolutionary War Service. In describing the move, Margaret said her father took with him, "fourteen horses, plenty of cattle, good rifles, his family, his bedding and his Bible." The youngest child at that time was John, less than a year old.
   En route to their new home, an incident occurred that suggests the hardy stock from which Margaret descended. While crossing the Cumberland River, Mrs. Davis was thrown from the spirited horse she was riding, and broke her arm. The party stopped only long enough for the men to splint her arm with a crude sort of bandage, and they journeyed on, with Mrs. Davis once more on her spirited mount and carrying one of her children on her lap.
   The family settled first at Daughtery's Station (sometimes spelled: Dorrity, etc.) on Clark's Run near Danville, Kentucky, where they made friends with James Allen and his family. The Davises and the Allens later moved farther down Clark's Run where they built the first two cabins in what was then a remote section of Kentucky. Three years later they moved to the vicinity of Harrod's Fort, (now Harrodsburg in Mercer County). Life in the wilds of Kentucky was quite a contrast to what the family had known in Virginia. During the first winter they went three months without bread of any kind. Dried venison or dried beef were substitutes. They wore moccasins in the absence of shoes, and Margaret's first Kentucky dress was fashioned from fabric her mother wove from the lint of wild nettle and buffalo wool.

Skirmishes with the Indians were frequent, and all the females learned to shoot rifles. Margaret related at least two incidents to her family years later. Once when she had been left at home alone the family returned to find a dead Indian outside the cabin and Margaret standing guard with a rifle, which is now in the possession of family members.

Another scare occurred while Margaret's father was out hunting and she and her mother were in the cabin with the young children. Indians came and tried to get in. Mrs. Davis shot out the front door while Margaret held a spear up the chimney in case they should attempt entry that way. They had to spend most of the night and all the next day in these positions without saying a word, with Margaret's young siblings on a quilt under the bed.

The Davises and their neighbors passed through the usual privations of pioneer life with the children receiving such education as the country afforded. The boys had the advantage of several years of instruction with the celebrated Dr. Priestly, the most noted scholar of that time in the "west." Among their classmates were Felix Grundy, Adam Huntsman, the Allens and others who later became men of prominence.

The Davises were members of the Old Mud Meeting House, which had been built in Mercer County by the Dutch Reform assembly and later amalgamated with Presbyterians and other denominations. In about 1785, at the strong urging of his wife, Jean, Joseph led a horse into Virginia and brought the first Presbyterian clergyman, Dr. David Rice to Mercer County. Jean and Joseph were pillars of the church and he led the singing at each service. However, once while celebrating the birth of one of his sons with friends it seems they had overindulged in the "flowing bowl." News of the celebration reached the pastor's ears and when Joseph approached him to arrange his son's baptism, the Reverend refused. Joseph offered no defense for his conduct, but on the following Sunday when the hymn was announced— silence prevailed. Everyone looked at Joseph who sat with chin in hand, elbow on his closed hymnal, and stared steadily at the pastor.

"Brother Davis, heist the tune!" the pastor called out. Joseph responded in his rich Scottish brogue, "I'll neither whistle nor sing, Reverend, whilst ye refuse to mark the little lambe because the old ram went astray." The next Sunday the child was duly christened, and the little church rang with triumphant tunes led by the exultant father.

By 1786 the Davis household boasted of 10 children, 4 of whom had been born in Kentucky. To avoid confusion, Margaret and her brothers changed the spelling of their name to Daveiss because there were so many families of that name in Kentucky.

Shortly after her 21st birthday, Margaret married 23-year-old William Hess, son of Henry and Margarethe Hess. He too was inspired with the same pioneer spirit and found Kentucky a land of promise. Their wedding ceremony took place the 8th of April, 1790 in Mercer County, Kentucky with the Reverend David Rice officiating and Joseph Davis as bondsman. The couple lived in Mercer County, then later in Madison County, Kentucky, both of which were created from Lincoln County, Kentucky. Will is listed as a taxpayer in Madison County beginning in 1794, and he and Margaret witnessed a deed of sale there in August of 1803.

The Hess family moved to Tennessee in March 1804, settling in Williamson County, in the town of Franklin. Will's name appears regularly on the county's tax lists beginning in 1805. The fact that Margaret's Mother's brother, Joseph Hamilton, was very prominent in the area may have had some bearing on their locating there. Tax lists for 1809 and 1810 show Will owned seven lots in the town of Franklin. Court Records also indicate that Will served frequently on Williamson County juries from 1807 to 1809, and that he served as Justice of the Peace in 1810.

In 1814 as the "War of 1812" was winding down, Will made a trip to New Orleans to sound out business prospects. In a letter on January 11 to his son Joseph, Will reported receiving a good offer and thought they could do business there. But his patriotic fervor was aroused by the military situation in which he found his countrymen. He joined in the fight to keep the British from taking New Orleans, turning down a commission so that he could be "finished" with his duty as soon as possible and return to his family. This letter written from the battlefield, bears out the facts of the conflict. Our outnumbered forces led by General Andrew Jackson, Commander in Chief, fought so bravely under the most trying conditions, with inadequate arms and scarce ammunition. General Packenham, Commander of the British forces was soundly defeated, and in fact perished—thanks to the battle acumen of Jackson and the valor of his troops.

The letter:

"Dear Son and Family,

After my best love to you all I can inform you I am in tolerable health only as I have been much exposed to cold. I was again permitted to come to town where I have been for 3 days. Tomorrow I return to camp. I thought all misfortune had done with me but here was a disappointment as I expected to make money and a good job was offered me. But the British must be fought. I can do good business when I be at liberty. I hope the British Army will not remain long here. There has been some firing every day for two weeks but last Sunday, the 8th day of the New Year, we had a general engagement and for about three or four hours the heavy firing lasted without much interruption the whole day. We had about five or six men killed, about seventeen wounded. We killed about 1100 of the British on the field and wounded and took prisoner about 800 men and those wounded dying every day. There are some of the British vessels in the mouth of the river. We expect another hard battle every day. We all wish hard soon is the last battle. The British had their two head generals killed and the third one badly wounded—about 19 other officers. Our men appear to be willing to fight although I am here I cannot give perfect statements. If I live I will write you but I pray my son, Joseph, and my son, Nelson, leave not home nor leave the family if you can help it as all their trust and confidence is in you. May the God of Heaven bless you all as a family. In the morning I return to camp. I could have had an appointment (commission) but was determined to be done with it as soon as possible therefore I would have none.

P.S. The British attempted to scale over the breastworks was the reason we killed so many of them. Till this scrap is over we cannot leave this place. To Joseph D. Hess—God bless every one of you.

Will Hess"

After victory was achieved, Will started home but because of illness stopped at the home of a cousin in Wilkerson County, Mississippi to recuperate. Word of his illness reached Margaret, and she set out with two of her children in a horse drawn wagon to bring him home. Unfortunately Will died before she reached him. She buried him there in Mississippi, then with her children started for home.

(Paraphrased from Margaret's own account): "The whole interior of the state of Mississippi was in the possession of Choctaw and Chickasaw Indians except a small district on the Tombigbee where the early settlers were Anglo-American, Spanish and French. General Wilkerson in 1798 had erected a military post on the first high land on the Mississippi River and called it Fort Adams. After leaving such 'civilization' as the Fort offered and passing through Indian Country, Margaret's son became ill so she stopped with Indians to let him recover. The squaws were sulky and would not talk with her, so she went out and sat on a log near an old warrior who was dressing deer skins, and talked with him. He would not reply but she knew he understood her. After a while he motioned for her to follow him. He drove her horses into his cornfield and allowed them to eat their fill. Margaret wanted a chicken for soup to feed her ailing child but the squaws refused to let her have one. It was a pressing need so the widowed mother 'obtained' one secretly. Then she borrowed a pot from one of the unsuspecting women to cook the fowl, and fed her son the much needed nourishment. Next morning, very early, the Indian woman called to retrieve her vessel. The chicken soup in it would have been a dead giveaway, so the quick thinking Margaret threw a shovel full of ashes in and stirred. The old squaw walked away muttering and shaking her head wondering what kind of mess she had cooked, and was never the wiser."

With son, Joseph and his family residing in Bedford County, Tennessee, Margaret decided to buy land and move her family there. The purchase of this land resulted in an historic trial. The man who sold Margaret this tract later moved the deed leaving her tract vacant. Finding this out, she sold a horse to get money to reenter it; went into the office, entered the land, stepped out and encountered a man coming in. That gentleman was planning to enter her tract for himself. A lawsuit resulted which she won but her adversary was granted a re-trial in Lincoln County. Margaret retained James K. Polk (later President Polk) to represent her but as result of injury caused by a fall from his horse, Polk did not arrive in time to defend her. Her adversary refused delay and urged an immediate trial. Margaret stated to the Judge that she had no lawyer, but with his permission would represent herself. Having proved her title by maps and charts, she began a three-hour defense after which there was not a dry eye in the house. These were not tears of pity, but of admiration for her command of the law, and the decision was immediately given in her favor. Her adversary walked up to his lawyer and said, "Well, Jenkins, ain't this the very devil." The Judge remarked at supper that evening that he had never known a case better managed or better presented. The secret of all this ability was due to a broken arm when Margaret was a young girl. While recuperating, she amused herself reading her brother's law books, and reciting to him. This brother was the prominent Joseph Hamilton Daveiss, first Attorney General of Kentucky, who led the prosecution against Aaron Burr for treason, and who died heroically at the Battle of Tippecanoe.

The 1820 Bedford County census shows Margaret (then about 50) with five children from the age of 10 and upwards at home to support and educate. It is difficult to imagine how she was able to provide for five children in those times. Her inherited characteristics plus the toughness and strength she developed as a child in the Kentucky wilderness no doubt helped her through. She not only provided essentials for these children, she sent all but one of her daughters to the prestigious Nashville Academy.

By 1830 Margaret had moved to Gibson County, Tennessee where sons, Nelson I., James A.W., and daughter, Narcissa were living. (Nelson, a Presbyterian minister, and Medical Doctor, was one of the founders of Trenton.) The following year Margaret witnessed an unusual solar event, which she described in her Bible. "I was in the town of Trenton in the State of Tennessee on the 14th day of August in the year 1831 on Sunday, when I saw the sun in full size a clere blue culler ontil it set the same night, the moon was blue ontil it set also. The next morning it being the 15th of said month the sun rose blue as the day before." Margaret was not the only one to comment on the phenomenon. "The Southern Statesman" newspaper carried stories of similar sightings by citizens of Jackson and Nashville, Tennessee, Russellville, Kentucky and Little Rock, Arkansas. For several weeks the newspaper ran items giving various explanations including one which attributed the sun's unusual appearance to "it's conjunction with the planet, Herschel."

Exceptional! Remarkable! Rare! Surprising! Margaret was called all these by her children. Her son, Walter

Margaret Daveiss Hess

Scott Hess remembered that she cared little for domestic affairs, but she was a most brilliant woman, of fine physique, of cheerful countenance. In conversation she was the peer of Andrew Jackson, James K. Polk, Adam Huntsman and Felix Grundy, all of whom were her warm personal friends.

When Margaret was in her 90th year she still loved to tell of the glad hearts in the Wilderness when the tidings of peace were received. The War of Independence had been won! A new impulse was given to immigration. Fields were opened and new settlements were formed all over the state. Struggles there were, sometimes trouble with the Indians, but the, "State had taken its firm, first step toward dominion over the soil, and no power and no difficulty could check its progress." [MDH]

The family still smiles when being told of the inevitable pot of hot chocolate she kept brewing on the back of the stove, and her quick response when chided for talking to herself, "Well I always did enjoy talking to a smart woman." Her granddaughters, Jane Hess Campbell, Susan and Willie Hess Dunlap, Lyde Thomas and Katherine Johnston, lovely ladies who inherited Margaret's zest for living, handed down many tales of this extraordinary woman.

Margaret Daveiss Hess died at the age of 92, having retained an active mind and body to the very end. She went to a photograph gallery to have pictures made for her grandchildren, "got a chill" and died a few days later with pneumonia. She had written complete instructions for her funeral in the cherished Bible she left to her son, James A.W. She specified that the service be opened with the singing of Watt's hymn, "Why Do You Mourn Departing Friends;" that the sermon be based on the first four chapters of Colossians, and that the service conclude with, "And Must This Feeble Body Die" to the tune of "Pisgah."

Margaret is buried in Oakland Cemetery in Trenton, Tennessee near the gravesite of her son, Nelson Irving Hess. A special Marker was erected in her memory August of 1958 in ceremonies attended by about 100 of her descendents. Her legacy and enduring influence live on generations later, as exemplified by one of her descendant's comments in a letter. "After I had visited her grave, I had to give a speech at my church. I had a real panic attack, as the crowd was quite large. I thought of Margaret being the first woman to argue a case in a court of law in the U.S. and that thought got me through. I said to myself that I had that blood in me and I could handle a speech—and I did!" Rose Allen Oliver, March 1991.

A portion of Margaret's Memoirs was published in the "Ladies Pearl," A Cumberland Presbyterian Magazine. The write up by Angeron Page appeared in the September 1860 edition, vol. 8, no. 1

There was at one time a women's legal society in New York named for Margaret Daveiss Hess, the first female to plead a case in court in the United States.

Notes for William Hess:

Parents of William were Henry and Margarethe Hess.

Listed in the "Pennsylvania German Pioneers," vol. 1, p. 497 we find Henry Hesse arrived from Germany on the good ship, "Snow Ketty," in the year 1752.

A January 1759 map published by Act of Parliament showing places of interest in Pennsylvania, includes large tracts of land taken up by Philadelphia speculators prior to 1730 in Saucom Valley and sold to early German settlers. Included in these records we find land sold to the Hesses.

After arrival in America, our Henry Hesse married Margarethe - last name unknown - settled in Easton, Pennsylvania, in the Forks of the Delaware. Henry served as Private 5th Class, Sixth Company, Northhampton County Militia. This information can be found in the Pennsylvania Archives, 5th Series, Vol. 8, p. 89.

Henry Hesse is listed in the first U.S. census (1790) in More Township, Northhampton County, Pennsylvania. Record of children found in:

"Some of the First Settlers of the Forks of the Delaware," published by the Rev. Henry Martyn Kieffer, D.D. 1760—1852. These are translations from German of the record books of the First Reformed Church of Easton, Pennsylvania.

William, born February 24, 1767—parents are Henry and Margarethe Hesse. Baptism on April 25. Sponsors Mr. and Mrs. William Hesse—p. 84

John Henry born January 4, 1769. Baptism February 12. Sponsors Henry Schneider and wife, Juliana—p. 90.

Magdalena, born September 12, 1777. Baptism January 4, 1778. Sponsors Frederick Hesse, and Magdalena Scholl, both single—p. 101.

It should be noted that there are many spellings of Hesse: Hay, Hest, Herr, Hisse, and Hass could all be variations according to Prof. William J. Hinks in "Extracts from Reformed Church Records" Nov. 3, 1943.

There were so many immigrants by this name in Pennsylvania, regardless of spelling that we are doubly grateful to Margaret for leaving a record of her husband, William's, early information.

An interesting rumor has circulated in many branches of our family that our German folks were connected at some point with a castle on the Rhine River, Hess Castle. So far we have not been able to establish a reliable link back to it. This is also the name of a community? or township? near the castle itself, probably this was a serfdom back in ye olden days. The reason we give any credence to the rumor at all is that so many far-flung family branches—unknown to each other until recently—had all been told this same tale, handed down through the generations.

Children of Margaret Daveiss and William Hess are:

73   i.   Joseph Daveiss[10] Hess, born May 11, 1791 in Mercer County, Kentucky. He married Sally D. Stovall October 01, 1816 in Rutherford County, Tennessee.

Notes for Joseph Daveiss Hess:

Little is known of Capt. Joseph Davis Hess, oldest son of Margaret and William. He married Miss Sally D. Stovall October 1st. in Rutherford County, Tennessee, and is listed in the records of surrounding counties as a land owner. Apparently his family stayed in Middle Tennessee. We would like to know more of this branch if anyone has information.

+   74   ii.   William Randolph Hess, born December 03, 1793 in Mercer County, Kentucky; died April 24, 1838.

+   75   iii.   Dr. Nelson Irving Hess, born March 29, 1795; died October 02, 1868 in Trenton, Gibson County, Tennessee.

76   iv.   Jane W. Hess, born January 17, 1797; married John Beard.

Jane and John Beard/Baird, Esq. had one son who became a Presbyterian minister. We, at this time, do not know his name or any other information.

+   77   v.   Margaret W. Hess, born November 17, 1798.

+   78   vi.   Nancy Adair Hess, born October 14, 1800 in Kentucky; died March 04, 1854 in Gibson County, Tennessee.

+   79   vii.   Narcissa F. Hess, born August 23, 1802.

+   80   viii.   Maria L. Hess, born December 03, 1805 in Williamson County, Tennessee, died in Malden, Missouri.

81   ix.   Louisiana M. Hess, born January 19, 1808.

Louisiana M. Hess was born January 10th or January 19th, a Sunday in 1808. She married a Mr. McKnight and the authors know nothing else about her at this time.

+ 82 x. James A.W. Hess, born November 20, 1810 in Williamson County, Tennessee; died February 06, 1885 in Gibson County, Tennessee.

62. James Harvey[9] Davis (Joseph[8], James[7], Nathaniel[6] Davis (2), Robert[5] Davis (1), Elizabeth[4] Hughes, Nicketti[3] Powhatan, Cleopatra[2], Chief[1] Powhatan) was born August 28, 1770. He married **Mary Risque**.

Possibly also had son named Joseph—not confirmed by the authors at this time.

Children of James Davis and Mary Risque are:
+ 83 i. Harvey[10] Davis.
   84 ii. John Davis. He married Miss Wallace.
   85 iii. Mary Davis. She married Mr. Jury.
   86 iv. Julia Davis. She married Mr. Hinch.

66. Jane[9] Davis (Joseph[8], James[7], Nathaniel[6] Davis (2), Robert[5] Davis (1), Elizabeth[4] Hughes, Nicketti[3] Powhatan, Cleopatra[2], Chief[1] Powhatan) was born August 08, 1777. She married **James Dunn** October 02, 1800. He was born in Lincoln County—now Boyle.

Children of Jane Davis and James Dunn are:
   87 i. Samuel D.[10] Dunn.
   88 ii. Sophia Dunn.
   89 iii. Mary Dunn.

67. John[9] Davis (Joseph[8], James[7], Nathaniel[6] Davis (2), Robert[5] Davis (1), Elizabeth[4] Hughes, Nicketti[3] Powhatan, Cleopatra[2], Chief[1] Powhatan) was born January 01, 1779 in Danville, Kentucky, and died November 17, 1852 in Daveiss County, Kentucky. He married **Sara Duncan** December 11, 1806 in Nelson County, Kentucky. She was born October 03, 1787, and died in Daveiss County, Kentucky.

Children of John Davis and Sara Duncan are:
   90 i. Joseph Hamilton[10] Davis, II.
   91 ii. John J. Davis. He married Sally Coleman.
   92 iii. Julia Davis. She married Benjamin B. Blincoe October 10, 1831.
   93 iv. Sally Ann Davis. She married Dr. Stephen Ogden April 20, 1822.
   94 v. Harriotte Davis. She married Dr. Henry B. Roberts.
+ 95 vi. Rose C. Davis, born 1830 in Daveiss County, Kentucky; died August 13, 1854 in Owensboro, Daveiss County, Kentucky.

69. William[9] Davis (Joseph[8], James[7], Nathaniel[6] Davis (2), Robert[5] Davis (1), Elizabeth[4] Hughes, Nicketti[3] Powhatan, Cleopatra[2], Chief[1] Powhatan) was born November 24, 1782. He married **Mary Montgomery** December 02, 1806.

Children of William Davis and Mary Montgomery are:

    96   i.   Camillus Cecil[10] Davis.

    97   ii.   William Montgomery Davis.

    98   iii.   Jane Hamilton Davis.

Generation No. 10

72. Charles Martin[10] Burks (William Pinkney[9], Richard[8], Samuel[7], Samuel[6], Mary[5] Davis, Elizabeth[4] Hughes, Nicketti[3] Powhatan, Cleopatra[2], Chief[1] Powhatan) was born in Shelby County, Tennessee.

Notes for Charles Martin Burks:
  Moved to Drew, Arkansas at very young age.

Children of Charles Martin Burks are:

    99 i.   Marietta[11] Burks, born July 24, 1878; died November 08, 1983.

Notes for Marietta Burks:
  Always called "Mamie." Married a Mr. Webb.

  + 100 ii.   Ida Sue Burks.

74. William Randolph[10] Hess (Margaret[9] Daveiss, Joseph[8] Davis, James[7], Nathaniel[6] Davis (2), Robert[5] Davis (1), Elizabeth[4] Hughes, Nicketti[3] Powhatan, Cleopatra[2], Chief[1] Powhatan) was born December 03, 1793 in Mercer County, Kentucky, and died April 24, 1838. He married **Sophia Weston Dyer** June 04, 1817.

Major William Randolph Hess was born the 3rd of December in 1793 in Mercer County, Kentucky. He was admitted to the bar when quite young, practiced in Shelbyville then was prominent among the lawyers who first settled Brownsville, Tennessee.

"Old Times in West Tennessee" by Joseph S. Williams, published in 1873 in Memphis had this to say about him: "Ingenious and amiable in aspect, square in build and medium in stature; his hair, for lack of a barber, usually fell low upon his broad shoulders. ...He had wit, learning and elocution, spritely in debate, with all the dignity of a professional man, yet he was modest and retiring. ...Few men in so brief a career attained to a higher degree of eminence. His genius and learning, however, were counterbalanced by a too great fondness for personal ease and self gratification."

Major Hess was Worshipful Master of Jackson Masonic Lodge in 1824—25. He died April 24, 1838.

Sophia was born April 14, 1800 in Hawkins County, Tennessee, the daughter of Major Joel Dyer earlier of Murfreesboro.

Child of William Hess and Sophia Dyer is:

  + 101 i.   Katherine Malvina[11] Hess, born March 19, 1818; died March 24, 1875.

75. Dr. Nelson Irving[10] Hess (Margaret[9] Daveiss, Joseph[8] Davis, James[7], Nathaniel[6] Davis (2), Robert[5] Davis (1), Elizabeth[4] Hughes, Nicketti[3] Powhatan, Cleopatra[2], Chief[1] Powhatan) was born March 29, 1795, and died October 02, 1868 in Trenton, Gibson County, Tennessee. He married **(1) Elizabeth Dyer**. He married **(2) Adeline Northcutt** 1829. She was born 1809, and died August 07, 1837. He married **(3) Catherine Hill**, daughter of John Hill. and Martha D. She was born 1813, and died September 12, 1895 in Clinton, Kentucky.

Notes for Dr. Nelson Irving Hess:

He first married Elizabeth Dyer [could have been Mary Elizabeth as there is reference to his first wife, Mary, in early records]. They had one child, Robert Henry, born in 1824 and died in 1825. He then married Adeline Northcutt, who was born in 1809, and died August 7, 1837. Their children were Elizabeth Hess who married Professor W.A. Jones, Mary Adeline Hess who married Col. Edward Crossland, Marian Wallace Hess who married a Mr. Jackson.

After Adeline's death Nelson married Catherine Hill (who had a sister living with them - age 49 - in the 1860 Trenton census) Their children were Nelson I. Hess II, John Hill Hess, Andrew Jackson "Hick" Hess, Sarah Isabelle Hess, James Ferdinand Hess, Louisiana Jane Hess, and Catherine Augusta Hess.

According to an oil portrait painted in his 30's or 40's, Dr. Hess was clean shaven with dark hair worn long, a very distinguished looking man. His features resemble those of his mother, Margaret Daveiss Hess, and his uncle, Joseph Hamilton Daveiss.

Nelson was a Doctor of Medicine as well as a Presbyterian minister. He began his medical practice in Jackson, Tennessee in 1825, then settled in Trenton and is considered one of that town's founders. He participated in Tennessee's second Constitutional Convention in 1834, was a Bank of Tennessee director, Gibson County commissioner in 1830, Trenton Postmaster in 1850 and early pastor of Trenton Presbyterian Church.

We in the family enjoy several accounts of his humor and will record one example:

The History of the Cumberland Presbyterian Church by McDonnold, published in 1888, p. 148 says, "The country west of the Tennessee River was bought from the Indians in 1819. It was settled rapidly. Many Cumberland Presbyterians were among its pioneers. An anecdote of the Rev. N.I. Hess, Cumberland Presbyterian minister, who had explored all of West Tennessee before it was bought from the Indians is here given. When the friends of the Mobile and Ohio R.R. were making a canvass to secure subscriptions to its stock they employed two orators, one a distinguished Congressman and the other the Rev. Hess. At each barbeque Hess would tell of some incident of his early travels and adventures in that very neighborhood before the country belonged to the White men, and would so adroitly use it as to leave the Congressman clear behind in popularity. The Congressman chafed at this and resolved on a remedy. He determined to transfer their canvass to the other side of their field where he supposed the pioneer tours of Hess had not extended. The plan was agreed to and a barbeque was prepared at a big spring on the other side of the district. The Congressman spoke first, and being confident of victory, he made a great effort. When Hess arose his first sentence was, 'just forty years ago, in company with two Red men of the forest, I drank water out of that spring,' and then with more than his wonted felicity, he painted the wonderful progress and grander destiny of West Tennessee."

Notes for Catherine Hill:

Died at the residence of relatives, Dr. and Mrs. W.A. Jordan of Clinton, Kentucky.

Children of Nelson Hess and Catherine Hill are:

+ 102   i.   Dr. Nelson Irving[11] Hess II, born April 25, 1841; died May 14, 1921.

+ 103   ii.   John Hill Hess, born November 09, 1842.
  104   iii.   Andrew Jackson "Hick" Hess, born October 01, 1844.
+ 105   iv.   Sarah Isabelle Hess, born October 17, 1846.
+ 106   v.   James Ferdinand Hess, born February 04, 1848; died 1928.
+ 107   vi.   Louisiana Jane Hess, born October 05, 1850; died September 21, 1894.
+ 108   vii.   Catherine Augusta Hess, born October 23, 1853.

Left: Margaret Hess Jones. **Right:** *Col. William Buchanan Jones*

Children of Nelson Hess and Adeline Northcutt are:
+ 109   i.   Elizabeth[11] Hess, born July 18, 1837 in Trenton, Tennessee; died June 08, 1896 in Malden, Missouri.
  110   ii.   Mary Adeline Hess, born December 18, 1830 in Trenton, Gibson County, Tennessee. She married Col. Edward Crossland.
+ 111   iii.   Marian Wallace Hess, born March 29, 1833; died October 22, 1857.

77. Margaret W.[10] Hess (Margaret[9] Daveiss, Joseph[8] Davis, James[7], Nathaniel[6] Davis (2), Robert[5] Davis (1), Elizabeth[4] Hughes, Nicketti[3] Powhatan, Cleopatra[2], Chief[1] Powhatan) was born November 17, 1798. She married **William Buchanan Jones** October 15, 1817. He was born 1797.

Notes for William Buchanan Jones:
   William Buchanan Jones was a lawyer, poisoned during the Carpet Bagger days of early Texas history.
Children of Margaret Hess and William Jones are:
  112   i.   Marian[11] Jones married (1) Spaniard; married (2) Dan Rice.

   Marian first married a wealthy Spaniard whose name we have not discovered. After his death, she married an entertainer of some note, Dan Rice. See information listed under his name.

   Dan Rice, called the king of circus clowns, owned and operated a showboat, which sailed the Mississippi presenting a series of entertainments. In the Memphis area he tied up along the bluff at the foot of Madison or Monroe. For his 1874 exhibit a Madame MaCarte had joined his troupe billed as a most daring bareback rider. An August 18, 1949 Commercial Appeal article, "Strange As It Seems," reminisced, "Dan Rice, a circus clown once gave $32,000 to President Lincoln for the benefit of wounded soldiers and their dependents."

  113   ii.   Hess Jones.
  114   iii.   Nancy Jones.

78. Nancy Adair[10] Hess (Margaret[9] Daveiss, Joseph[8] Davis, James[7], Nathaniel[6] Davis (2), Robert[5] Davis (1), Elizabeth[4] Hughes, Nicketti[3] Powhatan, Cleopatra[2], Chief[1] Powhatan) was born October 14, 1800 in Kentucky, and died March 04, 1854 in Gibson County, Tennessee. She married **Alexander Hamilton Cresap**, son of James Cresap and Polly Shellhorn. He was born February 12, 1805 in Old Town, Maryland, and died September 06, 1892.

Ancestry of Alexander:

Thomas Cresap was born in Skipton Yorkshire, England in 1694. He emigrated to America in 1710 - was a Colonel in the Prov. Militia, a Patriot. He married Hannah Johnson April 30, 1727. She was born in 1705 and died January 31, 1787 in Old Town, Hartford County, Maryland. Thomas died in Old Town Maryland in 1790. For more information consult the Maryland Archives, Volume 48, p. 16.

Their son, Michael Cresap, was born June 29, 1742 in Old Town, Maryland, married Mary Whitehead August 4, 1764 in St. Paul's Episcopal Church, Philadelphia, Pennsylvania. He was a Captain in the Revolutionary Army and was carrying troops to General Washington in Maryland when he became ill and died October 18, 1775 in New York where he was buried in the Trinity Church Yard with full Military Honors.

Michael's son, James Michael Cresap, was born 1773 in Old Town, Maryland, married Polly Shellhorn, and died 1823.

It is their son, Alexander Hamilton Cresap who married Nancy Adair Hess.

Child of Nancy Hess and Alexander Cresap is:

+ 115   i.   Nelson Adair[11] Cresap, born September 17, 1841 in Madison County, Alabama; died December 16, 1935 in Gibson County, Tennessee.

79. Narcissa F.[10] Hess (Margaret[9] Daveiss, Joseph[8] Davis, James[7], Nathaniel[6] Davis (2), Robert[5] Davis (1), Elizabeth[4] Hughes, Nicketti[3] Powhatan, Cleopatra[2], Chief[1] Powhatan) was born August 23, 1802. She married **(1) Kinchen Welborn**. She married **(2) Bill Erwin**.

Notes for Narcissa F. Hess:

Narcissa married first, Kinchen Welborn, who deserted her at some point. After a wait of seven years, she declared him dead and married Bill Erwin/Irwin. Mr. Welborn turned up suddenly to everyone's dismay. Narcissa's Mother, Margaret Daveiss Hess, instructed her sons to take care of him—and make a good job of it—if he caused any trouble for Narcissa and her husband, Bill. Apparently Mr. Welborn got the message.

Child of Narcissa Hess and Kinchen Welborn is:

+ 116   i.   William J. Nelson[11] Welborn.

Children of Narcissa Hess and Bill Erwin are:

   117   i.   Child[11] Erwin, born 1841.
   118   ii.   Sterling Brewer Erwin, born May 22, 1842.
   119   iii.   Child Erwin, born 1844.

80. Maria L.[10] Hess (Margaret[9] Daveiss, Joseph[8] Davis, James[7], Nathaniel[6] Davis (2), Robert[5] Davis (1), Elizabeth[4] Hughes, Nicketti[3] Powhatan, Cleopatra[2], Chief[1] Powhatan) was born December 03, 1805 in Williamson County, Tennessee, and died in Malden, Missouri. She married **William Irwin Price** January 02, 1839. He was born December 03, 1805 in North Carolina, and died in Malden, Missouri.

Children of Maria Hess and William Price are:

   120   i.   Lucy[11] Price.
+ 121   ii.   Maria Annie Price.
+ 122   iii.   Kate Price.
+ 123   iv.   William Hess Price, born July 24, 1842 in Gibson County, Tennessee; died July 08, 1912 in Malden, Missouri.

82.   James A.W.[10] **Hess** (Margaret[9] Daveiss, Joseph[8] Davis, James[7], Nathaniel[6] Davis (2), Robert[5] Davis (1), Elizabeth[4] Hughes, Nicketti[3] Powhatan, Cleopatra[2], Chief[1] Powhatan) was born November 20, 1810 in Williamson County, Tennessee, and died February 06, 1885 in Gibson County, Tennessee. He married **(1) Louisa B. Webb** December 08, 1831. She was born November 15, 1815, and died October 18, 1840. He married **(2) Gabrilla Lankford** September 01, 1841 in Denmark, Madison County, Tennessee, daughter of Thomas Lankford and Joanna Eley. She was born September 07, 1820 in Louisburg, Franklin County, North Carolina, and died July 02, 1897 in Old Shiloh, Gibson County, Tennessee.

Maj. James A.W. Hess

Notes for James A.W. Hess:

James Augustus Washington Hamilton Irwin Warren Montgomery Enos Hess, referred to in these writings as James A.W., was born on a farm in Middle Tennessee. At age 17 he moved to West Tennessee to help his brother-in-law survey part of the Chickasaw lands. In addition to this work he served for years as Sheriff, was Gibson County Surveyor in 1874, served as election commissioner in the 1876 Democratic primary, was a farmer and landowner. His military rank dates from the early days of the Civil War, when he was leader of the Home Guard.

In 1926 N.A. Cresap wrote of him, "The first survey for streets was made by Major James Hess, a surveyor who lived at Shiloh...and plotted out the streets almost as they are today."

He was spoken of very highly by his neice-in-law, Rebecca McLemore Welborn, in her paper, Rebecca's Journal written in 1864 and printed in the Tennessee Genealogical Magazine/Ansearchin' News - Summer 2000. She says, "—he has all the virtues that it takes to constitute an honest, honorable man,—" and other words of praise.

Hess Hall a dormitory at the University of Tennessee, Knoxville Campus was named in honor of a grandson, James Preston Hess, son of Walter Scott Hess and Mattie Preston.

At his death in 1885, James A.W. was buried at Shiloh, and then later was moved to his final resting place—Rose Hill Cemetery, Humboldt.

[The surveyor's compass and chain he used all his life are in the McClung Collection at Knoxville.]

Notes for Louisa B. Webb:

Children of James A.W. and Louisa who did not live to adulthood:
>   William Nelson Hess (b) Nov. 12, 1832   (d) Oct.13, 1836
>   Louisiana Narcissa Hess (b) Dec. 25, 1836 (d) Aug. 20, 1838
>   Louisa Hess   (b) Sept. 30, 1840   (d) Oct. 9, 1840

Notes for Gabrilla Lankford:

The earliest Lankford ancestor we find in America is William, who came from England about 1725 and settled in King and Queen County, Virginia. He later moved to Isle of Wight County, Virginia.

The child of William : Thomas Lankford married Elizabeth Weitzel November 9, 1769 in Southhampton County, Virginia.

Their children:

(1) Thomas Elisha Lankford, born 1773 in Southhampton County, Virginia and died 1834 in Madison County, Tennessee, married Joanna Eley, born April 8, 1777 in Franklin County, North Carolina, died 1846

Gabrilla Lankford Hess

in Denmark, Madison County, Tennessee, daughter of Josiah Eley and Charity Denby. Parents of Charity were James Denby [died April 20, 1795 in N.C.] and Patience Norfleet. Charity was born in Franklin County, N.C. and died there, after 1803. She and Josiah married about 1772. His parents were Michael Eley and Elizabeth Denson [daughter of William Denson and Amy Small]. Michael was born about 1710 in Isle of Wight County, Virginia and died there April 6, 1769. He married Elizabeth about 1738 in Virginia. She was born in Isle of Wight County and died there, after 1769.

*Michael served as Gentleman Justice [Justice of the Peace] appointed November 1, 1757 and as High Sheriff appointed November 5, 1767, Isle of Wight County, Virginia. Proof: Seventeenth Century Isle of Wight County, Virginia by John Bodie—p. 705.

*This is an excellent reference for those seeking membership in either D.A.R. or Colonial Dames of America. This line is proved to my generation. [MKA]

Parents of Michael were Robert Eley and Marthe Doughtie, daughter of James Doughtie. Robert was son of Robert who was son of Robert, the first of our line to come to America. This became very confusing - dealing with three generations of Robert Eleys and not much more to go on. [LJG]

(2) Jesse Lankford born 1777 in Southhampton County, Virginia and died March 3, 1849, married Miriam Duck. She was born in 1784 and died July 18, 1870 in Elm Hill, Southhampton County, Virginia. Our Cisco, Texas cousin, Eugene Lankford, lists Jesse's mother as Bettie Wester [most likely Bettie for Elizabeth and Wester as the way Weitzel sounded to the recorder - who died at Elm Hill about 1820]. Miriam had four children when she married Jesse: William, Martha, Nancy and Sally. She and Jesse had a son, William who never married. Miriam and Jesse remained at Elm Hill until their deaths, he at age 72 and she at age 86.

Children of James Hess and Louisa Webb are:

+ 124   i.   Margaret Eley[11] Hess, born January 30, 1835 in Shiloh, Gibson County, Tennessee; died December 04, 1869.

   125   ii.   Mary Augusta Hess, born May 27, 1839; died July 01, 1921. She married James A. Cox.

Newlyweds James A. and Mary Augusta "Gus" Hess Cox.

Notes for Mary Augusta Hess:

Nicknamed Gus, Mary Augusta lived with her half brother, Zach. Both were unmarried. Mr. Cox came often to the house to visit. She would tell her brother, "Mr. Cox came by to see you today. Finally

*The seven Hess sisters and one brother. **Top row from left**: Katherine "Kittie" Nelson Hess Johnson, Walter Scott Hess, Susan "Sue" Hess Dunlap, Willietta "Will" Hess Dunlap. **Bottom row from left**: Jane "Jennie E" Hamilton Hess Campbell, Eliza Ann "Lyde" Hess Thomas, Nancy "Nan" Henry Hess Bready, half-sister Mary Augusta "Gus" Hess Cox.*

Zach told her, "Gus don't you know Mr. Cox is coming to see you, not me." Soon after, Gus and Mr. Cox were married. She was 61, he 71. Gus was his sixth wife.

Children of James Hess and Gabrilla Lankford are:
+ 126   i.   Eliza Ann[11] Hess, born June 20, 1842.
   127   ii.   James Jones Hess, born July 08, 1843; died November 21, 1862 in Chattanooga, Tennessee.

Notes for James Jones Hess:
   James Jones Hess died November 21, 1862, in the Battle of Chattanooga during the War Between the States. Not married, died age 19, two weeks after entering the War.

   128   iii.   Nancy Henry Hess, born September 27, 1844; died November 23, 1916. She married Issac N. Bready.
+ 129   iv.   Susan Hess, born April 19, 1846.
+ 130   v.   Willietta Hess, born October 31, 1847; died August 22, 1928 in Gibson County, Tennessee.
   131   vi.   Thomas Lankford Hess, born May 17, 1849; died August 14, 1900.
+ 132   vii.   Katherine Nelson Hess, born December 04, 1850; died September 12, 1926.
+ 133   viii.   Jane Hamilton Hess, born August 27, 1852; died January 29, 1926 in Humboldt, Tennessee.

134 ix. Hessie Hess, born November 17,
          1854; died July 09, 1858.
+ 135 x. Walter Scott Hess, born June 30,
          1858; died October 09, 1933.

83. Harvey[10] Davis (James Harvey[9], Joseph[8], James[7], Nathaniel[6] Davis (2), Robert[5] Davis (1), Elizabeth[4] Hughes, Nicketti[3] Powhatan, Cleopatra[2], Chief[1] Powhatan)

Children of Harvey Davis are:
       136 i.   Annie[11] Davis.
+ 137 ii. Henrietta Davis.
+ 138 iii. Harvey Davis.

A 1924 visit to Mattie (top right) and Walter S. Hess (bottom right) by "Fayette" Dunlap, Kate, Sue, Will and Jane.

95. Rose C.[10] Davis (John[9], Joseph[8], James[7], Nathaniel[6] Davis (2), Robert[5] Davis (1), Elizabeth[4] Hughes, Nicketti[3] Powhatan, Cleopatra[2], Chief[1] Powhatan) was born 1830 in Daveiss County, Kentucky, and died August 13, 1854 in Owensboro, Daveiss County, Kentucky. She married **Nimrod Bryant Allen**. He was born 1822 in Mason County, Kentucky, and died in Daveiss County, Kentucky.

Child of Rose Davis and Nimrod Allen is:
+ 139 i. Nimrod Bryant[11] Allen, Jr., born November 08, 1852 in Daveiss County, Kentucky; died March 13, 1931 in West Palm Beach, Florida.

Generation No. 11

100. Ida Sue[11] Burks (Charles Martin[10], William Pinkney[9], Richard[8], Samuel[7], Samuel[6], Mary[5] Davis, Elizabeth[4] Hughes, Nicketti[3] Powhatan, Cleopatra[2], Chief[1] Powhatan) She married **Albert Newton Gilliam**.

Child of Ida Burks and Albert Gilliam is:
+ 140 i. Ellis C.[12] Gilliam, born September 15, 1910; died May 06, 1999.

101. Katherine Malvina[11] Hess (William Randolph[10], Margaret[9] Daveiss, Joseph[8] Davis, James[7], Nathaniel[6] Davis (2), Robert[5] Davis (1), Elizabeth[4] Hughes, Nicketti[3] Powhatan, Cleopatra[2], Chief[1] Powhatan) was born March 19, 1818, and died March 24, 1875. She married **(1) Charles G. Feild** 1839. She married **(2) James McConnell** December 07, 1852.

Children of Katherine Hess and Charles Feild are:
       141 i.   Willetta[12] Feild. She married Peter Brown.
+ 142 ii. Henry Allison Feild.
       143 iii. Thomas Blackburn Feild, born 1843; died 1862.

Children of Katherine Hess and James McConnell are:

    144   i. Lee[12] McConell.

    145   ii. Kitty McConell. She married James Young.

102. Dr. Nelson Irving[11] Hess II (Nelson Irving[10] Hess, Margaret[9] Daveiss, Joseph[8] Davis, James[7], Nathaniel[6] Davis (2), Robert[5] Davis (1), Elizabeth[4] Hughes, Nicketti[3] Powhatan, Cleopatra[2], Chief[1] Powhatan) was born April 25, 1841, and died May 14, 1921. He married **(1) Sallie Joyce** January 30, 1865. She was born February 10, 1845, and died November 22, 1865. He married **(2) Ida Rebecca Seay** November 20, 1867. She was born February 19, 1847, and died January 22, 1870. He married **(3) Rebecca Ellen Layton** December 15, 1870. She was born May 30, 1850, and died February 16, 1885. He married **(4) Sidney Nimon Layton** July 18, 1885. She was born December 27, 1858, and died May 30, 1945.

Notes for Dr. Nelson Irving Hess II:

    Served in Confederate Army April 1861 through April 1865. Was a surgeon with General Nathan Bedford Forrest's Cavalry - see war record. Graduated in Medicine in St. Louis, Missouri March 8, 1866. practiced 54 years in Gibson and Crockett counties.

Child of Dr. Hess II and Ida Seay is:

+ 146   i. Annie Catherine[12] Hess, born September 11, 1868; died December 22, 1946.

Children of Dr. Hess II and Rebecca Layton are:

+ 147   i. Edna Isabelle[12] Hess, born December 08, 1871.

    148   ii. Nelson Howell Hess, born February 12, 1873; died 1879.

+ 149   iii. Sallie Emma Hess, born March 20, 1875; died April 01, 1958.

    150   iv. Idella Harwell Hess, born August 27, 1877; died February 15, 1878.

+ 151   v. Dr. Frizzell Pride Hess, born February 07, 1879.

    152   vi. Burney Foster Hess, born July 13, 1881; died February 21, 1892.

Children of Dr. Hess II and Sidney Layton are:

    153   i. Sidney Nelson[12] Hess, born January 24, 1887. She married Wilson Wade Spence April 30, 1907; born February 27, 1884; died November 08, 1938.

    154   ii. Marion Elizabeth Hess, born July 18, 1889. She married B.S. Sorelle March 16, 1912; born October 21, 1884; died January 04, 1942.

    155   iii. Ella Vaden Hess, born March 17, 1891. She married L.H. Jones December 25, 1912; born November 26, 1885; died January 05, 1957.

+ 156   iv. Nelson Irvin Hess III, born January 31, 1893.

+ 157   v. Cas Goodloe Hess, born February 18, 1895.

+ 158   vi. Jamye Willard Hess, born October 20, 1897.

103. John Hill[11] Hess (Nelson Irving[10], Margaret[9] Daveiss, Joseph[8] Davis, James[7], Nathaniel[6] Davis (2), Robert[5] Davis (1), Elizabeth[4] Hughes, Nicketti[3] Powhatan, Cleopatra[2], Chief[1] Powhatan) was born November 09, 1842.

Child of John Hill Hess is:

    159   i. Irene[12] Hess.

Seated left to right: James Ferdinand Hess, John William Hess, Price Faris Hess.

105. Sarah Isabelle[11] Hess (Nelson Irving[10], Margaret[9] Daveiss, Joseph[8] Davis, James[7], Nathaniel[6] Davis (2), Robert[5] Davis (1), Elizabeth[4] Hughes, Nicketti[3] Powhatan, Cleopatra[2], Chief[1] Powhatan) was born October 17, 1846. She married **W.A. Jordan**.

Children of Sarah Hess and W. Jordan are:
    160   i. Kate[12] Jordan.
    161 ii. Horace Jordan.

106. James Ferdinand[11] Hess (Nelson Irving[10], Margaret[9] Daveiss, Joseph[8] Davis, James[7], Nathaniel[6] Davis (2), Robert[5] Davis (1), Elizabeth[4] Hughes, Nicketti[3] Powhatan, Cleopatra[2], Chief[1] Powhatan) was born February 04, 1848, and died 1928. He married **M. Price Faris** January 15, 1902. She was born 1877, and died 1934.

Children of James Hess and M. Faris are:
  + 162   i. John William "Jack"[12] Hess, born 1902; died 1940.
    163 ii. James Ferdinand Hess II.

107. Louisiana Jane[11] Hess (Nelson Irving[10], Margaret[9] Daveiss, Joseph[8] Davis, James[7], Nathaniel[6] Davis (2), Robert[5] Davis (1), Elizabeth[4] Hughes, Nicketti[3] Powhatan, Cleopatra[2],

Chief^1 Powhatan) was born October 05, 1850, and died September 21, 1894. She married **J.S. Cooper**.

Children of Louisiana Hess and J. Cooper are:
- 164   i.   Arthur F.^{12} Cooper.
- 165   ii.   Fanny L. Cooper.
- 166   iii.   Isabelle Cooper.

108. Catherine Augusta^{11} Hess (Nelson Irving^{10}, Margaret^9 Daveiss, Joseph^8 Davis, James^7, Nathaniel^6 Davis (2), Robert^5 Davis (1), Elizabeth^4 Hughes, Nicketti^3 Powhatan, Cleopatra^2, Chief^1 Powhatan) was born October 23, 1853. She married **Henry Clay O'Bryan**.

Child of Catherine Hess and Henry O'Bryan is:
- 167   i.   Evangeline^{12} O'Bryan. She married Fred C. Hurst.

109. Elizabeth^{11} Hess (Nelson Irving^{10}, Margaret^9 Daveiss, Joseph^8 Davis, James^7, Nathaniel^6 Davis (2), Robert^5 Davis (1), Elizabeth^4 Hughes, Nicketti^3 Powhatan, Cleopatra^2, Chief^1 Powhatan) was born July 18, 1837 in Trenton, Tennessee, and died June 08, 1896 in Malden, Missouri. She married **W.A. Edward Jones** February 16, 1857 in Trenton, Tennessee. He was born January 07, 1834 in LaGrange, Tennessee, and died November 30, 1883 in St. Francis, Ar.

"Lizzie" Hess, daughter of Adeline Northcutt and Dr. N.I. Hess, was married to Professor W.A. Jones in Trenton, Tennessee, 16 February 1857 at "Hesse-Castle," [home of the bride's parents]. Officiating was the Rev. Guilford Jones, President of Andrew College in Trenton.

Children of Elizabeth Hess and W. Jones are:
- 168   i.   Marian^{12} Jones, born January 14, 1858 in Union City, Tennessee; died December 18, 1885 in Malden, Missouri. She married Joseph A. McGaugh June 24, 1879 in Clarkton, Missouri.
- 169   ii.   Nelson Hess Jones, born February 04, 1865 in Trenton, Gibson County, Tennessee; died February 17, 1913 in Clarendon, Arkansas. He married Katie Dunn June 18, 1893 in Malden, Missouri; died July 08, 1899 in Malden, Missouri.
- 170   iii.   Edward Crossland Jones, born July 25, 1870 in Union City, Tennessee; died February 21, 1907 in Little Rock, Ar. He married Minnie Margaret Price November 29, 1897 in Union city, Tennessee; born March 10, 1872 in Trenton, Gibson County, Tennessee; died March 08, 1947 in Memphis, Shelby County, Tennessee.

111. Marian Wallace^{11} Hess (Nelson Irving^{10}, Margaret^9 Daveiss, Joseph^8 Davis, James^7, Nathaniel^6 Davis (2), Robert^5 Davis (1), Elizabeth^4 Hughes, Nicketti^3 Powhatan, Cleopatra^2, Chief^1 Powhatan) was born March 29, 1833, and died October 22, 1857. She married **Mr. Jackson**.

Child of Marian Hess and Mr. Jackson is:
- 171   i.   Marian W.^{12} Jackson, born October 12, 1857.

115.   Nelson Adair[11] **Cresap** (Nancy Adair[10] Hess, Margaret[9] Daveiss, Joseph[8] Davis, James[7], Nathaniel[6] Davis (2), Robert[5] Davis (1), Elizabeth[4] Hughes, Nicketti[3] Powhatan, Cleopatra[2], Chief[1] Powhatan) was born September 17, 1841 in Madison County, Alabama, and died December 16, 1935 in Gibson County, Tennessee.   He married **Martha Alice Love** December 23, 1875 in Humboldt, Tennessee.   She was born June 14, 1853 in Gibson County, Tennessee, and died September 26, 1902.

Notes for Nelson Adair Cresap:
   "Major" Nelson Adair Cresap was a 1st Lt. in the C.S.A. military.

Children of Nelson Cresap and Martha Love are:
   + 172   i.   Anna Bell[12] Cresap, born May 29, 1888 in Gibson County, Tennessee; died March 28, 1947 in Lake Comorant, Mississippi.
      173   ii.   Fannie Hess Cresap, born November 24, 1877; died June 28, 1879.
   + 174   iii.   Charles Edgar Cresap, born 1881 in Gibson County, Tennessee; died 1968.
   + 175   iv.   Katherine Louise Cresap, born 1879 in Trenton, Tennessee; died 1949.
      176   v.   Joe Sid Cresap, born 1884; died 1927 in Texas. He married Bessie Senter.
      177   vi.   James Lawson Cresap, born 1883; died 1927. He married Mary Russell Bower.
      178   vii.   Walter Augustus Cresap, born 1885; died 1918. He married Florence Taylor.

116.   William J. Nelson[11] **Welborn** (Narcissa F.[10] Hess, Margaret[9] Daveiss, Joseph[8] Davis, James[7], Nathaniel[6] Davis (2), Robert[5] Davis (1), Elizabeth[4] Hughes, Nicketti[3] Powhatan, Cleopatra[2], Chief[1] Powhatan) He married **Bernetta Crossland**.   She was born January 03, 1829, and died October 21, 1845.

Child of William Welborn and Bernetta Crossland is:
      179   i.   James K. Polk[12] Welborn, born 1845; died April 1865.

121.   Maria Annie[11] **Price** (Maria L.[10] Hess, Margaret[9] Daveiss, Joseph[8] Davis, James[7], Nathaniel[6] Davis (2), Robert[5] Davis (1), Elizabeth[4] Hughes, Nicketti[3] Powhatan, Cleopatra[2], Chief[1] Powhatan) She married **Mr. Stewart**.

Children of Maria Price and Mr. Stewart are:
      180   i.   Linnie[12] Stewart. She married Wiley Blakemore.

Notes for Wiley Blakemore:
   Mr. Wiley Blakemore was a carpenter who worked for John Elbert Campbell.

      181   ii.   Irene Stewart. She married Mister Russell.

122.   Kate[11] **Price** (Maria L.[10] Hess, Margaret[9] Daveiss, Joseph[8] Davis, James[7], Nathaniel[6] Davis (2), Robert[5] Davis (1), Elizabeth[4] Hughes, Nicketti[3] Powhatan, Cleopatra[2], Chief[1] Powhatan) She married **The Rev. William Thomas Bennett**, son of William Bennett and Rebecca Powell. He was born October 04, 1836 in Humboldt, Tennessee, and died August 18, 1879 in Humboldt, Tennessee.

Notes for Kate Price:

Catherine Louisa—called "Kate" graduated The Female Collegiate Institute of Trenton, Tennessee, June 21, 1861.

She married The Reverend William Thomas Bennett at the Shiloh Baptist Church, Shiloh, Tennessee. The service was performed by the bride's uncle, The Reverend Nelson I. Hess of Trenton.

Dr. Hess was the son of Margaret Daveiss Hess and both are mentioned elsewhere in this book. The Bennett Family Bible, containing their Marriage Certificate, is now in the possession of their great-granddaughter, Mary Elizabeth Tribble [Mrs. James Cox of Ft. Lauderdale, Florida].

Notes for The Rev. William Thomas Bennett:

Was Professor of Greek and Ancient Languages at Madison College, which was destroyed by Federal Forces during the War Between the States.

Later ordained into the Ministry, he traveled long distances over rough country and bad roads to carry the Gospel to remote country districts. Riding a large, fiery sorrel mule named Bucephalus, and with his co-worker, the Rev. Sion Skipper, he covered the northwestern counties of West Tennessee.

When war came the Rev. Sion joined the Northern Forces while William volunteered with the Confederate Army. He enlisted May 28, 1861, serving as Private in Company B, 12th Regiment, with Captain Ben Sanderford, until the Battle of Shiloh. He was promoted to Chaplain December 19, 1862, and was stationed in Union City, Tennessee and later in Columbus, Kentucky. He served with Colonel G.R.M. Russell, in the Battle of Belmont, and as Chaplain with General Nathan Bedford Forrest until the end of the war. This information, with other records, can be found with the Application for Membership by Mary Elizabeth Tribble Cox in the United Daughters of the Confederacy.

Soon after hostilities ended William visited his old friend and co-worker, the Rev. Skipper and was happy to find that political differences had not "cooled the Christian love that had united them."

He married a young lady he had known from childhood [Catherine Louisa "Kate" Price - descendent of Margaret Daveiss and William Hess] and resumed his ministerial work through heat, cold and many difficulties including failing health.

At age forty-three, the Reverend William Thomas Bennett died, leaving his wife and three surviving children: Howard Clifton (9), Estelle Rebecca (6), and Elsie (2). The other five children had died between 1866 and 1878.

Children of Kate Price and William Bennett are:

+ 182   i.   Elsie Bess[12] Bennett, born October 06, 1877 in Fruitland, Tennessee; died September 04, 1936 in Memphis, Tennessee.

+ 183   ii.   Estelle Rebecca Bennett, born August 19, 1874 in Humboldt, Tennessee; died August 19, 1953 in Vidalia, Georgia.

+ 184   iii.   Howard Clifton Bennett, born May 09, 1870 in Humboldt, Tennessee; died August 25, 1912 in Cleburne, Texas.

123. William Hess[11] Price (Maria L.[10] Hess, Margaret[9] Daveiss, Joseph[8] Davis, James[7], Nathaniel[6] Davis (2), Robert[5] Davis (1), Elizabeth[4] Hughes, Nicketti[3] Powhatan, Cleopatra[2], Chief[1] Powhatan) was born July 24, 1842 in Gibson County, Tennessee, and died July 08, 1912 in Malden, Missouri. He married **(1) Margaret Elizabeth Adamson** January 08, 1868 in Gibson County, Tennessee, daughter of William Adamson and Margaret Martin. She was born August 19, 1841 in

Pulaski, Tennessee, and died March 13, 1901 in Union City, Tennessee. He married **(2) Lizzie McGinnis** abt. 1905.

William Hess Price served in Co. K. 12th Tennessee Infantry Regiment, C.S.A. He enlisted in Humboldt, Tennessee in 1861 in Captain Cannon's Company, Colonel Russell's Regiment. The 12th Tennessee and the 47th were consolidated and known as the 12 and 47 Consolidated Regiment. W.H. Price was present when General Joseph E. Johnson surrendered his army to General Sherman at Greensboro, North Carolina, April 1865, and afterward returned home.

Margaret's people were from Scotland [Scotch Presbyterian] and when they came to this country they changed the spelling of their name from McAdamson to Adamson. They lived near Pulaski, Tennessee. Later her foster brother, Frederick Adamson and her step-mother moved to Trenton, Tennessee where they later died and were buried. [re: F.C. Price of Columbia, Ms.]

Children of William Price and Margaret Adamson are:

185   i.   Minnie Margaret[12] Price, born March 10, 1872 in Trenton, Gibson County, Tennessee; died March 08, 1947 in Memphis, Shelby County, Tennessee. She married (1) Edward Crossland Jones November 29, 1897 in Union city, Tennessee; born July 25, 1870 in Union City, Tennessee; died February 21, 1907 in Little Rock, Ar.. She married (2) Ed Lee Riley December 25, 1920.
186   ii.   Cuthbert Price, born November 27, 1876.
+ 187 iii. Annie Leslie Price, born May 09, 1879.
188   iv.   Vernon Price, born April 04, 1882.
+ 189 v.   Frederick Carlton Price, born August 10, 1884 in Troy, Tennessee; died July 07, 1965 in Columbia, Mississippi.

124. Margaret Eley[11] Hess (James A.W.[10], Margaret[9] Daveiss, Joseph[8] Davis, James[7], Nathaniel[6] Davis (2), Robert[5] Davis (1), Elizabeth[4] Hughes, Nicketti[3] Powhatan, Cleopatra[2], Chief[1] Powhatan) was born January 30, 1835 in Shiloh, Gibson County, Tennessee, and died December 04, 1869. She married **Macon Senter** October 16, 1852 in Shiloh, Gibson County, Tennessee, son of Alvin Senter and Janet. Children of Margaret Hess and Macon Senter are:

190   i.   Louisa Janet[12] Senter, born August 16, 1853.
191   ii.   Emma Jane Senter, born May 18, 1858 in Trenton, Gibson County, Tennessee.
192   iii. Ernest Senter, born May 27, 1867 in Trenton, Gibson County, Tennessee; died May 23, 1889.
193   iv.   Alvin Hess Senter, born November 21, 1869 in Trenton, Gibson County, Tennessee. He married Myrtle Bennett December 16, 1890 in Fruitland, Gibson County, Tennessee.

126. Eliza Ann[11] Hess (James A.W.[10], Margaret[9] Daveiss, Joseph[8] Davis, James[7], Nathaniel[6] Davis (2), Robert[5] Davis (1), Elizabeth[4] Hughes, Nicketti[3] Powhatan, Cleopatra[2], Chief[1] Powhatan) was born June 20, 1842. She married **James William Thomas** January 30, 1872 in Old Shiloh, son of James Thomas and Elizabeth Coppage. He was born February 12, 1825 in North Carolina, and died November 12, 1898 in Mt. Pleasant Cemetery, Gibson County, Tennessee.

Eliza Ann Hess's nickname was Lyde. She was James William Thomas's third wife, following Addie Chapman and Fanny Reeves.

Left: Eliza Ann "Lyde" Hess Thomas. Right: James William Thomas.

James William Thomas was a Confederate Veteran.

Children of Eliza Hess and James Thomas are:

+ 194   i.   Fannie Augusta[12] Thomas, born December 16, 1872.
+ 195   ii.   Benjamin Hess Thomas, born September 18, 1874.
+ 196   iii.   Ida Thomas, born November 24, 1877; died 1962 in Milan.

129. Susan[11] Hess (James A.W.[10], Margaret[9] Daveiss, Joseph[8] Davis, James[7], Nathaniel[6] Davis (2), Robert[5] Davis (1), Elizabeth[4] Hughes, Nicketti[3] Powhatan, Cleopatra[2], Chief[1] Powhatan) was born April 19, 1846. She married **William Newton Lafayette Dunlap** in November 7, 1872, son of Ebenezer Dunlap and Mary Harber. He was born October 05, 1842.

William Newton Lafayette Dunlap was always called "Fayette."

Children of Susan Hess and William Dunlap are:

+ 197   i.   Warner Ebenezer[12] Dunlap, born May 03, 1875; died January 16, 1948.
+ 198   ii.   Mary G. Dunlap, born October 14, 1876.
+ 199   iii.   Anna Kate Dunlap, born August 28, 1878.
   200   iv.   Sula E. Dunlap, born November 16, 1887. She married Walter Warmath November 23, 1921.
   201   v.   Tom W.S. Dunlap, born September 04, 1883.
   202   vi.   James Hess Dunlap, born April 08, 1880; died August 22, 1881.
   203   vii.   Florence L. Dunlap, born December 30, 1885; died November 16, 1888.

Ebenezer and Mary Harber Dunlap

The family of Winchester Monroe and Willietta Hess Dunlap. Left to right: Margaret Davies, Charles Quintard, Winchester "Chet" Monroe, Mary Katherine "Kitty," Willie Mai Chester (standing in back), Willietta, Thomas Walter, James Lafayette. (Notice the pictures of her parents, Maj. James A.W. and Gabrilla Hess on the wall.)

130. Willietta[11] Hess (James A.W.[10], Margaret[9] Daveiss, Joseph[8] Davis, James[7], Nathaniel[6] Davis (2), Robert[5] Davis (1), Elizabeth[4] Hughes, Nicketti[3] Powhatan, Cleopatra[2], Chief[1] Powhatan) was born October 31, 1847, and died August 22, 1928 in Gibson County, Tennessee. She married **Winchester Monroe Dunlap** December 23, 1875 in Gibson County, Tennessee, son of Ebenezer Dunlap and Mary Harber. He was born December 11, 1845 in Gibson County, Tennessee, and died August 16, 1938 in Gibson County, Tennessee.

Notes for Winchester Monroe Dunlap:

From notes written by Winchester M. Dunlap:

Grandfather, Robert Dunlap, moved with his family from North Carolina to Rutherford County, Tennessee about 1802 or 1803. Later he moved to Bedford County, Tennessee, then in 1821 settled in West Tennessee near what is now Jackson. There were very few settlements here at that time. Only Robert and two sons, John and Ebenezer, and one daughter, Margaret, made the change to West Tennessee.

Robert and Mary [called Polly] lived a short while near the Forked Deer River not far from the area later known as Gibson Wells. Later they bought a place about 2 miles north of Humboldt where they lived the remainder of their lives, rearing their seven children there.

Mary's parents, Elisha and Jane Harber, came from North Carolina in 1803, settled in Rutherford County, Tennessee, then moved to Gibson County, Tennessee in 1821.

An incident of interest: When this part of West Tennessee was settled there were no roads and the route between settlements was marked by "blazes" on trees [chipping away some of the bark]. Peggy Dunlap, aunt of Winchester, started from her home in what is now Madison County, to visit her mother, who lived a few miles north of what is now Gibson, Tennessee. She was riding a pony with her baby on her lap and a little dog following. After crossing the river she lost her way and stayed all night in the woods. Early next morning she heard a fowl crowing. At first light she set off to find it and in doing so came upon a man she knew who guided her to her mother's home. This gives us an idea of some of the challenges these early settlers faced.

Winchester Monroe Dunlap [called "Chet"] was buried in Rose Hill Cemetery, Humboldt, Tennessee.

Children of Willietta Hess and Winchester Dunlap are:

 - 204   i.   Margaret Davies[12] Dunlap, born October 25, 1876 in Gibson County, Tennessee; died November 26, 1928 in Gibson County, Tennessee.
 - + 205   ii.   James Lafayette Dunlap, born March 14, 1878 in Gibson County, Tennessee; died 1954.
 - + 206   iii.   Willie Mai Chester Dunlap, born November 14, 1879 in Gibson County, Tennessee; died December 26, 1940 in Gibson County, Tennessee.
 - 207   iv.   Mary Katherine Dunlap, born December 27, 1881; died January 18, 1958. She married Charles Jefferson Dodson November 24, 1926 in Humboldt, Tennessee.

Notes for Mary Katherine Dunlap:
Always called "Kitty."

 - 208   v.   Charles Quintard Campbell Dunlap, born December 07, 1884; died June 16, 1931. He married Katherine May McCary July 22, 1919 in Mobile. Alabama.
 - 209   vi.   Thomas Walter Dunlap, born July 27, 1887 in Gibson County, Tennessee; died August 04, 1901 in Gibson County, Tennessee.

132. Katherine Nelson[11] Hess (James A.W.[10], Margaret[9] Daveiss, Joseph[8] Davis, James[7], Nathaniel[6] Davis (2), Robert[5] Davis (1), Elizabeth[4] Hughes, Nicketti[3] Powhatan, Cleopatra[2], Chief[1] Powhatan) was born December 04, 1850, and died September 12, 1926. She married **Matthew Monroe Johnson**.

Notes for Katherine Nelson Hess:
Katherine Hess and Matthew Johnson had 12 children, 11 of whom married. They lived in Texas.

Children of Katherine Hess and Matthew Johnson are:

 - 210   i.   Gabrilla[12] Johnson.
 - 211   ii.   James Johnson.
 - 212   iii.   Nellie Johnson.
 - + 213   iv.   John Orgain Johnson.
 - 214   v.   Walter Johnson.
 - 215   vi.   Jennie Johnson.
 - 216   vii.   Matthew Johnson.
 - 217 viii.   Birdie Johnson.
 - 218   ix.   Mamie Johnson.
 - 219   x.   Winnie Johnson.

133. Jane Hamilton[11] **Hess** (James A.W.[10], Margaret[9] Daveiss, Joseph[8] Davis, James[7], Nathaniel[6] Davis (2), Robert[5] Davis (1), Elizabeth[4] Hughes, Nicketti[3] Powhatan, Cleopatra[2], Chief[1] Powhatan) was born August 27, 1852, and died January 29, 1926 in Humboldt, Tennessee. She married **John Elbert Campbell** January 07, 1879 in Gibson County, Tennessee, son of Levi Campbell and Lucinda Huffmaster. He was born April 06, 1851 in Grainger County, Tennessee, and died May 28, 1921 in Humboldt, Gibson County, Tennessee.

Jane Hamilton Hess Campbell and John Elbert Campbell

Jane was not a real beauty - her high cheekbones betrayed her Indian heritage, which came from Chief Powhatan.

She was a tomboy in her youth, loved horses, rode extremely well and often broke horses for her father, Major James A.W. Hess. Her husband, John E. Campbell, made her quit this wild career after she was thrown while pregnant with their first child. She was also a good shot. Son, Elbert, recalled a time when birds were ruining apples on their trees and "Mommy" shot them while the old pet coon stood by begging for them. "Elsie," the cat got her share too.

Jane was a devoted wife and mother, pleasant neighbor, thoughtful friend, wonderful cook (who did not want any children underfoot in the kitchen). Her bread, rolls, corn light bread, tea cakes and ginger cakes were the stuff of legend. In Sunday Church all the young folks fought to sit next to her for she had teacakes in her purse for weary children.

Early Sunday mornings sons, Zach and Elbert [Ross still lived at home] always showed up for breakfast, after which daughter, Lillian, played the piano and they all sang. One summer when they had closed the windows to keep the noise from the neighbors, Mrs. Matt Senter next door called on the phone and asked them to "open up again" as they really enjoyed the singing.

Jane was deathly afraid of storms, and instilled this fear in many of her children and grandchildren. She would take the hairpins from her hair, remove the stays from her corset, pile all the children in the feather bed and climb in with them. While the storm raged husband, John, sat under a light and read poetry.

Granddaughter, Lil Gardiner, recalls the telephone on their wall which you "cranked," and everybody on the line listened in—and she remembers their laundry woman who had a parrot she taught to say, "Lillian, Polly wants a cracker."

Early in her marriage, Jane started calling herself, Jennie E. instead of Jane Hamilton, because she thought it sounded "cute" with John E. They were a true love match and are buried side by side in Rose Hill Cemetery in Humboldt, Tennessee.

Levi Campbell and Lucinda Huffmaster, parents of John Elbert Campbell.

John Elbert Campbell was born April 6, 1851 in Rutledge, Grainger County, Tennessee in view of Clinch Mountain. His father, Levi, built and repaired the stagecoaches that ran between Knoxville, Tennessee and Abington, Virginia in the 1840's and 50's. In the 1950's Lil Gardiner, her mother, Lillian Johnson, cousin Marian Albright and Uncle Elbert Campbell, visited the old home place and were delighted to find it still kept in good condition by the Campbell/Wolfe cousins who owned it then. Beautiful woodwork, hand carved by Levi was still in place, and though his workshop had been moved to make way for the new road, it was still on the property. On our way we had detoured by Gatlinburg for lunch and had such delicious Country Ham, Elbert asked where they got it. The waitress replied, "Oh a little backwoods county nearby." "Where?" we asked. "Grainger County," was the reply. We each had a hard time keeping a straight face as we left the restaurant and headed for that little "backwoods" county and the home of our ancestors who turned out pretty well—thank you! John loved growing up here and called it his little mountain home. If he did everything attributed to him, he was quite a busy fellow.

At an early age, he cut cordwood for the old Peavine Railroad which ran by his family home. One day when he was chopping wood, he sliced the toes of one foot nearly off. He was home alone—in the country—no doctor nearby so he was on his own. Years later he told his children, and grandchildren how he held is toes in place and poured Copel's (Kopel's?) varnish over them and let it dry. It worked! They all saw the scar and heard the tale many times.

He was too young to fight in the War Between the States (no true Southerner calls it the Civil War), but his father and older brothers fought for the South. Even so, John had his war adventures, hiding the stock in the mountains and helping protect their food and valuables. The Yankees came to confiscate their food one day. John's Mother, Lucinda, stood at the smokehouse door and as fast as the men threw hams and slabs of bacon out, she threw them right back in. The soldiers finally got tired and went away. Another day a group of Yankees were killing all the geese in the yard. This alerted the cook, old "Aunt Laura West," and she just had time to dump the silver into the slop bucket she had prepared for the hogs. When the men entered the house, she was busily sweeping standing over the cellar door - so they never saw it. Thus she saved much of their food, and their silver.

The only livestock left on the farm was a team of oxen, which belonged to John, who was then 14. The Yankees drove them away to their camp in Knoxville. John walked all night from Rutledge to Knoxville and asked to see the Commandant. He told the Officer he had come to retrieve his oxen, as they had nothing left with which to plow and make a crop. The Commandant was so impressed that this 14 year old boy had walked so far he agreed to return the team to him and invited John to rest there that night and go home the next morning.

He received his High School education at Madison Academy in Grainger County, then attended the old Mossy Creek Academy - now Carson Newman in Jefferson County. He went through their entire curriculum in just over a year and then decided it was time to head west to make his fortune. He ran out of money at John's Creek in West Tennessee, and stopped at a Camp Meeting in Carroll County. There the McKinney family invited him to their home for dinner. He liked the country and later bought some land there for $2.00 an acre - close to Cedar Grove.

While staying with the McKinneys in Milan, John met "Chet" and "Fayette" Dunlap who were married to two of James A.W. Hess's daughters, Willietta and Susan. It was through them that he met another of Major Hess's daughters, Jane, and lost his heart forever.

John sold Lighting Rods with the Dunlap men; he sold tombstones and any thing else he could find to make some money. He always said his toughest customer was Mr. Austin Bailey. He wanted to sell him a large tombstone but every morning when he got to the Bailey's they were already out in the field. One morning he arrived at 1:00 AM and waited. Mr. Bailey was so impressed with his persistence that he bought two very large, very expensive sarcophagi.

After John and Jane married, they lived for a year with her father, Major James Augustus Washington Hamilton Irwin Warren Montgomery Enos Hess. Then John bought a farm at Old Shiloh in Gibson County, near High Hill School. This was at first a joke in the community. "John can't even grow peas on that old place, it's covered with nothing but sagegrass," was the general opinion. With good managing and hard work the land was improved and became a specimen farm in those years. It was named Oakwood Stock and Fruit Farm, and flourished with fruit trees of every kind, grapes of every variety, plums, Rose Beauty peaches, all kinds of berries, tomatoes and garden vegetables. One of the pear trees

John E and Jane Campbell with their first grandchild, Lillian Lannom Knowles.

Jane Hess Campbell with daughters. Left to right: Marian Lannom, Gay Long, Jane Hess, Lillian Johnson.

planted before 1900 was still bearing fruit in the late 1950's. His daughter, Marian Campbell (Lannom), wrote of this in journals and letters to relatives. She continues, "after family consumption there was a surplus which he processed in his canning factory and sold - mainly to Canada. He was one of the first fruit dealers to ship out of the country. He shipped tomatoes early and had to pay duty. J.D. Cody in Montreal was his buyer."

Jersey Red hogs, sheep, Holstein and Jersey cows were his specialty in stock. Zypelina was the first Jersey he purchased (from the Isle of Jersey], paying $300 for her. Everyone thought he was foolish. However, he sold and shipped her calves all over at very good prices. She and her offspring were never-failing prize winners at the Gibson County Fair in Trenton. Many in the family have silver pieces she won: butter dishes, cream sets, berry services, pickle stands and so many more. On judging day farmers were heard to lament, "Well, we might as well take our cows and go on home. Here comes Campbell with old Zyp."

His Plymouth chickens were shipped at good prices. Daughter, Marian, wrote of nights when great piles of eggs were wrapped separately in paper, placed carefully in egg baskets on cotton and muslin with a picture of a rooster and a hen pasted in the center. Next morning, off to the express office in Humboldt to be shipped. Miller maize was grown and processed in his gristmill as food for chicks, and the surplus sold and shipped. For years he subscribed to and wrote articles (out of his own experience) for Home and Farm magazine.

In May of 1899 or 1900, the family moved into the spacious four-story house John built on Fort Hill, which was on the outskirts of Humboldt. He called it "Fairview." It was built on the site of a

Family of Jane Hess Campbell and John Elbert Campbell
Pictured left to right. **Top row**: *Rev. Robert I. Long, Frances, Janie & Gay Long, Zach Campbell, Marian Johnson, Lillian Johnson, Corrinne Campbell, Lytle Bell & James Elbert Campbell, Herman Lannom.* **Second row**: *Grace Long, Robert Long, John E. Campbell, Jane Campbell holding Jane Johnson, Lillian Johnson, Lillian Lannom, Marian Lannom.* **Front row**: *John Ross Long, Dorothy Campbell, Juliet Campbell, Elizabeth Campbell, along with the un-named chicken.*

Confederate Fort, and at that time the trenches were still evident. The barracks were across the M&O Railroad on Mr. W.B. Seat's hill toward Gibson Wells. Then, sometime after 1918, he and Jane and their bachelor son, Ross, moved to a large house on 17th Avenue in Humboldt. Daughter, Lillian Johnson, had been widowed by this time and she and her three daughters, Lillian, Jane and Marian moved in with them. John acquired a sawmill and with his three sons in business with him, started a lumberyard and became a contractor and builder - often acting as his own architect. He built many fine residences. Lane Chapel, a colored church, was the first brick veneer building in Humboldt, and son, Elbert, had a hand in it. He was an expert mason.

John, Mr. George Bailey and Mr. O.C. Sharp were partners in the Humboldt Hotel built in 1917 and used until it was torn down for the Merchants State Bank in 1965. John was interested in the bank and owned stock which all of his children inherited. The bank has since merged with Union Planters (1987) and stockowners were given three and one half shares of U.P. for one M.S. share. Very nice!

He loved travel, reading was a passion with him, and he kept up with everything new. No chance was ever lost to have a photograph taken of his family. Lil Gardiner remembers that no matter what you were doing or how you were dressed, when a traveling photographer came round, you were summoned to the front yard, lined up and "shot." We are so grateful today to have all these wonderful pictures.

John E. was buried in Rose Hill Cemetery, Humboldt, Tennessee.

Children of Jane Hess and John Campbell are:
+ 220   i. Marian Lucinda[12] Campbell, born May 22, 1880 in Gibson County, Tennessee; died September 28, 1946 in Jackson, Tennessee.
+ 221   ii. Gabrilla Hess Campbell, born September 07, 1881 in Humboldt, Gibson County, Tennessee; died May 07, 1967 in Humboldt, Gibson County, Tennessee.
+ 222 iii. Levi Ross Campbell, born October 16, 1883 in Gibson County, Tennessee; died 1948 in Gibson County, Tennessee.
+ 223   iv. Lillian Jeanette Campbell, born June 30, 1885 in Gibson County, Tennessee; died May 15, 1961 in Humboldt, Gibson County, Tennessee.
+ 224   v. Zachariah Joseph Campbell, born August 18, 1887 in Gibson County, Tennessee; died March 25, 1957 in Humboldt, Gibson County, Tennessee.
+ 225   vi. James Elbert Campbell, born 1889 in Gibson County, Tennessee; died 1964 in Gibson County, Tennessee.

135. Walter Scott[11] Hess (James A.W.[10], Margaret[9] Daveiss, Joseph[8] Davis, James[7], Nathaniel[6] Davis (2), Robert[5] Davis (1), Elizabeth[4] Hughes, Nicketti[3] Powhatan, Cleopatra[2], Chief[1] Powhatan) was born June 30, 1858, and died October 09, 1933. He married **Mattie Preston** December 21, 1891.

Walter Scott Hess was educated at the International Order of Oddfellow's College in Humboldt, Tennessee, Walter was continually engaged in the field of education from the age of 18 years. He taught in Gibson County forty-two years, after which he and wife, Mattie, moved to Knoxville, Tennessee for the remainder of his life. He was a Democrat and a member of the Methodist Church.

His great nieces and nephews hated being in his classes because he was so strict and always "made examples" of them.

Children of Walter Hess and Mattie Preston are:
226   i. James Preston[12] Hess.

James Preston Hess graduated from the University of Tennessee, Knoxville where he was employed the whole of his working career. In 1924, Preston was head of the Vocational School, later moving up the chain to Secretary of the Board and Business Manager of the University, which positions he held for 33 years, until his retirement in 1965.

In 1961 the largest structure on the Campus [to that date] was completed, and named the James Preston Hess Residence Hall, in his honor. It cost 3 million dollars to build and housed 1,036 men. In an impressive ceremony, Governor Frank Clement dedicated the Hall, President Andrew Holt accepted, and paid tribute to Preston.

    227   ii. Mary Gabrilla Hess.

137. Henrietta[11] **Davis** (Harvey[10], James Harvey[9], Joseph[8], James[7], Nathaniel[6] Davis (2), Robert[5] Davis (1), Elizabeth[4] Hughes, Nicketti[3] Powhatan, Cleopatra[2], Chief[1] Powhatan) She married **Daniel Moore**.

Children of Henrietta Davis and Daniel Moore are:
    228   i. Mary[12] Moore.
    229   ii. Wallace Moore.
    230 iii. McBrayer Moore.

138. Harvey[11] **Davis** (Harvey[10], James Harvey[9], Joseph[8], James[7], Nathaniel[6] Davis (2), Robert[5] Davis (1), Elizabeth[4] Hughes, Nicketti[3] Powhatan, Cleopatra[2], Chief[1] Powhatan)

Child of Harvey Davis is:
  + 231   i. Theodore[12] Davis.

139. Nimrod Bryant[11] **Allen, Jr.** (Rose C.[10] Davis, John[9], Joseph[8], James[7], Nathaniel[6] Davis (2), Robert[5] Davis (1), Elizabeth[4] Hughes, Nicketti[3] Powhatan, Cleopatra[2], Chief[1] Powhatan) was born November 08, 1852 in Daveiss County, Kentucky, and died March 13, 1931 in West Palm Beach, Florida. He married **Cecelia Ann Ravenscroft** September 01, 1874 in Richland County, Illinois. She was born May 29, 1856 in Indiana, and died April 30, 1939 in Crawford County, Missouri.

Child of Nimrod Allen and Cecelia Ravenscroft is:
  + 232   i. Charles Grube[12] Allen, born May 25, 1882 in Richland County, Illinois; died September 16, 1948 in Vermillion County, Illinois.

Generation No. 12

140. Ellis C.[12] **Gilliam** (Ida Sue[11] Burks, Charles Martin[10], William Pinkney[9], Richard[8], Samuel[7], Samuel[6], Mary[5] Davis, Elizabeth[4] Hughes, Nicketti[3] Powhatan, Cleopatra[2], Chief[1] Powhatan) was born September 15, 1910, and died May 06, 1999. He married **Trena Berry** 1932.

Child of Ellis Gilliam and Trena Berry is:
+ 233   i.   Bobby Ellis[13] Gilliam, born August 18, 1934.

142. Henry Allison[12] Feild (Katherine Malvina[11] Hess, William Randolph[10], Margaret[9] Daveiss, Joseph[8] Davis, James[7], Nathaniel[6] Davis (2), Robert[5] Davis (1), Elizabeth[4] Hughes, Nicketti[3] Powhatan, Cleopatra[2], Chief[1] Powhatan) He married **(1) Margaret Barrett**.   He married **(2) Virginia Capps**. She was born August 06, 1845, and died April 09, 1923.

Child of Henry Feild and Virginia Capps is:
+ 234   i.   Virginia[13] Feild.

146. Annie Catherine[12] Hess (Dr. Nelson Irving[11] Hess II, Nelson Irving[10] Hess, Margaret[9] Daveiss, Joseph[8] Davis, James[7], Nathaniel[6] Davis (2), Robert[5] Davis (1), Elizabeth[4] Hughes, Nicketti[3] Powhatan, Cleopatra[2], Chief[1] Powhatan) was born September 11, 1868, and died December 22, 1946. She married **Andrew Jackson Phillips** January 12, 1887. He was born November 02, 1858, and died April 18, 1936.

Children of Annie Hess and Andrew Phillips are:
+ 235   i.   Andrew Nelson[13] Phillips, born December 08, 1887.
  236   ii.   Ora Mae Phillips, born February 16, 1890.
  237   iii. Elmer Clyde Phillips, born June 01, 1891.
  238   iv.   Alice Muzzette Phillips, born December 31, 1894.
  239   v.   Edna Frizzell Phillips, born April 14, 1897.
  240   vi.   Thomas Durell Phillips, born September 16, 1900.
  241   vii. Mabel Clair Phillips, born June 22, 1903.
  242   viii. Ida Seay Phillips, born April 10, 1907.
  243   ix.   James Robert Phillips, born October 31, 1908.

147. Edna Isabelle[12] Hess (Dr. Nelson Irving[11] Hess II, Nelson Irving[10] Hess, Margaret[9] Daveiss, Joseph[8] Davis, James[7], Nathaniel[6] Davis (2), Robert[5] Davis (1), Elizabeth[4] Hughes, Nicketti[3] Powhatan, Cleopatra[2], Chief[1] Powhatan) was born December 08, 1871. She married **(1) J.N. Cannon** June 28, 1892. He was born September 1831, and died December 30, 1896. She married **(2) W.R. Jones** October 01, 1899. He was born March 05, 1870, and died June 15, 1925. She married **(3) J.T. Wilborn** July 10, 1930. He died January 25, 1940.

Child of Edna Hess and W.R. Jones is:
  244   i.   Hess Almquist[13] Jones, born May 12, 1900; died November 02, 1929. He married Dorothy Beayrs April 25, 1928.

149. Sallie Emma[12] Hess (Dr. Nelson Irving[11] Hess II, Nelson Irving[10] Hess, Margaret[9] Daveiss, Joseph[8] Davis, James[7], Nathaniel[6] Davis (2), Robert[5] Davis (1), Elizabeth[4] Hughes, Nicketti[3] Powhatan, Cleopatra[2], Chief[1] Powhatan) was born March 20, 1875, and died April 01, 1958. She married **James Robert Farrow** May 02, 1897.

Child of Sallie Hess and James Farrow is:
+ 245   i.   Rebecca Caroline[13] Farrow, born May 12, 1909.

151.   Dr. Frizzell Pride[12] Hess (Dr. Nelson Irving[11] Hess II, Nelson Irving[10] Hess, Margaret[9] Daveiss, Joseph[8] Davis, James[7], Nathaniel[6] Davis (2), Robert[5] Davis (1), Elizabeth[4] Hughes, Nicketti[3] Powhatan, Cleopatra[2], Chief[1] Powhatan) was born February 07, 1879. He married **Fantine Hawkins** January 23, 1911.

Dr. Frizzell Pride Hess was a Doctor of Medicine who practiced in the Holly Grove Community of Haywood County near "Jones Station." His office was a building in the yard of his farm home.

Child of Dr. Frizzell Hess and Fantine Hawkins is:
246   i.   Juanita[13] Hess, born November 28, 1911. She married George H. Boyd March 14, 1940.

156.   Nelson Irvin[12] Hess III (Dr. Nelson Irving[11] Hess II, Nelson Irving[10] Hess, Margaret[9] Daveiss, Joseph[8] Davis, James[7], Nathaniel[6] Davis (2), Robert[5] Davis (1), Elizabeth[4] Hughes, Nicketti[3] Powhatan, Cleopatra[2], Chief[1] Powhatan) was born January 31, 1893. He married **Nell Louise Taylor** September 26, 1915.

Nelson Irvin Hess III was an engineer with Southern Bell Telephone and Telegraph Co. He was a Mason, a member of the Eastern Star and past Commander of the Sons of Confederate Soldiers. He was at the time of his death living in Memphis, Tennessee where he and his wife, Nell, were members of the Lindenwood Christian Church.

Children of Nelson Hess and Nell Taylor are:
+ 247   i.   Ella Louise[13] Hess, born July 16, 1916; died June 30, 1938.
+ 248   ii. Nelson Irvin Hess, IV. born February 22, 1919.

157.   Cas Goodloe[12] Hess (Dr. Nelson Irving[11] Hess II, Nelson Irving[10] Hess, Margaret[9] Daveiss, Joseph[8] Davis, James[7], Nathaniel[6] Davis (2), Robert[5] Davis (1), Elizabeth[4] Hughes, Nicketti[3] Powhatan, Cleopatra[2], Chief[1] Powhatan) was born February 18, 1895. He married **(1) Johnie Saine** July 16, 1912. She died January 05, 1915. He married **(2) Bessie Boylston** October 15, 1919.

Child of Cas Hess and Johnie Saine is:
249   i.   Sidney Katherine[13] Hess, born May 09, 1914. She married Earl Wilkinson July 14, 1936.

Children of Cas Hess and Bessie Boylston are:
250   i.   Mary Virginia[13] Hess, born August 18, 1921.
251   ii. William Nelson Hess, born July 01, 1925. He married Ann Conners; born April 02, 1955.

158.   Jamye Willard[12] Hess (Dr. Nelson Irving[11] Hess II, Nelson Irving[10] Hess, Margaret[9] Daveiss, Joseph[8] Davis, James[7], Nathaniel[6] Davis (2), Robert[5] Davis (1), Elizabeth[4] Hughes, Nicketti[3] Powhatan, Cleopatra[2], Chief[1] Powhatan) was born October 20, 1897. He married **Annie Walker** November 1917.

Children of Jamye Hess and Annie Walker are:
  252 i. Jayme Willard[13] Hess, Jr., born July 1918.
+ 253 ii. Annie Willard Hess.

162. John William "Jack"[12] Hess (James Ferdinand[11], Nelson Irving[10], Margaret[9] Daveiss, Joseph[8] Davis, James[7], Nathaniel[6] Davis (2), Robert[5] Davis (1), Elizabeth[4] Hughes, Nicketti[3] Powhatan, Cleopatra[2], Chief[1] Powhatan) was born 1902, and died 1940.

Child of John William "Jack" Hess is:
+ 254 i. Patricia[13] Hess, born 1929.

172. Anna Bell[12] Cresap (Nelson Adair[11], Nancy Adair[10] Hess, Margaret[9] Daveiss, Joseph[8] Davis, James[7], Nathaniel[6] Davis (2), Robert[5] Davis (1), Elizabeth[4] Hughes, Nicketti[3] Powhatan, Cleopatra[2], Chief[1] Powhatan) was born May 29, 1888 in Gibson County, Tennessee, and died March 28, 1947 in Lake Comorant, Mississippi. She married **Herbert Wilson Banks** July 19, 1911 in Trenton, Tennessee. He was born May 13, 1882, and died July 05, 1974.

Anna Bell was only 12 years old when her mother died, but because she behaved in such a lady-like manner at the time, was nicknamed "Lady" Anna, and called that ever after.

Children of Anna Cresap and Herbert Banks are:
+ 255 i. Martha Elizabeth[13] Banks, born June 09, 1915.
  256 ii. Charles Herbert Banks, born June 03, 1912 in Trenton, Tennessee; died 1987 in Brazil, Tennessee. He married Kathryn Stott; died 1989 in Brazil, Tennessee.
+ 257 iii. John Banks, born June 18, 1918 in Humboldt, Tennessee; died July 01, 1992.

174. Charles Edgar[12] Cresap (Nelson Adair[11], Nancy Adair[10] Hess, Margaret[9] Daveiss, Joseph[8] Davis, James[7], Nathaniel[6] Davis (2), Robert[5] Davis (1), Elizabeth[4] Hughes, Nicketti[3] Powhatan, Cleopatra[2], Chief[1] Powhatan) was born 1881 in Gibson County, Tennessee, and died 1968. He married **Lula Kimbrough**.

Children of Charles Cresap and Lula Kimbrough are:
  258 i. Sara Alice[13] Cresap, born 1907; died 1928. She married Evan Jarrell.
+ 259 ii. Charles Edgar Cresap, Jr., born 1918.

175. Katherine Louise[12] Cresap (Nelson Adair[11], Nancy Adair[10] Hess, Margaret[9] Daveiss, Joseph[8] Davis, James[7], Nathaniel[6] Davis (2), Robert[5] Davis (1), Elizabeth[4] Hughes, Nicketti[3] Powhatan, Cleopatra[2], Chief[1] Powhatan) was born 1879 in Trenton, Tennessee, and died 1949. She married **Solon Harrison** 1911.

Children of Katherine Cresap and Solon Harrison are:
+ 260 i. Nelson Cresap[13] Harrison, born May 25, 1912 in Trenton, Tennessee; died December 10, 1981.

+ 261   ii.   Mary Cassandra Harrison, born 1914 in Trenton, Tennessee.

+ 262   iii.   Frank Russell Harrison, born 1918; died 1972.

182. Elsie Bess[12] Bennett (Kate[11] Price, Maria L.[10] Hess, Margaret[9] Daveiss, Joseph[8] Davis, James[7], Nathaniel[6] Davis (2), Robert[5] Davis (1), Elizabeth[4] Hughes, Nicketti[3] Powhatan, Cleopatra[2], Chief[1] Powhatan) was born October 06, 1877 in Fruitland, Tennessee, and died September 04, 1936 in Memphis, Tennessee. She married **Daniel Lycurgus Ross** May 20, 1897 in Dyer, Tennessee. He was born in Cascilla, Mississippi, and died in Memphis, Tennessee.

Notes for Daniel Lycurgus Ross:

Received his Law Degree from the University of Mississippi. Went to Memphis, Tennessee in 1918 where he founded the International Sugar Feed Company.

Children of Elsie Bennett and Daniel Ross are:

263   i.   Howard Calvin[13] Ross, born September 19, 1899.

264   ii.   James L. Ross, born October 08, 1901 in Iuka, Mississippi; died in Memphis, Tennessee. He married Louise Browning.

Notes for James L. Ross:

Received B.A. Degree from University of Tennessee, Knoxville in 1923, graduated from University of Memphis Law School in 1929 and was admitted to the Bar. He had joined the National Bank of Commerce in Memphis in 1920, and was elected its President in 1957. He enjoyed membership in several civic and social organizations in Memphis and was a communicant of the Grace-St. Luke's Episcopal Church.

183. Estelle Rebecca[12] Bennett (Kate[11] Price, Maria L.[10] Hess, Margaret[9] Daveiss, Joseph[8] Davis, James[7], Nathaniel[6] Davis (2), Robert[5] Davis (1), Elizabeth[4] Hughes, Nicketti[3] Powhatan, Cleopatra[2], Chief[1] Powhatan) was born August 19, 1874 in Humboldt, Tennessee, and died August 19, 1953 in Vidalia, Georgia. She married **Enoch Eugene Tribble** September 21, 1892 in Fruitland, Tennessee, son of George Tribble and Mary Barmore. He was born January 18, 1870 in Guntown [Brice's Crossroads], Mississippi, and died October 20, 1936 in Chuluota, Florida.

Notes for Estelle Rebecca Bennett:

A teacher and a poet, Estelle was a leader in the First Baptist Church of DeLand, Florida and of Vidalia, Georgia, and a speaker in demand wherever she resided.

Her husband, "Gene" Tribble was an expert in telegraphy and in that field worked with the railroads all his life. Estelle made homes for him and their two children in Tennessee, Texas, Oklahoma, and finally in Chuluota, Florida. After Gene's death, Estelle sold their property and divided the rest of her time between her children and their families.

Children of Estelle Bennett and Enoch Tribble are:

+ 265   i.   Clifton Eugene[13] Tribble, born March 12, 1895 in Fruitland, Tennessee; died August 19, 1953 in Vidalia, Georgia.

266   ii.   Mary Estelle Tribble, born March 15, 1898 in Fruitland, Tennessee; died February 11, 1971 in DeLand, Florida. She married Curtis Milton Lowry; born August 25, 1900 in Uniondale, Pennsylvania; died 1982 in DeLand, Florida.

Notes for Mary Estelle Tribble:

Graduated "straight A student" from Enid High School, Enid Oklahoma in 1915, then entered Stetson in DeLand, Florida as English Major. When an English teacher resigned during her Senior year, Mary was invited to teach the class. She earned her Bachelor's Degree in 1923, her Master's in 1925, and was named Dean of Women of the University [at that time was the youngest Dean of Women in the United States]. She was named Professor Emeritus in 1964, having taught at Stetson more than forty years.

Notes for Curtis Milton Lowry:

Received his M.E.Degree at Bucknell University in Pennsylvania after which he taught Engineering and Mathematics at Stetson where he was very much loved by his students. He was a musician who played many different instruments, was on the Board of the bank with which he was associated, but was happiest when on his Cruiser sailing the St. John's River.

184. Howard Clifton[12] Bennett (Kate[11] Price, Maria L.[10] Hess, Margaret[9] Daveiss, Joseph[8] Davis, James[7], Nathaniel[6] Davis (2), Robert[5] Davis (1), Elizabeth[4] Hughes, Nicketti[3] Powhatan, Cleopatra[2], Chief[1] Powhatan) was born May 09, 1870 in Humboldt, Tennessee, and died August 25, 1912 in Cleburne, Texas. He married **Lillie Freeman** October 04, 1894 in Fruitland, Tennessee. She was born December 31, 1872 in Humboldt, Tennessee, and died May 22, 1960 in Kilgore, Texas.

Children of Howard Bennett and Lillie Freeman are:
    267   i.   Elsie Rebecca[13] Bennett, born 1894.
    268   ii.   Katie Lou Bennett, born 1895.
    269   iii. George Edmund Bennett, born 1903.
    270   iv. Howard Clifton Bennett, Jr., born 1905.

Notes for Howard Clifton Bennett, Jr.:

Dr. Howard Clifton Bennett, Jr. was for many years Minister of Kilgore Baptist Church, Kilgore, Texas where the Harvey Cliburn family were members. [Their son, Van Cliburn later became the internationally celebrated pianist]. Dr. Bennett's mother, Lillie Freeman, lived with them in Kilgore until her death in 1960.

Before retirement in 1976, he became President of East Texas Baptist College in Marshall, Texas where he, his wife, Mary Lee, and their three daughters made their home.

187. Annie Leslie[12] Price (William Hess[11], Maria L.[10] Hess, Margaret[9] Daveiss, Joseph[8] Davis, James[7], Nathaniel[6] Davis (2), Robert[5] Davis (1), Elizabeth[4] Hughes, Nicketti[3] Powhatan, Cleopatra[2], Chief[1] Powhatan) was born May 09, 1879. She married **Oliver Conrad Powell**.

Children of Annie Price and Oliver Powell are:
    271   i.   Oliver Carlton[13] Powell, born April 06, 1908 in Jonesboro, Arkansas.
+ 272   ii.   Oscar Lee Powell, born in Jonesboro, Arkansas.
+ 273   iii. Frances Powell, born in Jonesboro, Arkansas.
    274   iv. Martha Powell, born in Jonesboro, Arkansas. She married Thomas Flocco.

189. Frederick Carlton[12] Price (William Hess[11], Maria L.[10] Hess, Margaret[9] Daveiss, Joseph[8] Davis, James[7], Nathaniel[6] Davis (2), Robert[5] Davis (1), Elizabeth[4] Hughes, Nicketti[3] Powhatan, Cleopatra[2], Chief[1] Powhatan) was born August 10, 1884 in Troy, Tennessee, and died July 07, 1965 in Columbia, Mississippi. He married **Frances McKee** December 10, 1910 in Natchez, Mississippi, daughter of Jethro McKee and Mary Ballard. She was born December 16, 1889, and died June 21, 1960.

Children of Frederick Price and Frances McKee are:

    275   i.   Frederick Carlton[13] Price, Jr., born August 02, 1912 in Columbus, Mississippi; died 1950 in North Korea. He married Helene Cowand March 02, 1935; born 1913.

Notes for Frederick Carlton Price, Jr.:
Killed in battle.

+ 276   ii.   Jesse Cuthbert Price, born January 21, 1915 in Greenwood, Mississippi; died 1966 in Columbia, Mississippi.
+ 277   iii.   Irwin Vernon Price, born March 13, 1917 in Columbus, Mississippi; died 1983 in Houston, Texas.
+ 278   iv.   Margaret Frances Price, born July 24, 1922 in Columbus, Mississippi.
+ 279   v.   Charles William Price, born August 15, 1932 in Columbia, Mississippi.

194. Fannie Augusta[12] Thomas (Eliza Ann[11] Hess, James A.W.[10], Margaret[9] Daveiss, Joseph[8] Davis, James[7], Nathaniel[6] Davis (2), Robert[5] Davis (1), Elizabeth[4] Hughes, Nicketti[3] Powhatan, Cleopatra[2], Chief[1] Powhatan) was born December 16, 1872. She married **John Browning**.

Children of Fannie Thomas and John Browning are:

    280   i.   Cecil[13] Browning.
    281   ii.   Organ Browning.
    282   iii.   Elizabeth Browning.
    283   iv.   Lydia Sue Browning.

195. Benjamin Hess[12] Thomas (Eliza Ann[11] Hess, James A.W.[10], Margaret[9] Daveiss, Joseph[8] Davis, James[7], Nathaniel[6] Davis (2), Robert[5] Davis (1), Elizabeth[4] Hughes, Nicketti[3] Powhatan, Cleopatra[2], Chief[1] Powhatan) was born September 18, 1874. He married **Eleanor Glass**.

Benjamin Hess Thomas was a Gibson County Trustee.

Child of Benjamin Thomas and Eleanor Glass is:

    284   i.   Elizabeth[13] Thomas, Adopted child.

196. Ida[12] Thomas (Eliza Ann[11] Hess, James A.W.[10], Margaret[9] Daveiss, Joseph[8] Davis, James[7], Nathaniel[6] Davis (2), Robert[5] Davis (1), Elizabeth[4] Hughes, Nicketti[3] Powhatan, Cleopatra[2], Chief[1] Powhatan) was born November 24, 1877, and died 1962 in Milan. She married **Charles Clyde Browning** 1903 in Gibson County, Tennessee, son of Matthew Browning and Susan Springer. He was born

*Left: Ida Thomas, daughter of "Lyde" Hess Thomas. **Right:** Ida and Charles Clyde Browning in later years.*

January 25, 1879, and died 1967 in Gibson County, Tennessee.

Ida Thomas was a lifelong resident of Gibson County and a charter member of the Oakwood Baptist Church.

Charles Clyde Browning was a farmer in Gibson County.

Children of Ida Thomas and Charles Browning are:

+ 285   i.   Benjamin Hess[13] Browning, born November 06, 1903 in Gibson County, Tennessee; died January 15, 1979 in Gibson County, Tennessee.
  286   ii. Ward Eli Browning, born November 12, 1906.
+ 287   iii. Eleanor Louise Browning, born January 16, 1910.

Ben Hess (son of Ida and Charles) and Mary Nell Martin Browning.

197.   Warner Ebenezer[12] Dunlap (Susan[11] Hess, James A.W.[10], Margaret[9] Daveiss, Joseph[8] Davis, James[7], Nathaniel[6] Davis (2), Robert[5] Davis (1), Elizabeth[4] Hughes, Nicketti[3] Powhatan, Cleopatra[2], Chief[1] Powhatan) was born May 03, 1875, and died January 16, 1948. He married **Sallie May Kimbrough** July 30, 1901. She was born January 12, 1875, and died July 06, 1963 in Humboldt, Gibson County, Tennessee.

Children of Warner Dunlap and Sallie Kimbrough are:

+ 288   i.   Warner Ebenezer[13] Dunlap, Jr., born December 25, 1903 in Gibson County, Tennessee; died August 1979 in Stanton, Tennessee.

+ 289   ii.   Kimbrough Lafayette Dunlap, born July 26, 1907 in Humboldt, Gibson County, Tennessee; died 1987 in Humboldt, Gibson County, Tennessee.

   290   iii.   Thomas Duke Dunlap, born March 15, 1912 in Gibson County, Tennessee; died April 29, 2001. He married (1) Mary Elizabeth Raines. He married (2) Eloise Bryant Walden.

Tom Dunlap

Thomas Duke Dunlap received his B.S. Degree and Law Degree from the University of Tennessee, Knoxville. Following service in Naval Intelligence during World War II, he practiced law in Knoxville and Memphis and was Assistant U. S. Attorney. Later Tom joined his brother, Kimbrough, in strawberry farming in Humboldt where he became associated with Merchants State Bank. He left U.T. a gift of seven million dollars to establish a scholarship program for sophomores, juniors and seniors. He also made a bequest of one million dollars to be used for the building of an out-patient physical rehabilitation facility and conference center for Humboldt, Tennessee and the surrounding community. These gifts were announced at the time of his death in 2001.

198. Mary G.[12] Dunlap (Susan[11] Hess, James A.W.[10], Margaret[9] Daveiss, Joseph[8] Davis, James[7], Nathaniel[6] Davis (2), Robert[5] Davis (1), Elizabeth[4] Hughes, Nicketti[3] Powhatan, Cleopatra[2], Chief[1] Powhatan) was born October 14, 1876. She married **Dr. Benjamin S. Penn** May 1900.

Children of Mary Dunlap and Benjamin Penn are:

   291   i.   Frances[13] Penn.
   292   ii.   Mary Penn.

199. Anna Kate[12] Dunlap (Susan[11] Hess, James A.W.[10], Margaret[9] Daveiss, Joseph[8] Davis, James[7], Nathaniel[6] Davis (2), Robert[5] Davis (1), Elizabeth[4] Hughes, Nicketti[3] Powhatan, Cleopatra[2], Chief[1] Powhatan) was born August 28, 1878. She married **James M. Gates** August 22, 1911.

Child of Anna Dunlap and James Gates is:

   293   i.   Sue[13] Gates. She married Beech Hall October 1939.

205. James Lafayette[12] Dunlap (Willietta[11] Hess, James A.W.[10], Margaret[9] Daveiss, Joseph[8] Davis, James[7], Nathaniel[6] Davis (2), Robert[5] Davis (1), Elizabeth[4] Hughes, Nicketti[3] Powhatan, Cleopatra[2], Chief[1] Powhatan) was born March 14, 1878 in Gibson County, Tennessee, and died 1954. He married **Margaret Redd** March 10, 1909 in Durant, Mississippi.

Child of James Dunlap and Margaret Redd is:

   294   i.   Lina Peggy May[13] Dunlap, born February 28, 1910 in Memphis, Tennessee. She married Thomas Lee Robinson October 24, 1929 in Memphis, Tennessee.

206. Willie Mai Chester[12] Dunlap (Willietta[11] Hess, James A.W.[10], Margaret[9] Daveiss, Joseph[8] Davis, James[7], Nathaniel[6] Davis (2), Robert[5] Davis (1), Elizabeth[4] Hughes, Nicketti[3] Powhatan, Cleopatra[2], Chief[1] Powhatan) was born November 14, 1879 in Gibson County, Tennessee, and died December 26, 1940 in Gibson County, Tennessee. She married **Hulon Otis Warlick** January 29, 1902 in Humboldt, Tennessee, son of Pinkney Warlick and Mary Mitchum. He was born November 13, 1875 in Gibson County, Tennessee, and died August 29, 1945 in Gibson, County, Tennessee.

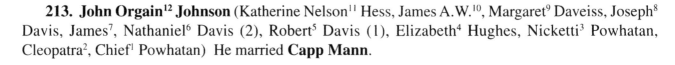

Willie Mai Chester Dunlap was always called "Chessie."

Children of Willie Dunlap and Hulon Warlick are:

+ 295   i.   Hulon Otis[13] Warlick, Jr., born January 18, 1903 in Humboldt, Gibson County, Tennessee; died September 24, 1964 in Memphis, Tennessee.

+ 296   ii.   Mildred Warlick, born September 11, 1904 in Humboldt, Gibson County, Tennessee; died May 17, 1999 in Humboldt, Gibson County, Tennessee.

+ 297   iii.   Monie Warlick, born September 23, 1910; died July 30, 1978.

Willie Mai "Chessie" Chester Dunlap Warlick

213. John Orgain[12] Johnson (Katherine Nelson[11] Hess, James A.W.[10], Margaret[9] Daveiss, Joseph[8] Davis, James[7], Nathaniel[6] Davis (2), Robert[5] Davis (1), Elizabeth[4] Hughes, Nicketti[3] Powhatan, Cleopatra[2], Chief[1] Powhatan) He married **Capp Mann.**

Children of John Johnson and Capp Mann are:

   298   i.   Jack[13] Johnson.

+ 299   ii.   Alsay Johnson, born September 02, 1916 in Brownsville, Tennessee; died January 08, 1995 in Shelbyville, Tennessee.

220. Marian Lucinda[12] Campbell (Jane Hamilton[11] Hess, James A.W.[10], Margaret[9] Daveiss, Joseph[8] Davis, James[7], Nathaniel[6] Davis (2), Robert[5] Davis (1), Elizabeth[4] Hughes, Nicketti[3] Powhatan, Cleopatra[2], Chief[1] Powhatan) was born May 22, 1880 in Gibson County, Tennessee, and died September 28, 1946 in Jackson, Tennessee. She married **Joseph Herman Lannom** February 25, 1903, son of W. Lannom and Elizabeth Hurt. He was born November 01, 1882 in Cades, Tennessee, and died July 29, 1949 in Jackson, Tennessee.

Herman and Marian Lannom, with daughter Lillian

Notes for Marian Lucinda Campbell:
     Marian was born at the family residence, Oakwood Stock Farm—Three miles north of Humboldt, Tennessee.

Enterprises owned and operated by Joseph Herman Lannom (husband of Marian Campbell) and Roy Johnson (husband of Marian's sister Lillian Campbell). The business was located on 14th Ave, Humbolt, later the site of Stovall Plumbing (lower left photo). Marian had a surrey with "fringe on top" which caused a pleasant stir as she drove around town.

She was educated at the Mississippi Synodical College for Women in Holly Springs, Mississippi, and was very gifted musically and artistically. She played nine musical instruments and taught music in Humboldt several years. Her granddaughter, Marian Albright, remembers Mrs. Myrtle Keenan of Humboldt telling of taking guitar lessons from Marian.

She painted beautifully in oil, watercolor, charcoal and pastels. Many in the family are fortunate to have one or more of her renderings.

An accomplished seamstress, she made beautiful clothes and costumes for her daughter, Lillian, and later for her three granddaughters. Many of these items were trimmed with her tatting, lace, and embroidery.

In February of 1903, she married Herman Lannom. Their one surviving child was Lillian Jeanette. Herman was in partnership with brother-in-law, Roy Johnson, in the Wagon and Fine Harness business, located on 14th Avenue (later the site of Stovall Plumbing). Lannom & Johnson & Co. expanded to include the sale of Willis Overland automobiles (one of the earlier distributorships in the state) in one side, and Plumbing fixtures and Supplies in the other.

When daughter Lillian left home for Nashville to attend Ward Belmont / Peabody College for Women / Vanderbilt, Mother Marian went with her. Mother and daughter set up housekeeping in an apartment where friends and family were always welcome. Lillian Johnson Gardiner was a frequent visitor in the Nashville apartment and can relate many fun stories of their times there. Father, Herman, kept the home fires burning and visited as often as he could. However being left on his own so much taught him to be very self sufficient in the kitchen, and he became known as one of the best cooks in the family. The ladies of the family often asked how he had cooked a certain dish, and he would reply, "Oh, I just used a little of such and a pinch of so and so, combined with a handful of that." He never measured anything and it drove the ladies crazy.

Sometime in the late 1920's Marian and daughter, Lillian, had an automobile accident in the vicinity of Linden, Tennessee. Marian's right hand was almost severed at the wrist, and was "re-attached" by a doctor there in Linden. She was told her hand would never be useful again. To an artist and musician this was unthinkable, so she sent Lillian to the Dime Store to purchase a rubber ball - and started her own therapy. She began by using her left hand to wrap her right hand around the ball, and continued this faithfully for hours, days, and weeks. Then as she gained motility could squeeze the ball slightly with her injured hand. This she practiced constantly, finally regaining the use of her hand, though she carried a very visible scar forever more.

In 1922, Lillian and two college friends toured Europe in the company of their chaperone, Mrs. Eleanora Wills Rutland. For 9 or 10 months they visited the various countries enjoying new experiences, beautiful music and wonderful food. The letters and gifts Lil sent home kept Marian entertained during her daughter's long absence.

After daughter Lillian married and grandchildren came along, Mammy, as Marian became known, was a strong influence in their lives. Each bedtime, she read Bible stories, Poetry, Classics and such. She entertained with games and wonderful figures fashioned from modeling clay.

Her love of God and the Presbyterian Church were obvious by the amount of time she spent in many aspects of church activity, including writing articles for the Christian Observer.

After a series of heart problems, she suffered a major attack, which caused her death in 1946. Gone but not forgotten by those remaining who knew and loved this versatile and talented woman.

She is buried in Rose Hill Cemetery, Humboldt, Tennessee.

In early years, Joseph Herman Lannom sold buggies and fine harness. When automobiles became available sold Willis Overland cars in partnership with his brother-in-law, Roy Johnson (married to Herman's wife's sister, Lillian). They also sold plumbing fixtures and supplies. Their business was located on 14th Avenue in Humboldt.

Herman and wife, Marian Campbell, had one daughter, Lillian. He was a devoted and loving father and grandfather.

Granddaughter, Marian Knowles (Albright) remembers his Christmas morning ritual of waking everyone calling out, "Christmas Gift, Christmas Gift." After presents were opened, he would make molasses candy in a big iron skillet. We never thought to get the recipe and have been unable to duplicate it since his death. "I got up early every morning and went with Grandfather to gather eggs and such garden vegetables as were in season. None of the women wanted children in the kitchen, but he would stand me in a chair, pull me up to the cabinet and help me 'cook' to my heart's content. I sat on his knee those long ago evenings listening to World War II news on the radio and he would explain, as best he could, the comments of Gabriel Heater, Walter Winchell and others bringing news of the 'front'."

Herman died of a stroke and complications of Alzheimer's disease in 1949. He is buried in Rose Hill Cemetery, Humboldt, Tennessee.

Child of Marian Campbell and Joseph Lannom is:
+ 300   i.   Lillian Jeanette[13] Lannom, born July 03, 1905 in Humboldt, Gibson County, Tennessee; died October 18, 1987 in Atlanta, Georgia.

221. Gabrilla Hess[12] Campbell (Jane Hamilton[11] Hess, James A.W.[10], Margaret[9] Daveiss, Joseph[8] Davis, James[7], Nathaniel[6] Davis (2), Robert[5] Davis (1), Elizabeth[4] Hughes, Nicketti[3] Powhatan, Cleopatra[2], Chief[1] Powhatan) was born September 07, 1881 in Humboldt, Gibson County, Tennessee, and died May 07, 1967 in Humboldt, Gibson County, Tennessee. She married **Robert Ira Long** 1901 in Humboldt, Gibson County, Tennessee, son of John Long and Frances Powers. He was born September 02, 1873 in Bladon Springs, Alabama, and died August 26, 1938 in New Orleans, Louisiana.

Children of Gabrilla Campbell and Robert Long are:
+ 301   i.   Frances Powers[13] Long, born June 24, 1902 in Slidell, Louisiana; died April 22, 1978 in Florida.
+ 302   ii.   Jane Hess Long, born November 01, 1904 in Ripley, Tennessee; died February 21, 1995 in Akron, Ohio.
+ 303   iii.   Robert Ira Long, born February 17, 1907 in Ripley, Tennessee; died November 11, 1985 in Maryville, Tennessee.
+ 304   iv.   Grace Campbell Long, born June 27, 1910 in Ripley, Tennessee.
   305   v.   John Ross Long, born October 14, 1912 in Ripley, Mississippi. He married Louise Mathis in Humboldt, Gibson County, Tennessee.

Notes for John Ross Long:
Back in the days of Selective Military Service, John had served his required year and returned home to Humboldt. As he recalls, just a few days later while he was taking a nap, Griffin Boyte, Wallis

Gay Long with brother James Elbert Campbell.

Family of Gabrilla "Gay" and Rev. Robert Ira Long. Left to right: Robert, Grace, John Ross, Frances, Janie and Campbell.

and Ralph Jones came running to his house saying, "Mr. John! You've got to go back—they've bombed Pearl Harbor." Sure enough in a day or so he got his "Greetings" from the President. He was drafted into the Quartermaster's Corps at Ft. Benning where he and the other new recruits were treated to all the K.P., Guard Duty, Patrol and other nasties. When the opportunity came for him to be moved to the Company Command, he jumped at it. There he learned all the "in's and outs" and made himself so indispensable he would never have to pull K.P. duty again. When it was time to ship out he traveled by train to San Diego, then by tramp steamer [30 days] to the Island of Fiji. He was in the Ordinance Branch supporting the Americal Division [America—Caledonia]. Later his outfit went to Guadalcanal, then on to the Island of Bouganville where he spent three years. This was a backwater kind of place, according to John, so they were quite surprised to hear that General McArthur was coming there to "view the front." Patrols were sent out every day for a week or more before his visit to clear out the enemy and insure protection for the General.

John's First Sergeant, a man from Dothan, Alabama, suffered a broken leg and John was appointed his "substitute" though he was only a Private, or Corporal at the time. He laughingly called himself a Second Sergeant, but carried out his duties efficiently.

John's mother had written that a cousin, James Elbert [Jim] Campbell was also on Bouganville, building airstrips with the 451st C.B.'s. John looked him up and they had a reunion. Jim said he had heard the rumor that his outfit was going home. John thought not, and sure enough he later found out they had gone just the other way—to Okinawa.

At some point a supply ship had been sunk off the coast of their island and the Company retrieved any goods they could salvage. John's outfit was told to go and pick up what canned goods they wanted. The labels had all washed off the cans so they had no idea what their bounty was. It turned out to be Apricots—all Apricots! When John was discharged and returned to Humboldt, all the friends and relatives wanted to entertain him to dinner. A cousin, Juliet Campbell [Mrs. Charles Lewis], invited him to eat with her family. For ages she had been hoarding a special surprise for a special occasion. You can imagine John's feelings when she, with glowing face, presented him with a bowl of—Apricots!

John has been a staunch member of the First Presbyterian Church in Humboldt, active in the Senior Citizen's Group and Lion's Club. In younger days he was a Scout leader. He has always been an important citizen of this community.

Notes for Louise Mathis:

Louise married first Garland Warmath and they had two sons, Walter, a gifted musician and John who married Beverly. They have two daughters, Georgia and Jana, and several grandchildren.

+ 306   vi.   Campbell Garth Long, born February 15, 1919 in Ripley, Mississippi; died February 17, 1996 in Temple, Oklahoma.

222. Levi Ross[12] Campbell (Jane Hamilton[11] Hess, James A.W.[10], Margaret[9] Daveiss, Joseph[8] Davis, James[7], Nathaniel[6] Davis (2), Robert[5] Davis (1), Elizabeth[4] Hughes, Nicketti[3] Powhatan, Cleopatra[2], Chief[1] Powhatan) was born October 16, 1883 in Gibson County, Tennessee, and died 1948 in Gibson County, Tennessee. He married **Eryn Kathleen Smith** 1929.

Levi Ross Campbell was executive administrator of his father, J.E. Campbell's considerable estate. This entailed managing farms, the lumberyard, bank stocks and a host of other responsibilities.

Levi Ross Campbell was born October 16, 1883, the third of six children born to John Elbert and Jane Hamilton [Jennie] Hess Campbell. He attended High Hill School and entered the University of

Levi Ross Campbell, Sr. and Eryn Kathleen Smith Campbell

Tennessee at Knoxville to study Civil Engineering. He excelled at his studies and graduated from U.T. in 1905. While there he played football, basketball and ran track. At Dudley Field at Vanderbilt in 1905, he received medals for the 120 and 220 hurdles, the running broad jump and the running high jump. [This was under the auspices of the Southern Intercollegiate Athletic Association—the Southeastern Conference was not formed until the early 1930's]. Interestingly, he never mentioned the medals and they were kept in a trunk in the attic and not found until after his death.

After graduation he returned to Humboldt where he enjoyed the life of a young bachelor until his father admonished him to settle down. Ross entered his father's contracting business and became engaged in building houses and selling building materials. He and his brother, Zach, continued the business after John E. died.

In 1929, at age 45 he married Eryn Kathleen Smith of the Pope Community in Madison County. Kathleen had taught school and was then working for Sanford Brothers in Chattanooga as a stenographer. They first made their home in the old Campbell house at 17th and Osborne in Humboldt then in 1941 built their new residence at 2811 East Main.

In 1932 he was elected President of the Merchants State Bank in Humboldt and served in that capacity until his death. [He informed the bank board that he did not intend to be "tied to a desk," so he was called upon as needed while Mr. George McDearmon ran the day-to-day affairs.] For this service he was paid the princely sum of $300.00 per year.

In 1936 his only child, L. Ross Campbell, Jr. was born—May 8th—during the Strawberry Festival.

After a devastating fire in 1941 the lumberyard was sold to Lashlee-Rich and Ross continued to buy and sell Real Estate, an avocation he enjoyed until his death in 1948.

He served as an Elder in the First Presbyterian Church for many years, was a member of the American Bankers Association and the Humboldt Rotary Club.

Child of Levi Campbell and Eryn Smith is:

+ 307   i.   Levi Ross[13] Campbell, JR., born May 08, 1936 in Memphis, Tennessee.

223.   Lillian Jeanette[12] Campbell (Jane Hamilton[11] Hess, James A.W.[10], Margaret[9] Daveiss, Joseph[8] Davis, James[7], Nathaniel[6] Davis (2), Robert[5] Davis (1), Elizabeth[4] Hughes, Nicketti[3] Powhatan, Cleopatra[2], Chief[1] Powhatan) was born June 30, 1885 in Gibson County, Tennessee, and died May 15, 1961 in Humboldt, Gibson County, Tennessee. She married **Tyree Leroy Johnson** December 28, 1908 in Fairview, Fort Hill, Humboldt, Tennessee, son of Andrew Johnson and Lula Tyree. He was born November 17, 1879 in Gibson County, Tennessee, and died December 05, 1918 in Humboldt, Gibson County, Tennessee.

Tyree Leroy "Roy" and Lillian Campbell Johnson

Lillian was born at the family residence, Oakwood Stock Farm, three miles north of Humboldt in Old Shiloh, Gibson County, Tennessee. She first attended Old Shiloh School where her mother's brother, Walter Hess, was headmaster. This was not a happy experience as he used his nieces and nephews as examples and they were always "on show." She completed her education at the Mississippi Synodical College for Women in Holly Springs, following in the footsteps of her two older sisters, Marian and Gabrilla. According to Lillian, the first train ride to college seemed to take her a million miles from home.

Like her siblings, Lillian was gifted musically, especially in piano. She was still pianist for the Men's Bible Class of the Presbyterian Church in Humboldt the year she died.

About 1907 she was asked to play for a camp meeting at Cades, Tennessee. There she was a guest in the home of Dr. Cyrus Tyree where she met his nephew, Tyree Leroy Johnson. They fell in love and were married the next year at Fairview, the spacious home her parents had built on Fort Hill (then the outskirts of Humboldt). Being a fine seamstress, she with the help of her sister, Marian, fashioned her own wedding gown, a beautiful accomplishment now in the possession of her daughter, Lillian Gardiner. Mrs. Gardiner also has a baby dress made for her by her mother.

Lillian and "Roy" were blessed with three daughters, and although they were very much in love, their marriage ended prematurely with Roy's death in 1918.

At that time Lillian moved in with her parents who had recently removed to Humboldt from their country home, Fairview. She was one of the first women to drive a car in this area. Her father, J.E.

Campbell bought an automobile and was quite happy to let daughter, Lillian, drive him on his many business errands. She helped him in many areas of enterprise.

She was ever an inspiration to her children, grandchildren, friends and relatives. Lillian died following a stroke June 1971 in Humboldt, Gibson County, Tennessee.

At an early age, Roy was a member of the first Highway Commission for the State of Tennessee and had many prominent friends all over the state. He and brother-in-law Herman Lannom were in business together in Humboldt. They first sold buggies and fine harnesses, then Willis Overland automobiles. Also they sold plumbing fixtures and supplies.

Roy was very handsome, fun-loving and great with children, but quite protective of his three sisters, and his three daughters, of whom he was very proud.

Once when Roy was hunting ducks at Reelfoot Lake he was bragging to some of the guys about how many he had shot. The man next to him asked, "Do you know who I am?" to which Roy replied, "No." The man said, "Well I'M the game warden." Roy asked, "Do you know who I am? I'm the biggest darned liar in West Tennessee."

During the flu epidemic in 1918, his only brother, Cyrus, died and was buried in Leland, Mississippi. Against all advice Roy determined to attend the funeral where he, too, contracted the disease and died ten days later at the age of 37. During his funeral every store in Humboldt closed.

Children of Lillian Campbell and Tyree Johnson are:

    308   i.   Lillian Jeanette[13] Johnson, born August 15, 1910. She married Laurence Bridges Gardiner December 1944 in Humboldt, Gibson County, Tennessee; born July 21, 1906 in Memphis, Shelby County, Tennessee; died October 02, 1994 in Memphis, Tennessee.

Notes for Lillian Jeanette Johnson:

Lillian, the first of three daughters born to Lillian and Roy, was the apple of her father's eye. He was always ready to play with her and show her off. One chilly morning he wanted to stroll her around the block in her buggy. Grandmother [Jane Hess Campbell] thought it was too cold for the baby and tried to talk Roy out of it. Roy was adamant; he wanted to take Lil out! So, Grandmother carefully wrapped a stick of firewood in Lil's blankets and admonished Roy not to "uncover the baby" for any reason. Off went a proud Papa strolling a stick of firewood happily around town.

Though her father died when Lil was eight, grandparents, aunts, uncles, and cousins as well as her mother and sisters, Jane and Marian, surrounded her. The family moved into the busy household of her grandparents, Jane and John E. Campbell and there was always something going on or someone visiting. Lil remembers that she and her sisters were lectured often on being kind to, and setting a good example for whichever relatives were "company" at the time.

After graduating from Humboldt High School, Lillian studied at Peabody College and Vanderbilt University 1928-1931, then Falls Business College also in Nashville 1931-32. She was for quite some time employed with the prestigious Law Firm of Norman and Keefe in Nashville, then later with the Department of Agriculture.

When World War II started and the Milan Arsenal was being built, Lil came home and took a position there. She started in the office of the builders-Oman Brothers of Nashville. Later she worked in the plant office when Proctor and Gamble took over the "project," then moved into the Office of the Controller. She progressed to Secretary of the Commanding Officer, Col. Knight and his successor, finally ending up as head of Personnel after the plant was up and going. In 1944 she left to be married.

During the next years Lil was a great help to her husband, Laurence, as he started a business of Managing Jersey Cattle Sales on a national scale. The job was very demanding, but had as its reward traveling this country and meeting interesting people all along the way.

Between travels, Lil became more and more involved with Genealogy and took an active role in many organizations. She originated "Ansearchin' News," the Magazine of the Tennessee Genealogical Society, which is still in publication today. She joined with her husband and others in organizing the Memphis Genealogical Society, co-authored several genealogical reference books, was Branch President, then State President of the National League of American Pen Women, Parliamentarian of her Chapter of the Colonial Dames of America. She was State President and later National President of the Huguenot Society—just to name a FEW of her many accomplishments—there are many more credits to her name, both in genealogical and in civic circles.

Through the years both she and husband, Laurence, have been generous with their time, talents and money in furthering the work of their Church [Independent Presbyterian], and in supporting the University of Tennessee as well as many other worthwhile "philanthropies."

As a child, Laurence Bridges Gardiner had food allergies, and the doctor suggested his family try fresh milk. They bought a Jersey cow. Laurence loved the cow and the milk. At age 10, he took over the milking and sold surplus milk. He also raised Carneau pigeons [a hobby which he continued the rest of his life] and for several years sold squab to the Memphis Hotels. He became an exhibitor [of his pigeons], and general flunkey at the old Tri-State Fair, which became the Mid-South Fair. For 75 years he served in the capacities of Certificate Holder, Vice President, Director of the Jersey Program, etc. The Fair honored him as its longest serving member with "Laurence B. Gardiner Day" in 1987.

He graduated from the University of Tennessee, Knoxville, in the field of Animal Husbandry. He was a member of Phi Kappa Phi and won the Purina Bowl for his work with Dairy cattle. He was a lifelong supporter of U.T. and served on various Boards and Committees.

Laurence Bridges and Lillian Jeanette Johnson Gardiner

After graduation he worked three years for the University in their Dairy Department. In 1932 he accepted the position of Southeastern Field Representative for the American Jersey Cattle Club and with the job came a second hand Dodge automobile. Laurence, NEVER having had a driving lesson, drove to North Carolina, South Carolina, Florida, Alabama, Mississippi, Tennessee and Kentucky meeting with dairy extension people in all the colleges.

One year, while visiting the West Tennessee Strawberry Festival in Humboldt, Tennessee, with a colleague, Tom McCord, he attended the Street Dance [which in those years was held in Bells], and there ran into Lillian Johnson, who worked with Tom in the Department of Agriculture at that time. Lil laughingly recalls that she and Laurence "met at a street dance between the Railroad and the Red light in Bells, Tennessee." A few years later Lillian and Laurence were married in the home of her uncle, L. Ross Campbell, Sr. in Humboldt, with friends and family present.

Laurence Gardiner receiving the DAR Medal of Honor with wife Lillian looking on.

Laurence then formed the "Pure Bred Jersey Sales Nationwide" and organized his own business, managing auctions of Registered Jersey cattle all over the United States.

He had long been interested in genealogy, researching family lines wherever he traveled. He became well known in this field, lecturing on the subject, and helping others research their history. He held memberships in the "Sons of the American Revolution," "The Jamestown Society," "First Families of Virginia," "Tennessee Genealogical Society" - [charter member], "Huguenot Society of the Founders of Manakin in the Colony of Virginia" [which established a scholarship in his and Lillian's honor], and he was a recipient of the D.A.R.'s Medal of Honor as an outstanding exemplar of the routine duties of citizenship including patriotism, leadership, trustworthiness, and service to the community.

Laurence was President of The Elmwood Cemetery Association for 17 years and was elected its first President Emeritus. He was for 45 years a member of the Downtown Kiwanis Club in Memphis. For 50 years a Deacon at Idlewild Presbyterian Church, he later became a charter member of Independent Presbyterian Church.

He continued researching ancestral lines for family and friends until a stroke disabled him in his mid 80's. At age 88 Laurence died at home with Lillian at his side. He is buried in Elmwood Cemetery.

+ 309   ii.   Jane Bright Johnson, born March 02, 1914 in Humboldt, Gibson County, Tennessee.
+ 310   iii.   Marian Lucille Johnson, born February 10, 1916 in Humboldt, Gibson County, Tennessee.

224. Zachariah Joseph[12] Campbell (Jane Hamilton[11] Hess, James A.W.[10], Margaret[9] Daveiss, Joseph[8] Davis, James[7], Nathaniel[6] Davis (2), Robert[5] Davis (1), Elizabeth[4] Hughes, Nicketti[3] Powhatan, Cleopatra[2], Chief[1] Powhatan) was born August 18, 1887 in Gibson County, Tennessee, and died March 25, 1957 in Humboldt, Gibson County, Tennessee. He married **Allie Corrinne Boling** December 18, 1910 in Jackson, Tennessee. She was born October 14, 1890 in Gibson County, Tennessee, and died June 18, 1961 in Humboldt, Gibson County, Tennessee.

Zach was born with beautiful blonde curly hair, which his mother did not want cut. One day her bachelor brother, Thomas Lankford Hess, took him to the barber shop, and bribing him with bananas, had the golden locks sheared. His mother cried and cried.

Zach managed the family lumberyard. He was pleasant, gracious, dignified and thoughtful, was active in the Presbyterian Church. He always enjoyed a good wager.

Family Memories from Childhood, written by his granddaughter, Susan Lewis Atkins Schoenemann, in 2000:

"Papa and Mama Campbell [Zachariah Joseph Campbell and Corrinne Boling Campbell]"

"Papa and Mama Campbell were inseparable, sharing everything. After meals they would take turns washing and drying the dishes. Papa would don his oversized, blue striped apron, tying it under his armpits; Mama wore a ruffled one. They seemed to enjoy each others company most of all. Their neighbors the Wrays, [across the street] commented that they enjoyed listening when Mama's and Papa's favorite television show was on just to hear them laughing. This was well before air-conditioning and everyone kept their windows open in fine weather.

Also pre air-conditioning, neighbors visited on the front porch. Papa would swing my cousins and me in one of those big, green porch swings by sitting in front of us and pushing our feet in turn. I can still feel his gentle hands.

He always smelled of Old Spice and peppermint.

At Papa's funeral, Mama said to me through her tears, 'He's the sweetest man who ever lived.' Three years later Mama was re-united with him. After lunch one day Mama was resting in Aunt Pink's bedroom at our house. She looked up, raised her arms toward Heaven and was gone. Happy at last!" [S.S.]

Children of Zachariah Campbell and Allie Boling are:
+ 311　i.　Dorothy Nesbitt[13] Campbell, born August 21, 1912 in Humboldt, Gibson County, Tennessee; died June 11, 1998 in Covington, Tipton County, Tennessee.
+ 312　ii.　Juliet Miriam Campbell, born July 22, 1915 in Humboldt, Gibson County, Tennessee.
+ 313　iii.　Janice Campbell, born February 19, 1920 in Humboldt, Gibson County, Tennessee; died April 21, 1990 in Memphis Shelby County, Tennessee.
　314　iv.　Zachariah Joseph Campbell, Jr., born September 11, 1924 in Humboldt, Gibson County, Tennessee; died 1979 in Memphis Shelby County, Tennessee. He married (1) Madelyn. He married (2) Eugenia Johnston 1947.

Notes for Zachariah Joseph Campbell, Jr.:
Employed with Crump Industrial Insurance Company in Memphis, Tennessee.

225.　James Elbert[12] Campbell (Jane Hamilton[11] Hess, James A.W.[10], Margaret[9] Daveiss, Joseph[8] Davis, James[7], Nathaniel[6] Davis (2), Robert[5] Davis (1), Elizabeth[4] Hughes, Nicketti[3] Powhatan, Cleopatra[2], Chief[1] Powhatan) was born 1889 in Gibson County, Tennessee, and died 1964 in Gibson County, Tennessee. He married **Lytle Bell Cannon** August 24, 1911 in Murfreesboro, Tennessee, daughter of Edward Cannon and Sarah Lytle. She was born 1891 in Murfreesboro, Tennessee, and died 1977 in Humboldt, Gibson County, Tennessee.

James Elbert Campbell was a brick mason, surveyor, and did important industrial reports for Chamber of Commerce in Humboldt, Tennessee.

Children of James Campbell and Lytle Cannon are:
+ 315　i.　Elizabeth Lytle[13] Campbell, born February 13, 1913.
+ 316　ii.　James Elbert Campbell, Jr., born May 10, 1921.
+ 317　iii.　Jack Cannon Campbell, born July 03, 1927; died July 2002 in Birmingham, Alabama.
+ 318　iv.　Robert Hess Campbell, born March 04, 1937; died June 18, 1997.

231. Theodore[12] **Davis** (Harvey[11], Harvey[10], James Harvey[9], Joseph[8], James[7], Nathaniel[6] Davis (2), Robert[5] Davis (1), Elizabeth[4] Hughes, Nicketti[3] Powhatan, Cleopatra[2], Chief[1] Powhatan) He married **Miss Twyman**.

Child of Theodore Davis and Miss Twyman is:
+ 319   i.   John[13] Davis.

232. Charles Grube[12] **Allen** (Nimrod Bryant[11], Rose C.[10] Davis, John[9], Joseph[8], James[7], Nathaniel[6] Davis (2), Robert[5] Davis (1), Elizabeth[4] Hughes, Nicketti[3] Powhatan, Cleopatra[2], Chief[1] Powhatan) was born May 25, 1882 in Richland County, Illinois, and died September 16, 1948 in Vermillion County, Illinois. He married **Blanche Eula Holmes** November 05, 1904 in Fayette County, Illinois. She was born September 10, 1886 in Marion County, Illinois, and died May 20, 1971 in Marion County, Illinois.

Child of Charles Allen and Blanche Holmes is:
+ 320   i.   William Nimrod[13] Allen, born November 13, 1907 in Salem, Marion County, Illinois; died August 25, 1979 in Martin, Weakley County, Tennessee.

Generation No. 13

233. Bobby Ellis[13] **Gilliam** (Ellis C.[12], Ida Sue[11] Burks, Charles Martin[10], William Pinkney[9], Richard[8], Samuel[7], Samuel[6], Mary[5] Davis, Elizabeth[4] Hughes, Nicketti[3] Powhatan, Cleopatra[2], Chief[1] Powhatan) was born August 18, 1934. He married **Margaret Tindall**.

Notes for Bobby Ellis Gilliam:
A professional Geologist in Shreveport, Louisiana.

Children of Bobby Gilliam and Margaret Tindall are:
+ 321   i.   Bobby Stephen[14] Gilliam.
+ 322   ii.   Mark Ellis Gilliam.
+ 323   iii. William Craig Gilliam.

234. Virginia[13] **Feild** (Henry Allison[12], Katherine Malvina[11] Hess, William Randolph[10], Margaret[9] Daveiss, Joseph[8] Davis, James[7], Nathaniel[6] Davis (2), Robert[5] Davis (1), Elizabeth[4] Hughes, Nicketti[3] Powhatan, Cleopatra[2], Chief[1] Powhatan) She married **Allen Walton**.

Child of Virginia Feild and Allen Walton is:
+ 324   i.   Virginia[14] Walton.

235. Andrew Nelson[13] **Phillips** (Annie Catherine[12] Hess, Dr. Nelson Irving[11] Hess II, Nelson Irving[10] Hess, Margaret[9] Daveiss, Joseph[8] Davis, James[7], Nathaniel[6] Davis (2), Robert[5] Davis (1), Elizabeth[4] Hughes, Nicketti[3] Powhatan, Cleopatra[2], Chief[1] Powhatan) was born December 08, 1887. He married **Marie Ellis** June 14, 1922.

Child of Andrew Phillips and Marie Ellis is:
    325   i.   Andrew Nelson[14] Phillips, Jr., born October 22, 1932.

245. Rebecca Caroline[13] Farrow (Sallie Emma[12] Hess, Dr. Nelson Irving[11] Hess II, Nelson Irving[10] Hess, Margaret[9] Daveiss, Joseph[8] Davis, James[7], Nathaniel[6] Davis (2), Robert[5] Davis (1), Elizabeth[4] Hughes, Nicketti[3] Powhatan, Cleopatra[2], Chief[1] Powhatan) was born May 12, 1909. She married **Luke Tooms** June 16, 1932. He was born April 04, 1900, and died December 19, 1949.

Children of Rebecca Farrow and Luke Tooms are:
+ 326   i.   Dr. Robert Edwin[14] Tooms, born October 26, 1933.
    327   ii.   Leighton Hess Tooms, born June 26, 1938.

247. Ella Louise[13] Hess (Nelson Irvin[12], Dr. Nelson Irving[11] Hess II, Nelson Irving[10] Hess, Margaret[9] Daveiss, Joseph[8] Davis, James[7], Nathaniel[6] Davis (2), Robert[5] Davis (1), Elizabeth[4] Hughes, Nicketti[3] Powhatan, Cleopatra[2], Chief[1] Powhatan) was born July 16, 1916, and died June 30, 1938.

Child of Ella Louise Hess is:
+ 328   i.   Roselle Louise[14] Hess, born June 01, 1937.

248. Nelson Irvin[13] Hess, IV. (Nelson Irvin[12], Dr. Nelson Irving[11] Hess II, Nelson Irving[10] Hess, Margaret[9] Daveiss, Joseph[8] Davis, James[7], Nathaniel[6] Davis (2), Robert[5] Davis (1), Elizabeth[4] Hughes, Nicketti[3] Powhatan, Cleopatra[2], Chief[1] Powhatan) was born February 22, 1919. He married **Maxine Broome** 1939.

Children of Nelson Hess and Maxine Broome are:
    329   i.   Nelson Irvin[14] Hess, V., born June 30, 1942.
    330   ii.   Preston Fletcher Hess, born October 11, 1949.
    331   iii. Malcohlm Hess, born September 15, 1954.

253. Annie Willard[13] Hess (Jamye Willard[12], Dr. Nelson Irving[11] Hess II, Nelson Irving[10] Hess, Margaret[9] Daveiss, Joseph[8] Davis, James[7], Nathaniel[6] Davis (2), Robert[5] Davis (1), Elizabeth[4] Hughes, Nicketti[3] Powhatan, Cleopatra[2], Chief[1] Powhatan) She married **Gaylon Bowen**.

Children of Annie Hess and Gaylon Bowen are:
    332   i.   Sidney Louise[14] Bowen.
    333   ii.   George Walker Bowen.

254. Patricia[13] Hess (John William "Jack"[12], James Ferdinand[11], Nelson Irving[10], Margaret[9] Daveiss, Joseph[8] Davis, James[7], Nathaniel[6] Davis (2), Robert[5] Davis (1), Elizabeth[4] Hughes, Nicketti[3] Powhatan, Cleopatra[2], Chief[1] Powhatan) was born 1929.

Patricia Hess (daughter of "Jack" Hess) and Col. Dressler-.

She married (1) **Will Gibson** 1948. He was born 1922. She married (2) **Colonel Dressler**. He died November 2001 in Cape Coral, Florida.

Martha Elizabeth Banks "Bitsy" Bell (center) with cousins Juliet Lewis and Jim Campbell at a family reunion, 1999.

Notes for Colonel Dressler:
Fought in Viet Nam. Died of complications due to Agent Orange.

Child of Patricia Hess and Will Gibson is:
+ 334   i. David[14] Gibson, born August 07, 1955 in Mt. Carmel, Illinois.

255. Martha Elizabeth[13] **Banks** (Anna Bell[12] Cresap, Nelson Adair[11], Nancy Adair[10] Hess, Margaret[9] Daveiss, Joseph[8] Davis, James[7], Nathaniel[6] Davis (2), Robert[5] Davis (1), Elizabeth[4] Hughes, Nicketti[3] Powhatan, Cleopatra[2], Chief[1] Powhatan) was born June 09, 1915. She married **William Clinton Bell**. He was born June 18, 1912 in Mississippi, and died June 29, 1980 in Humboldt, Tennessee.

Children of Martha Banks and William Bell are:
+ 335   i. William Clinton[14] Bell, Jr., born December 15, 1951.
+ 336 ii. David Banks Bell, born November 01, 1953.

257. John[13] **Banks** (Anna Bell[12] Cresap, Nelson Adair[11], Nancy Adair[10] Hess, Margaret[9] Daveiss, Joseph[8] Davis, James[7], Nathaniel[6] Davis (2), Robert[5] Davis (1), Elizabeth[4] Hughes, Nicketti[3] Powhatan, Cleopatra[2], Chief[1] Powhatan) was born June 18, 1918 in Humboldt, Tennessee, and died July 01, 1992. He married **Sue Standifer**.

Children of John Banks and Sue Standifer are:
337   i. Susan Walton[14] Banks, born June 23, 1951.

Notes for Susan Walton Banks:
At the time of this writing, Susan is unmarried and living in Nashville, Tennessee. She is the neice of Ms. Fannie Walton.

+ 338 ii. Kathryn Banks, born February 07, 1954.

259. Charles Edgar[13] **Cresap, Jr.** (Charles Edgar[12], Nelson Adair[11], Nancy Adair[10] Hess, Margaret[9] Daveiss, Joseph[8] Davis, James[7], Nathaniel[6] Davis (2), Robert[5] Davis (1), Elizabeth[4] Hughes, Nicketti[3] Powhatan, Cleopatra[2], Chief[1] Powhatan) was born 1918. He married **Bess Sanford**.

Children of Charles Cresap and Bess Sanford are:
339   i. Charles Edgar[14] Cresap III.

Notes for Charles Edgar Cresap III:
    At the time of this writing, Charles Cresap III, is living in Vicksburg, Mississippi. He has 2 children.

    340   ii.   Bardy Cresap.

260.   Nelson Cresap[13] Harrison (Katherine Louise[12] Cresap, Nelson Adair[11], Nancy Adair[10] Hess, Margaret[9] Daveiss, Joseph[8] Davis, James[7], Nathaniel[6] Davis (2), Robert[5] Davis (1), Elizabeth[4] Hughes, Nicketti[3] Powhatan, Cleopatra[2], Chief[1] Powhatan) was born May 25, 1912 in Trenton, Tennessee, and died December 10, 1981. He married **Frances Marian Williams** July 16, 1931. She was born January 26, 1912.
Child of Nelson Harrison and Frances Williams is:
    + 341   i.   Nelson Cresap[14] Harrison, Jr., born September 10, 1936.

261.   Mary Cassandra[13] Harrison (Katherine Louise[12] Cresap, Nelson Adair[11], Nancy Adair[10] Hess, Margaret[9] Daveiss, Joseph[8] Davis, James[7], Nathaniel[6] Davis (2), Robert[5] Davis (1), Elizabeth[4] Hughes, Nicketti[3] Powhatan, Cleopatra[2], Chief[1] Powhatan) was born 1914 in Trenton, Tennessee. She married **George Travis Hamilton** 1936.

Mary Cassandra's nickname was "Dit."

Children of Mary Harrison and George Hamilton are:
    342   i.   George Travis[14] Hamilton, Jr., born 1940; died 1969.
    + 343   ii.   Kate Cresap Hamilton, born 1941; died 1976.

262.   Frank Russell[13] Harrison (Katherine Louise[12] Cresap, Nelson Adair[11], Nancy Adair[10] Hess, Margaret[9] Daveiss, Joseph[8] Davis, James[7], Nathaniel[6] Davis (2), Robert[5] Davis (1), Elizabeth[4] Hughes, Nicketti[3] Powhatan, Cleopatra[2], Chief[1] Powhatan) was born 1918, and died 1972. He married **Lady Ruth Allen**.

Child of Frank Harrison and Lady Allen is:
    + 344   i.   Russell Allen[14] Harrison, born 1948 in Mayfield, Kentucky.

265.   Clifton Eugene[13] Tribble (Estelle Rebecca[12] Bennett, Kate[11] Price, Maria L.[10] Hess, Margaret[9] Daveiss, Joseph[8] Davis, James[7], Nathaniel[6] Davis (2), Robert[5] Davis (1), Elizabeth[4] Hughes, Nicketti[3] Powhatan, Cleopatra[2], Chief[1] Powhatan) was born March 12, 1895 in Fruitland, Tennessee, and died August 19, 1953 in Vidalia, Georgia. He married **Julia Elizabeth Herlong** July 15, 1919 in Lake City, Florida, daughter of George Herlong and Julia Clark. She was born January 16, 1896 in Fort White, Florida, and died September 1991 in Ft. Lauderdale, Florida.

Notes for Clifton Eugene Tribble:
    Followed his father's profession as a telegrapher. He was a linguist, musician and had a beautiful singing voice, loved Baseball and the game of Bridge. He enjoyed writing prose and poetry and had planned to write fiction when he retired.

Following a fatal heart attack suffered at his home, Clifton Eugene Tribble died August 19, 1953 and less than an hour later his mother Estelle Bennett Tribble, who was visiting, died of a heart attack. There was a double funeral in Vidalia after which Estelle was buried with her husband in Chuluota, Florida and Eugene was interred at Pine Crest Cemetery in Vidalia.

Notes for Julia Elizabeth Herlong:

Elizabeth was born four years after the Herlong brothers [including her father, George Yarbrough Herlong] their families and their parents, the Reverend Vastine Andrew and Mary Weaver Herlong moved from Edgefield County, South Carolina. They purchased pine land in North Florida, calling the settlement Herlong's and building a sawmill and all their homes around it.

After studying to become a teacher at the University of Florida, Gainesville, she accepted her first position at Seville, Florida where she met and married Clifton Tribble. They reared a daughter, Mary Elizabeth and later in life moved to Vidalia, Georgia where Clifton died. She then lived with Mary Elizabeth and her husband, Jim Cox, in Ft. Lauderdale until her death following a stroke in 1991. Her funeral was in the First Baptist Church in Vidalia with her nephew, the Right Reverend Bertram Nelson Herlong officiating. "Bert" flew from Detroit where he was Dean of the Episcopal Cathedral before being named Bishop of the Central Diocese of Tennessee.

Child of Clifton Tribble and Julia Herlong is:
+ 345   i.   Mary Elizabeth[14] Tribble, born November 11, 1927 in DeLand, Florida.

272. Oscar Lee[13] Powell (Annie Leslie[12] Price, William Hess[11], Maria L.[10] Hess, Margaret[9] Daveiss, Joseph[8] Davis, James[7], Nathaniel[6] Davis (2), Robert[5] Davis (1), Elizabeth[4] Hughes, Nicketti[3] Powhatan, Cleopatra[2], Chief[1] Powhatan) was born in Jonesboro, Arkansas. He married **Marie Hines**.

Child of Oscar Powell and Marie Hines is:
346   i.   Edward Lee[14] Powell.

273. Frances[13] Powell (Annie Leslie[12] Price, William Hess[11], Maria L.[10] Hess, Margaret[9] Daveiss, Joseph[8] Davis, James[7], Nathaniel[6] Davis (2), Robert[5] Davis (1), Elizabeth[4] Hughes, Nicketti[3] Powhatan, Cleopatra[2], Chief[1] Powhatan) was born in Jonesboro, Arkansas. She married **Thomas Clinton Droake**.

Children of Frances Powell and Thomas Droake are:
347   i.   Clinton[14] Droake.
348   ii.   Wayne Droake.

276. Jesse Cuthbert[13] Price (Frederick Carlton[12], William Hess[11], Maria L.[10] Hess, Margaret[9] Daveiss, Joseph[8] Davis, James[7], Nathaniel[6] Davis (2), Robert[5] Davis (1), Elizabeth[4] Hughes, Nicketti[3] Powhatan, Cleopatra[2], Chief[1] Powhatan) was born January 21, 1915 in Greenwood, Mississippi, and died 1966 in Columbia, Mississippi. He married **Flora Bill Regan** November 26, 1934 in Poplarville, Mississippi, daughter of Howard Regan and Myrtie Lowe. She was born 1915, and died 1983.

Children of Jesse Price and Flora Regan are:
349   i.   Jesse Cuthbert[14] Price, Jr., born 1945; died 1948.

+ 350   ii.   Judith Ann Price, born 1949.
+ 351   iii.   Patricia Regan Price, born 1951.

277. Irwin Vernon[13] **Price** (Frederick Carlton[12], William Hess[11], Maria L.[10] Hess, Margaret[9] Daveiss, Joseph[8] Davis, James[7], Nathaniel[6] Davis (2), Robert[5] Davis (1), Elizabeth[4] Hughes, Nicketti[3] Powhatan, Cleopatra[2], Chief[1] Powhatan) was born March 13, 1917 in Columbus, Mississippi, and died 1983 in Houston, Texas. He married **Ruby Rawls** May 26, 1939 in Leland, Mississippi, daughter of Jabus Rawls and Oneida Applewhite. She was born 1917.

Notes for Irwin Vernon Price:
     May be spelled Erwin Vernon Price. We have found both spellings in the family. LJG-MKA

Children of Irwin Price and Ruby Rawls are:
+ 352   i.   Frances O.[14] Price, born 1940.
   353   ii.   Mary Margaret Price, born 1943. She married Kenneth Scott.
   354   iii.   Ann Louise Price, born 1949. She married Wayne Wright.

278. Margaret Frances[13] **Price** (Frederick Carlton[12], William Hess[11], Maria L.[10] Hess, Margaret[9] Daveiss, Joseph[8] Davis, James[7], Nathaniel[6] Davis (2), Robert[5] Davis (1), Elizabeth[4] Hughes, Nicketti[3]

Margaret Price Perkins (far right) with cousins Tom Dunlap and this book's authors, Marian Albright (standing) and Lillian Gardiner, at the celebration of Lil's 85th birthday.

Powhatan, Cleopatra², Chief¹ Powhatan) was born July 24, 1922 in Columbus, Mississippi. She married **Edgar S. Perkins** February 22, 1942 in Columbia, Mississippi, son of Charlie Perkins and Sallie Vester. He was born March 09, 1921 in Corinth, Mississippi, and died November 07, 1977 in Corinth, Mississippi.

Children of Margaret Price and Edgar Perkins are:

+ 355   i.   Rebecca Anne¹⁴ Perkins, born August 10, 1944.
+ 356   ii.   Carlton Gregory Perkins, born May 04, 1948 in Corinth, Mississippi.
+ 357   iii.   Elliot Scott Perkins, born May 02, 1957.

279. Charles William¹³ Price (Frederick Carlton¹², William Hess¹¹, Maria L.¹⁰ Hess, Margaret⁹ Daveiss, Joseph⁸ Davis, James⁷, Nathaniel⁶ Davis (2), Robert⁵ Davis (1), Elizabeth⁴ Hughes, Nicketti³ Powhatan, Cleopatra², Chief¹ Powhatan) was born August 15, 1932 in Columbia, Mississippi. He married **Margaret Hoppen** January 30, 1958 in Bogalusa, Louisiana, daughter of Harry Hoppen and Thelma Webber.

Children of Charles Price and Margaret Hoppen are:

358   i.   Charles William¹⁴ Price, Jr., born 1960.
359   ii.   David Price, born 1964.

285. Benjamin Hess¹³ Browning (Ida¹² Thomas, Eliza Ann¹¹ Hess, James A.W.¹⁰, Margaret⁹ Daveiss, Joseph⁸ Davis, James⁷, Nathaniel⁶ Davis (2), Robert⁵ Davis (1), Elizabeth⁴ Hughes, Nicketti³ Powhatan, Cleopatra², Chief¹ Powhatan) was born November 06, 1903 in Gibson County, Tennessee, and died January 15, 1979 in Gibson County, Tennessee. He married **Mary Nell Martin** November 27, 1921 in Gibson County, Tennessee. She was born July 11, 1904 in Gibson County, Tennessee, and died January 27, 1974 in Gibson County, Tennessee.

Children of Benjamin Browning and Mary Martin are:

360   i.   Mary Helen¹⁴ Browning, born September 11, 1924.
+ 361   ii.   Geraldine Browning, born March 28, 1929 in Gibson County, Tennessee.
362   iii.   Charles Robert Browning, born January 18, 1931.

287. Eleanor Louise¹³ Browning (Ida¹² Thomas, Eliza Ann¹¹ Hess, James A.W.¹⁰, Margaret⁹ Daveiss, Joseph⁸ Davis, James⁷, Nathaniel⁶ Davis (2), Robert⁵ Davis (1), Elizabeth⁴ Hughes, Nicketti³ Powhatan, Cleopatra², Chief¹ Powhatan) was born January 16, 1910. She married **Wiliam Gordon "Jack" Cooke**.

Children of Eleanor Browning and Wiliam Cooke are:

+ 363   i.   William Robert¹⁴ Cooke, born January 11, 1932.
+ 364   ii.   Charles Browning Cooke, born April 07, 1933.

288. Warner Ebenezer¹³ Dunlap, Jr. (Warner Ebenezer¹², Susan¹¹ Hess, James A.W.¹⁰, Margaret⁹ Daveiss, Joseph⁸ Davis, James⁷, Nathaniel⁶ Davis (2), Robert⁵ Davis (1), Elizabeth⁴ Hughes, Nicketti³ Powhatan, Cleopatra², Chief¹ Powhatan) was born December 25, 1903 in Gibson County, Tennessee, and died August 1979 in Stanton, Tennessee. He married **Dorothy Holland Tucker** November 11, 1927. She was born December 06, 1901 in Stanton, Tennessee, and died 1998 in Stanton, Tennessee.

Notes for Warner Ebenezer Dunlap, Jr.:

After graduation from college Warner went to work for the Tennessee Highway Department before there was an adequate road system in the state, and was very instrumental in planning the highways we now enjoy. He retired as Chief Engineer of the Department - at age 70. He and his wife moved to Stanton, Tennessee and lived their remaining years in her ancestral home there.

Child of Warner Dunlap and Dorothy Tucker is:
    365   i.   May Alma[14] Dunlap.

289. Kimbrough Lafayette[13] Dunlap (Warner Ebenezer[12], Susan[11] Hess, James A.W.[10], Margaret[9] Daveiss, Joseph[8] Davis, James[7], Nathaniel[6] Davis (2), Robert[5] Davis (1), Elizabeth[4] Hughes, Nicketti[3] Powhatan, Cleopatra[2], Chief[1] Powhatan) was born July 26, 1907 in Humboldt, Gibson County, Tennessee, and died 1987 in Humboldt, Gibson County, Tennessee. He married **Anna Sue Craddock** July 05, 1927, daughter of Ben Craddock and Lucy Graves. She was born October 25, 1906 in Gibson County, Tennessee.

Notes for Kimbrough Lafayette Dunlap:

Graduated from Humboldt High School in 1924, attended U.T. Knoxville College of Engineering, and Union University in Jackson, Tennessee.

At the time of his marriage to Anna Sue Craddock [Sudie] in 1927, Kimbrough was working for Mr. Charles Cresap in charge of the road construction crew building and paving the highway from Alamo to Trenton. Later he bought into the insurance business with Walter Warmath, and on Walter's death purchased the remaining share from Walter's widow, Sula Dunlap Warmath. At that time [1930] the name was changed from Warmath and Dunlap to Kimbrough L. Dunlap Insurance Agency. About 1937 Kimbrough accepted a position with Prudential to reorganize the Nashville office and moved there for a stay of a few months. This lengthened into years. Both sons were born there, and Kimbrough stayed until he entered the United States Navy in 1944 with a rank of Lieutenant. Kimbrough, Jr. has a copy of the ship's log kept by his father from 1944 until the war ended—the ship did not return to the U.S. during that time.

After the war Kimbrough and Robert Guy James went into partnership in the fruit business and by 1947 Kimbrough added the frozen strawberry business—working out of the old Donovan Hotel at the "Crossing." Later he added frozen vegetable processing under the Snow Crop label.

According to son, Kimbrough, sometime in the 60's Kimbrough looked around and realized that everyone who had been in the fruit business was dead, and if he wanted to live to enjoy his grandchildren he had better find a less stressful way to make a living. So, back to the insurance business, adding a Real Estate operation in 1967 and in 1968 Kimbrough, Jr. joined him in partnership, moving his family to Humboldt from Montgomery, Alabama.

Kimbrough died in 1987 and is buried in Rose Hill Cemetery, Humboldt.

Children of Kimbrough Dunlap and Anna Craddock are:
    + 366   i.   Kimbrough Lafayette[14] Dunlap, Jr., born May 28, 1941 in Nashville, Tennessee.
    + 367   ii.   Dr. Warner Benjamin Dunlap, born July 01, 1943 in Nashville, Tennessee.

295. Hulon Otis[13] **Warlick, Jr.** (Willie Mai Chester[12] Dunlap, Willietta[11] Hess, James A.W.[10], Margaret[9] Daveiss, Joseph[8] Davis, James[7], Nathaniel[6] Davis (2), Robert[5] Davis (1), Elizabeth[4] Hughes, Nicketti[3] Powhatan, Cleopatra[2], Chief[1] Powhatan) was born January 18, 1903 in Humboldt, Gibson County, Tennessee, and died September 24, 1964 in Memphis, Tennessee. He married **Frances Webb Smith** June 15, 1930 in Grace Episcopal Church, Paducah, Kentucky. She was born May 10, 1906, and died June 02, 1991.

Children of Hulon Warlick and Frances Smith are:

+ 368   i.   Hulon Otis[14] Warlick, born August 14, 1931 in Memphis, Tennessee.
+ 369   ii. Katherine Webb Warlick, born August 05, 1934.
+ 370   iii. Frances Goulder Warlick, born November 26, 1938 in Memphis, Tennessee.
  371   iv. Anne Dunlap Warlick, born October 02, 1942 in Memphis, Tennessee.

296. Mildred[13] **Warlick** (Willie Mai Chester[12] Dunlap, Willietta[11] Hess, James A.W.[10], Margaret[9] Daveiss, Joseph[8] Davis, James[7], Nathaniel[6] Davis (2), Robert[5] Davis (1), Elizabeth[4] Hughes, Nicketti[3] Powhatan, Cleopatra[2], Chief[1] Powhatan) was born September 11, 1904 in Humboldt, Gibson County, Tennessee, and died May 17, 1999 in Humboldt, Gibson County, Tennessee. She married **Winfred F. Jones** December 25, 1928 in Humboldt, Tennessee, son of George Jones and Alice Miller. He was born September 12, 1901 in Greer, South Carolina, and died November 09, 1995 in Gibson County, Tennessee.

Mildred graduated from Humboldt High School in 1922, and from the University of Tennessee, Knoxville in 1926. She was a High School teacher for 9 years.

Winfred F. Jones "Ted" grew up in South Carolina and lived in several mill towns where his father was employed as a Superintendent. He attended Clemson College 2 years, then began playing professional baseball for the Texas League and Cotton States League—playing ball in the summers and working in the mills during the winter months.

His family moved to Humboldt, Tennessee where his father was Superintendent of the Avondale Mill. At the time of his marriage to Mildred Warlick in 1928, Ted was working at the Trenton, Tennessee Mill.

In 1936, Ted and his brother William Ralph Jones, Sr. started Jones Manufacturing Company, a textile mill, in Humboldt. In 1986, the W.F. Jones family sold their interest in the company to the W.R. Jones family.

Ted and wife, Mildred, were active members of the First Baptist Church of Humboldt, where she taught Sunday School for 60 years. They both enjoyed golf, fishing and bridge. Ted became a member of the Southern Senior Golf Association in the mid fifties and for many years they enjoyed traveling throughout the South to these Golf Tournaments.

They are buried in Rose Hill Cemetery, Humboldt, Tennessee.

Mildred Warlick and W.F. "Ted" Jones

Children of Mildred Warlick and Winfred Jones are:

+ 372   i.   Winfred F.[14] Jones, Jr., born April 18, 1936 in Humboldt, Gibson County, Tennessee.

+ 373   ii.   Rena Jones, born December 31, 1937 in Humboldt, Gibson County, Tennessee.

Monie Warlick and Riley Clark

297. Monie[13] Warlick (Willie Mai Chester[12] Dunlap, Willietta[11] Hess, James A.W.[10], Margaret[9] Daveiss, Joseph[8] Davis, James[7], Nathaniel[6] Davis (2), Robert[5] Davis (1), Elizabeth[4] Hughes, Nicketti[3] Powhatan, Cleopatra[2], Chief[1] Powhatan) was born September 23, 1910, and died July 30, 1978. She married **Riley Clark** May 10, 1936 in Humboldt, Tennessee. He was born February 16, 1911, and died September 18, 1990.

Children of Monie Warlick and Riley Clark are:

+ 374   i.   Kitty Ann[14] Clark, born December 22, 1940.

+ 375   ii.   Riley Clark, Jr., born August 05, 1943 in Humboldt, Gibson county, Tennessee; died 1986 in Charlotte, North Carolina.

+ 376   iii.   Charles Warlick Clark, born July 29, 1952 in Humboldt, Gibson County, Tennessee.

299. Alsay[13] Johnson (John Orgain[12], Katherine Nelson[11] Hess, James A.W.[10], Margaret[9] Daveiss, Joseph[8] Davis, James[7], Nathaniel[6] Davis (2), Robert[5] Davis (1), Elizabeth[4] Hughes, Nicketti[3] Powhatan, Cleopatra[2], Chief[1] Powhatan) was born September 02, 1916 in Brownsville, Tennessee, and died January 08, 1995 in Shelbyville, Tennessee. He married **Sue Paine Welch** May 21, 1955 in Starkville, Mississippi, daughter of Julian Welch and Adelaide Sevier. She was born January 04, 1929 in Savannah, Tennessee.

Notes for Alsay Johnson:

After receiving his education in the Brownsville public schools and B.A. from Cumberland University in Lebanon, Tennessee, Alsay taught in Kennett, Missouri, Brownsville, Tennessee, Orleans, France, Heidelberg, Germany, Shelbyville, Tennessee and the Webb School, Bell Buckle, Tennessee.

Notes for Sue Paine Welch:

Educated in the Savannah public schools, received a B.S. Degree from University of Tennessee, Knoxville; M.D. from U.T., Knoxville in 1953...Internship at Medical College of Virginia in Richmond; Residency in Cardiology and Internal Medicine at Kennedy V.A. Hospital in Memphis, Tennessee. Retired from the medical field in 1997 and spends her time traveling and visiting with children and grandchildren in Texas, Alabama and California.

Children of Alsay Johnson and Sue Welch are:

377   i.   Jane Sevier[14] Johnson, born March 22, 1956 in Orleans, France.

Editor; archaeological firm.

+ 378   ii.   John Mann Johnson, born April 26, 1957 in Orleans, France.
+ 379   iii.   Julia Claiborne Johnson, born May 12, 1959 in Heidelberg, Germany.

300. Lillian Jeanette[13] **Lannom** (Marian Lucinda[12] Campbell, Jane Hamilton[11] Hess, James A.W.[10], Margaret[9] Daveiss, Joseph[8] Davis, James[7], Nathaniel[6] Davis (2), Robert[5] Davis (1), Elizabeth[4] Hughes, Nicketti[3] Powhatan, Cleopatra[2], Chief[1] Powhatan) was born July 03, 1905 in Humboldt, Gibson County, Tennessee, and died October 18, 1987 in Atlanta, Georgia. She married **Joseph Walter Knowles** March 12, 1932 in Jackson, Tennessee, son of Homer Knowles and Lona Teague. He was born January 20, 1904 in Luray, Henderson County, Tennessee, and died January 12, 1982 in Atlanta, Georgia.

Walter and Lillian Lannom Knowles. **Left:** *early 1940s.* **Right:** *1970s.*

Lillian died in Atlanta, Georgia and is buried in Ridgecrest Cemetery, Jackson, Tennessee. See notes on her mother, Marian Campbell Lannom, for additional information.

Joseph Walter Knowles graduated from Jackson High School; attended Union University.

While in High School he "jerked sodas" at a drugstore in East Jackson. One day a young boy came in trying to sell a typewriter - Walter said he'd buy it if he could pay it out on "time"—5 cents a week. The young man was Phillip Rodgers [they were both about 15] and they formed a life long friendship. Later they both worked as clerks at Bond Shoe Store. Then Walter took a position as salesman for Wilson Brothers Men's Clothing based in Chicago. Early in the 1930's he bought half interest in McCall Hughes Men's Clothing Store in Jackson, Tennessee. At the death of his business partner, Addison Johnston, Walter purchased the remaining stock and became its sole owner.

His store became a gathering place for the "men about town" and he always had a group of handsome young college men clerking.

Due to repeated sinus and ear infections as a child, he suffered hearing loss, which prevented him from active duty during World War II, however he joined the State Guard, which took over the duties of our National Guard while they were serving in the military.

Walter was a member of the Cumberland Presbyterian Church where he served as Deacon and Elder. He was a respected business leader, President of the Jackson Lions Club, of which he was a charter member, and was active in several other Civic Organizations. He was a devoted husband and father.

Walter was diagnosed with lung cancer in 1979 and after a valiant fight died of pneumonia in 1982. He is buried in Ridgecrest Cemetery, Jackson, Tennessee.

Children of Lillian Lannom and Joseph Knowles are:

+ 380   i.   Jane Clementine[14] Knowles, born October 20, 1933 in Jackson, Madison County, Tennessee.
+ 381   ii.   Marian Lucinda Campbell Knowles, born July 27, 1936 in Jackson, Madison County, Tennessee.
+ 382   iii. Lillian Alice Knowles, born December 21, 1941 in Jackson, Tennessee.

301. Frances Powers[13] Long (Gabrilla Hess[12] Campbell, Jane Hamilton[11] Hess, James A.W.[10], Margaret[9] Daveiss, Joseph[8] Davis, James[7], Nathaniel[6] Davis (2), Robert[5] Davis (1), Elizabeth[4] Hughes, Nicketti[3] Powhatan, Cleopatra[2], Chief[1] Powhatan) was born June 24, 1902 in Slidell, Louisiana, and died April 22, 1978 in Florida. She married **Roy Aldrich** 1930 in Slidell, Louisiana. He was born September 01, 1899.

Notes for Roy Aldrich:
Presbyterian minister. Started Detroit Bible College in Detroit, Michigan.

Children of Frances Long and Roy Aldrich are:

383   i.   Roy[14] Aldrich, Jr., born October 18, 1930 in Detroit, Michigan. He married Patricia.
384   ii.   Shirley Ann Aldrich, born June 05, 1944 in Detroit, Michigan. She married Kenneth Leroy Schafer.

302. Jane Hess[13] Long (Gabrilla Hess[12] Campbell, Jane Hamilton[11] Hess, James A.W.[10], Margaret[9] Daveiss, Joseph[8] Davis, James[7], Nathaniel[6] Davis (2), Robert[5] Davis (1), Elizabeth[4] Hughes, Nicketti[3] Powhatan, Cleopatra[2], Chief[1] Powhatan) was born November 01, 1904 in Ripley, Tennessee, and died February 21, 1995 in Akron, Ohio. She married **Ivan Clarence Kuhns**. He was born May 08, 1891, and died July 1987.

Ivan was a veteran of World War 1. He was employed by the Western Maryland RailwayTransit.

Children of Jane Long and Ivan Kuhns are:

305   i.   Ivan Clarence[14] Kuhns, born September 26, 1935.

Notes for Ivan Clarence Kuhns:
Ivan, Jr. was Sports journalist for the Newark Star Ledger in New Jersey for 34 years. He married Helen Potter in May of 1986. They divorced in 1988.

+ 386   ii.   Robert Lydon Kuhns, born September 24, 1936.
387   iii. Lydon Marshall Kuhns, born March 02, 1946; died February 19, 1998.

Notes for Lydon Marshall Kuhns:
Lydon Marshall Kuhns was a freelance editor of various commercial publications, and an unpublished author. He was unmarried.

303. Robert Ira[13] Long (Gabrilla Hess[12] Campbell, Jane Hamilton[11] Hess, James A.W.[10], Margaret[9] Daveiss, Joseph[8] Davis, James[7], Nathaniel[6] Davis (2), Robert[5] Davis (1), Elizabeth[4] Hughes, Nicketti[3] Powhatan, Cleopatra[2], Chief[1] Powhatan) was born February 17, 1907 in Ripley, Tennessee, and died November 11, 1985 in Maryville, Tennessee. He married **Helen Sweet** June 26, 1930 in Garden Plain, Illinois. She was born November 06, 1904 in Garden Plain, Illinois, and died August 17, 2001 in Brenham, Texas.

Robert Ira Long was a Presbyterian minister.

Children of Robert Long and Helen Sweet are:
> 388 i. Nancy Gay[14] Long, born September 21, 1932 in Moberly, Missouri. She married George Michael Shoup June 05, 1951 in Houston, Texas.

Notes for George Michael Shoup:
> Goes by his middle name, Michael.

> 389 ii. Robert Ira Long III, born October 28, 1934 in Water Valley, Mississippi. He married Marion Mona Francis June 12, 1956 in Tacoma Park, Maryland.
> 390 iii. Helen Sweet Long, born October 27, 1938 in Water Valley, Mississippi. She married David Paris Young June 10, 1960 in Ferguson, Missouri.
> 391 iv. James Campbell Long, born August 26, 1944 in Clinton, Missouri. He married Susan Jane Small August 06, 1966 in Ferguson, Missouri.

304. Grace Campbell[13] Long (Gabrilla Hess[12] Campbell, Jane Hamilton[11] Hess, James A.W.[10], Margaret[9] Daveiss, Joseph[8] Davis, James[7], Nathaniel[6] Davis (2), Robert[5] Davis (1), Elizabeth[4] Hughes, Nicketti[3] Powhatan, Cleopatra[2], Chief[1] Powhatan) was born June 27, 1910 in Ripley, Tennessee. She married **Harold Anders Hoeglund** June 30, 1932 in Slidell, Louisiana, son of John Hoeglund and Amelia Nelson. He was born May 26, 1905 in McPherson, Kansas, and died April 03, 1979 in Pueblo, Colorado.

Notes for Grace Campbell Long:
> School teacher.

Notes for Harold Anders Hoeglund:
> School teacher.

Children of Grace Long and Harold Hoeglund are:
> + 392 i. Jean[14] Hoeglund, born October 15, 1939 in Kitchican, Alaska.
> + 393 ii. Anne Hoeglund, born May 11, 1941 in Emporia, Kansas.
> + 394 iii. Gabrilla Hoeglund, born July 30, 1944 in Humboldt, Gibson County, Tennessee.
> + 395 iv. Karen Sue Hoeglund, born September 07, 1950 in Yakima, Washington.
> 396 v. John Nelson Hoeglund, born January 31, 1954 in Yakima, Washington. He married Sonja Tande August 21, 1987 in Holland Lake Lodge, Condon, Montana.

Grace Long Hoeglund

306. Campbell Garth[13] **Long** (Gabrilla Hess[12] Campbell, Jane Hamilton[11] Hess, James A.W.[10], Margaret[9] Daveiss, Joseph[8] Davis, James[7], Nathaniel[6] Davis (2), Robert[5] Davis (1), Elizabeth[4] Hughes, Nicketti[3] Powhatan, Cleopatra[2], Chief[1] Powhatan) was born February 15, 1919 in Ripley, Mississippi, and died February 17, 1996 in Temple, Oklahoma. He married **Betty Carpenter** May 18, 1944 in Henryville, Indiana, daughter of Oliver Carpenter and Mary Murphy. She was born September 24, 1924 in Jackson County, Indiana.

Campbell Garth Long was a Presbyterian minister.

Children of Campbell Long and Betty Carpenter are:

> 397   i.   Campbell Garth[14] Long, born August 12, 1945 in Logansport, Indiana. He married Carolyn Sue Hamburter May 31, 1970 in Layton, Oklahoma.
> 398   ii.   Barbara Jean Long, born February 14, 1947 in Logansport, Indiana. She married Ducarrol Munroe November 15, 1969 in Temple, Oklahoma.
> 399   iii.   Beverly Ann Long, born May 25, 1950 in Logansport, Indiana. She married James Eddy Bennett July 10, 1968 in Temple, Oklahoma.
> 400   iv.   Brenda Kay Long, born January 13, 1952 in Logansport, Indiana. She married (1) Mike Brooks June 12, 1970 in Temple, Oklahoma. She married (2) David Pinner June 10, 1978 in Temple, Oklahoma.
> 401   v.   John Oliver Long, born September 20, 1956 in Comanche, Oklahoma. He married Alisa Tucker May 19, 1978 in Temple, Oklahoma.

307. Levi Ross[13] **Campbell, Jr.** (Levi Ross[12], Jane Hamilton[11] Hess, James A.W.[10], Margaret[9] Daveiss, Joseph[8] Davis, James[7], Nathaniel[6] Davis (2), Robert[5] Davis (1), Elizabeth[4] Hughes, Nicketti[3] Powhatan, Cleopatra[2], Chief[1] Powhatan) was born May 08, 1936 in Memphis, Tennessee. He married **Carolyn Ann Boswell** July 16, 1966, daughter of William Boswell and Frances Hooks. She was born March 27, 1939 in Memphis, Tennessee.
Levi Ross Campbell, Jr. is a banker in Memphis, Tennessee.

Children of Levi Campbell and Carolyn Boswell are:

> + 402   i.   Levi Ross Campbell, III born February 09, 1968.
> + 403   ii.   Dr. Dorothy Kathleen Campbell, born January 15, 1971 in Memphis, Tennessee.

309. Jane Bright[13] **Johnson** (Lillian Jeanette[12] Campbell, Jane Hamilton[11] Hess, James A.W.[10], Margaret[9] Daveiss, Joseph[8] Davis, James[7], Nathaniel[6] Davis (2), Robert[5] Davis (1), Elizabeth[4] Hughes, Nicketti[3] Powhatan, Cleopatra[2], Chief[1] Powhatan) was born March 02, 1914 in Humboldt, Gibson County, Tennessee. She married **(1) Elmer Hunt**. He was born August 18, 1908 in Louisiana. She married **(2) Walker Hassell Smith** 1954 in Oxford, Mississippi. He was born February 02, 1911 in Oxford, Mississippi, and died October 02, 1990 in Amelia Island, Florida.

Jane Bright Johnson graduated from Humboldt High School in June of 1931 and married Elmer [Mutt] Hunt that

Jane Johnson Hunt, 1953.

same month. Their two children were born in 1933 and 1937. In 1940, using money she had recieved for helping with the census, Jane went to Nashville to learn the florist business.

From the Geny family, whose Geny's Flower Shop was a thriving business, she learned floral design, wedding planning, and funeral arrangements. Back in Humboldt, Jane began her own business - Jane's Flowers - working first from her home, then building her own shop on Main Street. Being indus-

Walker Hassell Smith and Jane Johnson Hunt Smith

trious and innovative and as Bright as her middle name suggested, she soon built a large clientele.

In addition to operating the flower shop, and selling her homemade divinity, Jane worked her husband's truck farm, personally hauling the crops into Humboldt to be processed. She found ways to increase the efficiency of the processing situation - from the unloading sheds all the way to dispersal to consumers. She remembers well an experience late one evening as she arrived at the sheds with son, Roy, and daughter, Jane, asleep in the car. When she pulled up to have her load of cabbages weighed, it was discovered, to her horror, and the delight of the audience of men, that the trailer had not been attached to the car and there was nothing to show for a very long day's work.

The family's activities during the war years were related to home, school and church. There were radio programs on Sunday nights, bicycle rides to her mother's house, with a watermelon in the basket and children riding behind. Practice "airraid blackouts" made life even more interesting.

Jane became President of the Humboldt Women's Club, organized a City Library Board, contributed to the planning, building and opening of the public library, and was a member of the Gibson County Library Board.

As her Floral business flourished, Jane's reputation as a premier floral artist spread and she was a much sought after speaker, teacher and organizer, traveling extensively in the United States, Canada and Cuba, was elected to the FTD Board of Directors 1953-54, its only woman director and was responsible for public relations. She organized the Gibson County Florist Association and was a board member of the Southeastern Florist Association.

Jane and Mutt divorced in 1951 and in 1954 she married Walker Hassell Smith, a colleague and owner/operator of the Oxford Floral Company and Greenhouses in Oxford, Mississippi. Hassell was a widower with a daughter, Lou Alice, age six. In September of 1958 their household increased with the birth of Lillian Susan Walker Smith.

Hassell added a Finance Company to his other enterprises with offices in Oxford and Holly Springs.

Convinced that Oxford was ready for a major downtown motel, the Smiths decided to relocate their home and use that site for a Downtowner Motor Inn. The Smiths donated their antebellum home, Cedar Oaks, to the Oxford-Lafayette Historic Homes, Inc. and it was moved to the site where its architect's [William Turner] home once stood. In 1964 the Downtowner Inn was completed, later becoming the Holiday Inn with an addition including a penthouse residence for the Smiths.

Hassell expanded his businesses to include World Travel Agency and was named Director of Cruise Operations for Star Cruises.

The Smiths and Roy Hunt bought the first concominuim to be sold on Amelia Island Plantation off the coast of Jacksonville, Florida. Later Jane and Hassell built a lovely home on Amelia Island, with a front view of the golf course and overlooking scenic marshlands from the rear. For years friends and family members enjoyed Southern hospitality in their home and in their Condo.

In October of 1989, Hassell died of complications following a stroke he had suffered in 1978. A memorial service was held for him at the Amelia Island Chapel, [an Interdenominational Community Church he had helped organize and of which he was a charter member], followed with burial at St. Peter's Cemetery in Oxford, Mississippi.

Jane later sold the Amelia Island home and moved to Gainesville, Florida where she lives at this time - just across the street from her son, Roy.

Notes for Elmer Hunt:
In the lumber business in Humboldt, Tennessee.

Notes for Walker Hassell Smith:
Graduated from the University of Mississippi in 1933 with a Business Major in Accounting. Was drafted into the U.S. Military in 1941, released [because of age] but called back to active duty in 1942, accepted for Officer Candidate School, from which he emerged a Second Lieutenant. He was assigned to the Western Defense Command in Los Angeles, California, promoted to First Lieutenant becoming aide to Commanding General, Paul Baade - a position he kept until the war ended.

Battle experiences in Europe included five major campaigns; he received a battlefield promotion from Captain to Major by General Patton and knew all the commanders of all the armies in Europe including Generals Bradley and Eisenhower. After victory in Europe, he toured major U.S. cities with General Baade - marching and cheering in parades and in speeches - before leaving the military in 1946.

For more information on Hassell, see notes for Jane Bright Johnson.

Children of Jane Johnson and Elmer Hunt are:
+ 404   i.   Elmer Leroy[14] Hunt, born August 10, 1933.
  405   ii.   Jane Johnson Hunt, born March 11, 1937. She married Dr. James Cloud McLin; born 1934 in Memphis, Tennessee; died September 15, 1997 in Jacksonville, Florida.

Jane Johnson Hunt attended Randolph-Macon Women's College, graduated from University of Mississippi in 1959 with B.A. Degree. Dean's List and sorority officer while there. Has had a variety of interesting and demanding jobs including Interior Design projects, Banking, Office Management, Public Relations and Advertising. From 1972 until 1979, Jane traveled with her husband, Jim, on various international assignments. Since 1987 she has been with Sarvis, Inc. in Jacksonville, Florida where she holds the position of Executive Assistant to the president of the company, and is Administrative Director of Conference Center at the Avenues [owned by the President of Sarvis].

Dr. James Cloud McLin was born in Memphis and reared in Earle, Arkansas. He began piano lessons in Memphis at the age of four and made his orchestral debut at age twelve playing the Grieg Concerto with the Memphis Symphony. He received the highest ranking in the National Piano Playing Auditions and was the first student to do so. He also held the Young Artist Diploma and Paderewski Medal from the National Guild of Piano Teachers. After graduation from Rhodes College [then Southwestern] in Memphis, he won a Rotary Fellowship to the Royal Conservatory in Brussels, Belgium.

While serving as Director of Product and Musical Development with the Hammond Corporation, he was responsible for several performance features commonly found today on electronic keyboards. He was co-inventor of the Autochord and pioneered several other developments in musical technology. After a career in business and consulting, Dr. McLin resumed his musical pursuits at Florida State

University School of Music, and in December of 1996 received a doctorate in piano performance under Edward Kilenyi.

After a long and valiant battle with cancer, Jim died at the age of 63.

Child of Jane Johnson and Walker Smith is:

      406   i.   Lillian Susan Walker[14] Smith, born September 14, 1958. She married Ray Sahag April 08, 1989 in Amelia Island, Florida; born August 13, 1957.

Notes for Lillian Susan Walker Smith:

Walker and husband, Ray, work together as very well known and respected coaches of professional tennis athletes. They reside and work in the Jackson, Mississippi area but attract clients from all over the United States.

Walker earned a B.S. Degree from Colorado College, Colorado Springs, Colorado in 1982 and immediately began honing her special coaching expertise. From Junior Tennis Camp Instructor in Deerfield, Ma. to Co-designer of the annual program, daily lectures on new research and pertinent topics for Staff and all Nick Bollettieri Tennis Academy students in Bradenton, Florida, she has shown a consistent innovative gift which has served her students well.

Ray graduated from Jacksonville State University with a B.S. in General Management and since has instructed Junior and Adult classes in various aspects of the Tennis Profession. One of his fields of expertise is racquet stringing and customizing. At present he is the Head Professional, and Director of the Junior Elite Program at the Bridges Tennis Center in Jackson, Mississippi.

310. Marian Lucille[13] Johnson (Lillian Jeanette[12] Campbell, Jane Hamilton[11] Hess, James A.W.[10], Margaret[9] Daveiss, Joseph[8] Davis, James[7], Nathaniel[6] Davis (2), Robert[5] Davis (1), Elizabeth[4] Hughes, Nicketti[3] Powhatan, Cleopatra[2], Chief[1] Powhatan) was born February 10, 1916 in Humboldt, Gibson County, Tennessee. She married **Captain James Russell Graves** August 01, 1935 in Humboldt, Gibson County, Tennessee, son of William Graves and Mary Walton. He was born September 25, 1916 in Milan, Gibson County, Tennessee.

Marian was born in Humboldt, Tennessee, graduated from Humboldt High School and attended the University of Tennessee from 1933 until her marriage to Russell Graves in 1935. While attending the University she pledged Chi Omega and is still supporting the sorority.

After a 20-year career with the State of Tennessee Department of Employment, in Chattanooga, where she and Russell made their home, Marian retired with the title of Manager 1. She then joined her husband traveling in their motor home until settling in Memphis, Tennessee.

Their son, James Russell Graves, Jr., was born in Humboldt where Marian was living with her mother during part of Russell's military duty. Their daughter, Juliet Campbell Graves was born in Union City, Tennessee where Russell along with two of his brothers owned and operated Graves Flying School.

Marian Johnson and Russell Graves

Notes for Captain James Russell Graves:

Born in Milan, Tennessee, Russell moved, with his family, to a farm near Humboldt when a baby. He graduated from Humboldt High School and married his childhood sweetheart, Marian Johnson. In 1942 he and Marian moved to Chattanooga, Tennessee where he enjoyed a long career in the map-making division of the Tennessee Valley Authority. This career was interrupted by World War II, during which he served his country as a bomber pilot in the Army Air Corps. After discharge, he joined the Air Force Reserves, then later the Tennessee Air National Guard. This enabled him to fly small planes based in Chattanooga when and where he wanted. In 1969 he retired with the rank of Captain.

Russell continued his association with the T.V.A. until retirement in 1976. At that time he and Marian bought a motor home and "saw the U.S.A." until 1988 when they settled in Memphis, Tennessee where they now reside. They visit frequently with Marian's sister, Lillian [Mrs. Laurence] Gardiner, and a wide circle of friends. They are active members of the Trinity Methodist Church.

Children of Marian Johnson and James Graves are:

    407   i.   James Russell[14] Graves, born August 26, 1944 in Humboldt, Gibson County, Tennessee.

Notes for James Russell Graves:

After graduating from high School in Chattanooga, Tennessee in 1962, James Russell Graves, Jr. [Russ] served a four-year enlistment in the United States Air Force during the Viet Nam War. His duty took him out of bases in Viet Nam and King Salmon A.F. B. in Alaska.

Most of Russ's working years were with Greyhound Bus Company, mainly in Wyoming. At this writing, he is living in Memphis where he retired following a heart attack, but he has plans to build and live on property he owns in Sedalia, Missouri.

  + 408   ii.   Juliet Campbell Graves, born July 18, 1948 in Union City, Tennessee.

311. Dorothy Nesbitt[13] Campbell (Zachariah Joseph[12], Jane Hamilton[11] Hess, James A.W.[10], Margaret[9] Daveiss, Joseph[8] Davis, James[7], Nathaniel[6] Davis (2), Robert[5] Davis (1), Elizabeth[4] Hughes, Nicketti[3] Powhatan, Cleopatra[2], Chief[1] Powhatan) was born August 21, 1912 in Humboldt, Gibson County, Tennessee, and died June 11, 1998 in Covington, Tipton County, Tennessee. She married **Richard Mann Currie** June 26, 1934. He was born August 11, 1908 in Brownsville, Haywood County, Tennessee, and died September 09, 1989 in Covington, Tipton County, Tennessee.

Notes for Dorothy Nesbitt Campbell:

The first child of Zach and Corrinne Campbell, Dorothy Nesbit Campbell was born August 21, 1912 in Humboldt, Tennessee. She had three younger siblings, Juliet Campbell Lewis, Janice Campbell Roy and Zach Campbell, Jr.

Dorothy grew up in Humboldt, attended Huntington College, and graduated with an honors degree in Library Science from the University of Tennessee in Knoxville.

On June 24, 1934, Dorothy married Richard Mann Currie of Brownsville, Tennessee, whom she met and courted at the annual Taylor Kinfolks Camp Meeting. They had two children, Corrinne Campbell Currie and Richard Mann Currie, Jr.

Dorothy was a devout member of the United Methodist Church, a devoted wife and mother, a renowned cook, an avid gardener, and an exemplary grandmother to her five grandchildren. She lived every day of her happy life following the words of the Apostle, Paul, found in Colossians 3:12-14. Dorothy died in Covington, Tennessee and was buried at Tabernacle, Brownsville, Tennessee.

Notes for Richard Mann Currie:
    Buried at Tabernacle, Brownsville, Tennessee.

Children of Dorothy Campbell and Richard Currie are:
+ 409   i.   Corrinne Campbell[14] Currie, born January 14, 1936 in Humboldt, Gibson County, Tennessee.
+ 410   ii.   Richard Mann Currie, Jr., born April 09, 1943 in Cape Giradeau, Missouri.

Richard Mann and Dorothy Campbell Currie

Dorothy Campbell Currie with her cousins.

Names listed left to right.

Left: *Lillian Johnson Gardiner, Marian Johnson Graves, Dorothy Campbell Currie, John Ross Long.*

Below: *Marian Johnson Graves, Lillian Johnson Gardiner, Dorothy Campbell Currie, Mary Frances and James Campbell.*

312. Juliet Miriam[13] Campbell (Zachariah Joseph[12], Jane Hamilton[11] Hess, James A.W.[10], Margaret[9] Daveiss, Joseph[8] Davis, James[7], Nathaniel[6] Davis (2), Robert[5] Davis (1), Elizabeth[4] Hughes, Nicketti[3] Powhatan, Cleopatra[2], Chief[1] Powhatan) was born July 22, 1915 in Humboldt, Gibson County, Tennessee. She married **Charles Robertson Lewis** December 31, 1933 in Humboldt, Tennessee. He was born January 13, 1914 in Civil District 4, Edison, Gibson County, Tennessee, and died July 23, 2001 in Humboldt, Gibson County, Tennessee.

Notes for Juliet Miriam Campbell:

Family Memories from Childhood, by Susan Lewis Schoenemann, written in 2000:

Mother and Daddy [Juliet and Charles Lewis]

"Mother and Daddy were sweethearts from the 7th grade on, and still are. Daddy was the boss, and 'brought home the bacon.' Mother worked full time too, as a homemaker.

Mother was the focal point of my life from birth. She comforted me when I was afraid or ill, baked my favorite cookies to welcome me home from school, listened attentively as I recited poetry, sang or practiced piano, she chauffeured me, prayed for me, took part in my interests and there were a multitude of other considerations and sacrifices on my behalf that only mothers understand. Mother always put herself last and put God and family first, such as developing a liking for the 'ribby' chicken back, [being the rejected piece]. I can truly say that I have never heard a discouraging or disparaging word from her mouth. Reading Bible stories to me at bedtime and listening to my prayers were habitual...after all, my parents knelt beside their bed to pray together until my father could no longer kneel.

Daddy was always working hard to support us, but Sunday would find him at church with all of us following. Daddy liked to eat, and Granny Lewis liked to cook, so all was well. Once a year we made the day-long trip to Memphis to visit the Zoo, and eat at Pappy's and Jimmy's Restaurant. Daddy let me sit next to him because I could never finish a seafood platter and 'needed help.'

Evenings, when I would finally wind down and fall asleep, Daddy would carry me to bed. Mother told me years later that I was Daddy's 'baby bird.' When I gave birth to my son I understood. I recall Mother and Daddy standing outside the delivery room door observing through the window until Lewis was born. When they were allowed admittance, Daddy walked over to my bed and squeezed my big toe on my right foot. Without speaking, Daddy had said to me, 'Well done'."

Both Susan and her father, Charles, passed away in 2001.

Charles Robertson and Juliet Miriam Campbell Lewis shortly after marriage in 1933 (left) and in 1998, celebrating their 65th anniversary.

Notes for Charles Robertson Lewis:

Owned and operated a lumber and construction business in Humboldt, Tennessee.

Children of Juliet Campbell and Charles Lewis are:

411   i.   Charles Robertson[14] Lewis, Jr., born July 24, 1938 in Humboldt, Gibson County, Tennessee.

Notes for Charles Robertson Lewis, Jr.:

Worked with his father in the construction business. His specialty is metal work.

+ 412   ii.   Austin Campbell Lewis, born January 19, 1943 in Humboldt, Gibson County, Tennessee.

Juliet Campbell Lewis and Marian Graves at a family reunion in 1999.

+ 413   iii.   Susan Lewis, born April 15, 1947 in Humboldt, Gibson County, Tennessee; died May 20, 2001 in Humboldt, Gibson County, Tennessee.

+ 414   iv.   Bailey Edison Lewis, born June 29, 1953 in Humboldt, Gibson County, Tennessee.

313.   Janice[13] Campbell (Zachariah Joseph[12], Jane Hamilton[11] Hess, James A.W.[10], Margaret[9] Daveiss, Joseph[8] Davis, James[7], Nathaniel[6] Davis (2), Robert[5] Davis (1), Elizabeth[4] Hughes, Nicketti[3] Powhatan, Cleopatra[2], Chief[1] Powhatan) was born February 19, 1920 in Humboldt, Gibson County, Tennessee, and died April 21, 1990 in Memphis Shelby County, Tennessee. She married **Dr. Jesse Max Roy** August 29, 1940. He was born October 21, 1914 in Jackson, Madison County, Tennessee, and died June 17, 1973 in Forrest City, St. Francis County, Arkansas.

Dr. Jesse Max Roy was a Doctor of Medicine who owned and operated a medical clinic in Forest City, Arkansas.

Children of Janice Campbell and Jesse Roy are:

415   i.   Judy Ann[14] Roy, born September 10, 1943. She married Harlan Hoffman.

+ 416   ii.   William Max Roy, born September 10, 1943; died July 29, 1993 in Memphis Shelby County, Tennessee.

+ 417   iii.   Linda Joyce Roy, born December 23, 1946 in Memphis Shelby County, Tennessee.

315.   Elizabeth Lytle[13] Campbell (James Elbert[12], Jane Hamilton[11] Hess, James A.W.[10], Margaret[9] Daveiss, Joseph[8] Davis, James[7], Nathaniel[6] Davis (2), Robert[5] Davis (1), Elizabeth[4] Hughes, Nicketti[3] Powhatan, Cleopatra[2], Chief[1] Powhatan) was born February 13, 1913. She married **Marion Lloyd Riley, Jr.** February 26, 1943 in Humboldt, Gibson County, Tennessee. He was born January 18, 1912, and died 1987.

During World War II, Marion Lloyd Riley, Jr., was a photographer in the United States Navy aboard the aircraft carrier, Enterprise, in the Pacific Theatre. Stayed in Service until retirement.

Child of Elizabeth Campbell and Marion Riley is:

418   i.   Marion Lloyd[14] Riley, born 1945.

316. James Elbert[13] Campbell, Jr. (James Elbert[12], Jane Hamilton[11] Hess, James A.W.[10], Margaret[9] Daveiss, Joseph[8] Davis, James[7], Nathaniel[6] Davis (2), Robert[5] Davis (1), Elizabeth[4] Hughes, Nicketti[3] Powhatan, Cleopatra[2], Chief[1] Powhatan) was born May 10, 1921. He married **Mary Frances Wray** December 27, 1945 in Humboldt, Gibson County, Tennessee, daughter of Andrew Wray and Mary Sullivan. She was born 1921 in Humboldt, Gibson County, Tennessee.

Notes for James Elbert Campbell, Jr.:

A graduate of University of Tennessee, Knoxville school of Engineering, served during World War II in the United States Naval Construction Battalion in the Pacific Theatre.

Owns and operates [with his sons, Jim, Charles and John] the Williams Steel Company in Jackson, Tennessee.

Children of James Campbell and Mary Wray are:

+ 419   i.   James Elbert[14] Campbell,III, born February 20, 1950 in Humboldt, Gibson County, Tennessee.
+ 420   ii. Charles Wray Campbell, born January 08, 1952 in Humboldt, Gibson County, Tennessee.
+ 421   iii. John Lytle Campbell, born April 01, 1957 in Humboldt, Gibson County, Tennessee.

317. Jack Cannon[13] Campbell (James Elbert[12], Jane Hamilton[11] Hess, James A.W.[10], Margaret[9] Daveiss, Joseph[8] Davis, James[7], Nathaniel[6] Davis (2), Robert[5] Davis (1), Elizabeth[4] Hughes, Nicketti[3] Powhatan, Cleopatra[2], Chief[1] Powhatan) was born July 03, 1927, and died July 2002 in Birmingham, Alabama. He married **Faye Joan Mills** October 15, 1949. She was born 1928.

Jack Cannon Campbell graduated from Middle Tennessee State University, Murfresboro, Tennessee. During World War II, was in the United States Naval Construction Battalion. Resided in Birmingham, Alabama where he was a lumber broker.

Children of Jack Campbell and Faye Mills are:

+ 422   i.   Joseph Cannon[14] Campbell, born 1954.
+ 423   ii. Faye Lynn Campbell, born June 27, 1953 in Tupelo, Mississippi.
+ 424   iii. Kathy Rae Campbell, born 1958.

318. Robert Hess[13] Campbell (James Elbert[12], Jane Hamilton[11] Hess, James A.W.[10], Margaret[9] Daveiss, Joseph[8] Davis, James[7], Nathaniel[6] Davis (2), Robert[5] Davis (1), Elizabeth[4] Hughes, Nicketti[3] Powhatan, Cleopatra[2], Chief[1] Powhatan) was born March 04, 1937, and died June 18, 1997. He married **Sandra Williams** March 25, 1956 in Humboldt, Gibson County, Tennessee. She was born June 19, 1937.

Robert Hess Campbell graduated Mississippi State in Civil Engineering. Was in the Corps of Engineers in charge of Mississippi River Barge navigation. Worked out of Washington during the later years of his career. Died of complications due to colon cancer.

Children of Robert Campbell and Sandra Williams are:

+ 425   i.   Robert Hess[14] Campbell, Jr., born 1957.

+ 426 ii. William Thomas Campbell, born 1959.
+ 427 iii. Mark Sanders Campbell, born 1964.

319. John[13] Davis (Theodore[12], Harvey[11], Harvey[10], James Harvey[9], Joseph[8], James[7], Nathaniel[6] Davis (2), Robert[5] Davis (1), Elizabeth[4] Hughes, Nicketti[3] Powhatan, Cleopatra[2], Chief[1] Powhatan)

Children of John Davis are:
    428 i. John[14] Davis.
    429 ii. Harriet Davis. She married Dr. John Roberts.

Notes for Harriet Davis:
    Harriet and Dr. John Roberts were living in Owensboro, Kentucky in 1902.

320. William Nimrod[13] Allen (Charles Grube[12], Nimrod Bryant[11], Rose C.[10] Davis, John[9], Joseph[8], James[7], Nathaniel[6] Davis (2), Robert[5] Davis (1), Elizabeth[4] Hughes, Nicketti[3] Powhatan, Cleopatra[2], Chief[1] Powhatan) was born November 13, 1907 in Salem, Marion County, Illinois, and died August 25, 1979 in Martin, Weakley County, Tennessee. He married **Ruby Mae O'Brian** February 28, 1932 in Arkadelphia, Clark County, Arkansas. She was born July 1913 in Tonti, Marion County, Illinois.

Ruby Mae O'Brian was the second wife of William Nimrod Allen.

Child of William Allen and Ruby O'Brian is:
+ 430 i. Rose Lee[14] Allen, born December 08, 1945 in Eureka Springs, Arkansas.

Generation No. 14

321. Bobby Stephen[14] Gilliam (Bobby Ellis[13], Ellis C.[12], Ida Sue[11] Burks, Charles Martin[10], William Pinkney[9], Richard[8], Samuel[7], Samuel[6], Mary[5] Davis, Elizabeth[4] Hughes, Nicketti[3] Powhatan, Cleopatra[2], Chief[1] Powhatan) He married **Lana Weeks**.

Child of Bobby Gilliam and Lana Weeks is:
    431 i. Bobby Stephen[15] Gilliam, Jr..

322. Mark Ellis[14] Gilliam (Bobby Ellis[13], Ellis C.[12], Ida Sue[11] Burks, Charles Martin[10], William Pinkney[9], Richard[8], Samuel[7], Samuel[6], Mary[5] Davis, Elizabeth[4] Hughes, Nicketti[3] Powhatan, Cleopatra[2], Chief[1] Powhatan) married **Anita Bliss**.

Children of Mark Gilliam and Anita Bliss are:
    432 i. Corey A.[15] Gilliam.
    433 ii. Katen Gilliam.

323. William Craig[14] Gilliam (Bobby Ellis[13], Ellis C.[12], Ida Sue[11] Burks, Charles Martin[10], William Pinkney[9], Richard[8], Samuel[7], Samuel[6], Mary[5] Davis, Elizabeth[4] Hughes, Nicketti[3] Powhatan, Cleopatra[2], Chief[1] Powhatan) married **Martha Hogan**.

Children of William Gilliam and Martha Hogan are:
    434   i.   Michael Craig[15] Gilliam.
    435   ii.   William Blake Gilliam.

324. Virginia[14] Walton (Virginia[13] Feild, Henry Allison[12], Katherine Malvina[11] Hess, William Randolph[10], Margaret[9] Daveiss, Joseph[8] Davis, James[7], Nathaniel[6] Davis (2), Robert[5] Davis (1), Elizabeth[4] Hughes, Nicketti[3] Powhatan, Cleopatra[2], Chief[1] Powhatan) She married **Berry Brooks**.

A descendent of Col. William R. Hess, Virginia was one of our more colorful cousins. A world traveler, she collected rare and beautiful objects from all over the globe. Not only did she enjoy sharing her treasures, but loved telling of her many adventures. She was married to the famous "big game hunter," Berry Brooks.

Child of Virginia Walton and Berry Brooks is:
  + 436   i.   Virginia[15] Brooks.

Virginia Walton Brooks, Queen of Memphis in 1974 Cotton Carnival.

326. Dr. Robert Edwin[14] Tooms (Rebecca Caroline[13] Farrow, Sallie Emma[12] Hess, Dr. Nelson Irving[11] Hess II, Nelson Irving[10] Hess, Margaret[9] Daveiss, Joseph[8] Davis, James[7], Nathaniel[6] Davis (2), Robert[5] Davis (1), Elizabeth[4] Hughes, Nicketti[3] Powhatan, Cleopatra[2], Chief[1] Powhatan) was born October 26, 1933. He married **Geraldine Ricks**.

Child of Robert Tooms and Geraldine Ricks is:
    437   i.   Robert Cole[15] Tooms, born May 11, 1958.

328. Roselle Louise[14] Hess (Ella Louise[13], Nelson Irvin[12], Dr. Nelson Irving[11] Hess II, Nelson Irving[10] Hess, Margaret[9] Daveiss, Joseph[8] Davis, James[7], Nathaniel[6] Davis (2), Robert[5] Davis (1), Elizabeth[4] Hughes, Nicketti[3] Powhatan, Cleopatra[2], Chief[1] Powhatan) was born June 01, 1937. She married **J. Thomas Medford** June 25, 1953.

Child of Roselle Hess and J. Thomas Medford is:
    438   i.   Susan Louise[15] Medford, born March 20, 1954. She married Thomas Irvin; born August 02, 1957.

334. David[14] **Gibson** (Patricia[13] Hess, John William "Jack"[12], James Ferdinand[11], Nelson Irving[10], Margaret[9] Daveiss, Joseph[8] Davis, James[7], Nathaniel[6] Davis (2), Robert[5] Davis (1), Elizabeth[4] Hughes, Nicketti[3] Powhatan, Cleopatra[2], Chief[1] Powhatan) was born August 07, 1955 in Mt. Carmel, Illinois. He married **Karen Peterson** August 10, 1992 in Springfield, Illinois, daughter of Byron Peterson and Nancy Aldredge. She was born November 09, 1957 in Jeffersonville, Indiana.

Child of David Gibson and Karen Peterson is:
    439   i. Laura[15] Gibson, born July 07, 1994.

335. William Clinton[14] **Bell, Jr.** (Martha Elizabeth[13] Banks, Anna Bell[12] Cresap, Nelson Adair[11], Nancy Adair[10] Hess, Margaret[9] Daveiss, Joseph[8] Davis, James[7], Nathaniel[6] Davis (2), Robert[5] Davis (1), Elizabeth[4] Hughes, Nicketti[3] Powhatan, Cleopatra[2], Chief[1] Powhatan) was born December 15, 1951. He married **Susan Denise Robinson** June 15, 1985 in Jackson, Tennessee.

Children of William Bell and Susan Robinson are:
    440   i. William Clinton[15] Bell III, born March 30, 1991.
    441 ii. Bailey Andrews Bell, born February 19, 1993.
    442 iii. Parker Banks Bell, born August 31, 1994.
    443 iv. Palmer Robinson Bell, born May 13, 1997.
    444 v. Hayes Hamilton Bell, born February 19, 1999.

336. David Banks[14] **Bell** (Martha Elizabeth[13] Banks, Anna Bell[12] Cresap, Nelson Adair[11], Nancy Adair[10] Hess, Margaret[9] Daveiss, Joseph[8] Davis, James[7], Nathaniel[6] Davis (2), Robert[5] Davis (1), Elizabeth[4] Hughes, Nicketti[3] Powhatan, Cleopatra[2], Chief[1] Powhatan) was born November 01, 1953. He married **Gail Bradley**. She was born February 09, 1954 in Aberdeen, Mississippi.

Children of David Bell and Gail Bradley are:
    445   i. Andrew Charles[15] Bell, born February 15, 1983 in Houston, Texas.
    446 ii. Allison Banks Bell, born September 20, 1984 in Houston, Texas.

338. Kathryn[14] **Banks** (John[13], Anna Bell[12] Cresap, Nelson Adair[11], Nancy Adair[10] Hess, Margaret[9] Daveiss, Joseph[8] Davis, James[7], Nathaniel[6] Davis (2), Robert[5] Davis (1), Elizabeth[4] Hughes, Nicketti[3] Powhatan, Cleopatra[2], Chief[1] Powhatan) was born February 07, 1954. She married **Alan Douglas**.

Notes for Kathryn Banks:
    Kathryn and Alan Douglas live in Lexington, Kentucky

Children of Kathryn Banks and Alan Douglas are:
    447   i. Alan Banks[15] Douglas, born December 31, 1982.
    448 ii. Porter Douglas, born January 25, 1984.
    449 iii. Kathryn Douglas, born January 07, 1986.

341. Nelson Cresap[14] Harrison, Jr. (Nelson Cresap[13], Katherine Louise[12] Cresap, Nelson Adair[11], Nancy Adair[10] Hess, Margaret[9] Daveiss, Joseph[8] Davis, James[7], Nathaniel[6] Davis (2), Robert[5] Davis (1), Elizabeth[4] Hughes, Nicketti[3] Powhatan, Cleopatra[2], Chief[1] Powhatan) was born September 10, 1936. He married **Marigayle DeLoach**. She was born January 22, 1940.

Nelson Cresap Harrison, Jr. received a B.S. Degree in Mechanical Engineering from the University of Tennessee, Knoxville in 1959, and a Masters in Automotive Engineering in Detroit. In 1969 he received a Degree in Medicine from the U.T. Med. School in Memphis. Nelson practiced in Humboldt and Jackson, Tennessee until his retirement.

Marigayle "Gayle" DeLoach received a B.A. Degree from Lambuth College in Jackson, Tennessee, and a Masters Degree in Counseling from Memphis State University. She set up the Elementary Guidance Program in Humboldt City Schools and also practiced privately there.

Children of Nelson Harrison and Marigayle DeLoach are:
- 450   i.   Nelson Cresap[15] Harrison III, born January 03, 1967.
- 451   ii.   Paul Hunter DeLoach Harrison, born December 21, 1970. He married Shannon Lea Owens May 11, 1996; born July 17, 1978.
- 452   iii.   William Edward Hayden Harrison, born September 1972. He married Monica Renee Cates August 10, 1996; born November 24, 1972.

343. Kate Cresap[14] Hamilton (Mary Cassandra[13] Harrison, Katherine Louise[12] Cresap, Nelson Adair[11], Nancy Adair[10] Hess, Margaret[9] Daveiss, Joseph[8] Davis, James[7], Nathaniel[6] Davis (2), Robert[5] Davis (1), Elizabeth[4] Hughes, Nicketti[3] Powhatan, Cleopatra[2], Chief[1] Powhatan) was born 1941, and died 1976. She married **Charles Winford Orr** 1964.

Children of Kate Hamilton and Charles Orr are:
- 453   i.   Cassandra Cresap[15] Orr, born 1966.
- 454   ii.   Charles Leigh Orr, born 1969.

344. Russell Allen[14] Harrison (Frank Russell[13], Katherine Louise[12] Cresap, Nelson Adair[11], Nancy Adair[10] Hess, Margaret[9] Daveiss, Joseph[8] Davis, James[7], Nathaniel[6] Davis (2), Robert[5] Davis (1), Elizabeth[4] Hughes, Nicketti[3] Powhatan, Cleopatra[2], Chief[1] Powhatan) was born 1948 in Mayfield, Kentucky. He married **Debra Gafford** 1969.

Children of Russell Harrison and Debra Gafford are:
- 455   i.   Kenneth[15] Harrison, born 1970.
- 456   ii.   Malyna Sue Harrison, born 1972.

345. Mary Elizabeth[14] Tribble (Clifton Eugene[13], Estelle Rebecca[12] Bennett, Kate[11] Price, Maria L.[10] Hess, Margaret[9] Daveiss, Joseph[8] Davis, James[7], Nathaniel[6] Davis (2), Robert[5] Davis (1), Elizabeth[4] Hughes, Nicketti[3] Powhatan, Cleopatra[2], Chief[1] Powhatan) was born November 11, 1927 in DeLand, Florida. She married **James Claude [Jim] Cox** June 17, 1951 in Vidalia, Georgia, son of James Cox and Mildred Daniels. He was born May 27, 1926 in Mayport, Florida.

Notes for Mary Elizabeth Tribble:

An honor graduate of Vidalia High School, Mary Elizabeth continued her education at Stetson University where she received a Bachelor of Arts degree in 1945, majoring in piano and English. She met James Claude Cox at Stetson in 1947 and they were married in 1951. They moved to Fort Lauderdale where she taught at the Bennett Elementary School. In 2002 she gave the Keynote Address at the luncheon celebrating the school's 50th anniversary.

They had two sons and the family belonged to the First Baptist Church of Fort Lauderdale where she and Jim taught Sunday School and she sang in the choir before moving in 1982 to the Coral Ridge Presbyterian Church. They built their present home in Fort Lauderdale in 1960, but continue to maintain the home in Vidalia, Georgia.

In 2001 Mary Elizabeth and Jim celebrated their fiftieth wedding anniversary among friends and family in Vidalia.

Notes for James Claude [Jim] Cox:

The son of James Bertran and Mildred Daniels Cox, Jim graduated Moore Haven High School, Moore Haven, Florida in 1943. He enlisted at age seventeen in the U.S.Navy, during WWII, serving as Radioman. He enrolled in the Business School at Stetson University in 1946, received his Bachelor of Science Degree from Florida Southern College in Lakeland in 1950 and in 1966 completed his graduate degree at the School of Banking at Rutgers University.

Jim retired in June, 1991, after a career of 41 years in banking and finance. A community leader, he has been an active member in many civic and social organizations. Among others, he is a member of the Sons of the Revolution, [National No. 111352].

Children of Mary Tribble and James Cox are:

+ 457   i.   James Clifton[15] Cox, born August 27, 1957 in Fort Lauderdale, Florida.

+ 458 ii. Jeffrey Curtis Cox, born June 23, 1966 in Fort Lauderdale, Florida.

350. Judith Ann[14] Price (Jesse Cuthbert[13], Frederick Carlton[12], William Hess[11], Maria L.[10] Hess, Margaret[9] Daveiss, Joseph[8] Davis, James[7], Nathaniel[6] Davis (2), Robert[5] Davis (1), Elizabeth[4] Hughes, Nicketti[3] Powhatan, Cleopatra[2], Chief[1] Powhatan) was born 1949. She married **F. Robert Oldham**.

Children of Judith Price and F. Oldham are:

459   i.   Jennifer[15] Oldham.

460   ii. Courtney Oldham.

461 iii. Jessica Suzanne Oldham.

351. Patricia Regan[14] Price (Jesse Cuthbert[13], Frederick Carlton[12], William Hess[11], Maria L.[10] Hess, Margaret[9] Daveiss, Joseph[8] Davis, James[7], Nathaniel[6] Davis (2), Robert[5] Davis (1), Elizabeth[4] Hughes, Nicketti[3] Powhatan, Cleopatra[2], Chief[1] Powhatan) was born 1951. She married **Mel Puckett**.

Children of Patricia Price and Mel Puckett are:

462   i.   Brent[15] Puckett.

463   ii. Regan Puckett.

464 iii. Eric Puckett.

352. Frances O.[14] Price (Irwin Vernon[13], Frederick Carlton[12], William Hess[11], Maria L.[10] Hess, Margaret[9] Daveiss, Joseph[8] Davis, James[7], Nathaniel[6] Davis (2), Robert[5] Davis (1), Elizabeth[4] Hughes, Nicketti[3] Powhatan, Cleopatra[2], Chief[1] Powhatan) was born 1940. She married **Wallace Moore**.

Child of Frances Price and Wallace Moore is:
        465   i.   Lynn[15] Moore.

355. Rebecca Anne[14] Perkins (Margaret Frances[13] Price, Frederick Carlton[12], William Hess[11], Maria L.[10] Hess, Margaret[9] Daveiss, Joseph[8] Davis, James[7], Nathaniel[6] Davis (2), Robert[5] Davis (1), Elizabeth[4] Hughes, Nicketti[3] Powhatan, Cleopatra[2], Chief[1] Powhatan) was born August 10, 1944. She married **Jim L. Yonge** in Corinth, Mississippi.

Children of Rebecca Perkins and Jim Yonge are:
        466   i.   Lisa[15] Yonge, born 1967.
        467   ii. Courtney Yonge, born 1969.
        468   iii. Eric Yonge, born 1974.

356. Carlton Gregory[14] Perkins (Margaret Frances[13] Price, Frederick Carlton[12], William Hess[11], Maria L.[10] Hess, Margaret[9] Daveiss, Joseph[8] Davis, James[7], Nathaniel[6] Davis (2), Robert[5] Davis (1), Elizabeth[4] Hughes, Nicketti[3] Powhatan, Cleopatra[2], Chief[1] Powhatan) was born May 04, 1948 in Corinth, Mississippi. He married **Brenda McAnnally**.

Child of Carlton Perkins and Brenda McAnnally is:
        469   i.   Alison Leigh[15] Perkins, born 1973.

357. Elliot Scott[14] Perkins (Margaret Frances[13] Price, Frederick Carlton[12], William Hess[11], Maria L.[10] Hess, Margaret[9] Daveiss, Joseph[8] Davis, James[7], Nathaniel[6] Davis (2), Robert[5] Davis (1), Elizabeth[4] Hughes, Nicketti[3] Powhatan, Cleopatra[2], Chief[1] Powhatan) was born May 02, 1957. He married **Maria Tsagarakis**. She was born 1959.

Child of Elliot Perkins and Maria Tsagarakis is:
        470   i.   Kelli Rebecca[15] Perkins, born 1984.

361. Geraldine[14] Browning (Benjamin Hess[13], Ida[12] Thomas, Eliza Ann[11] Hess, James A.W.[10], Margaret[9] Daveiss, Joseph[8] Davis, James[7], Nathaniel[6] Davis (2), Robert[5] Davis (1), Elizabeth[4] Hughes, Nicketti[3] Powhatan, Cleopatra[2], Chief[1] Powhatan) was born March 28, 1929 in Gibson County, Tennessee. She married **John Lovelace White, Jr.** May 19, 1945 in Gibson County, Tennessee, son of John White and Lillian McCuan. He was born October 30, 1921 in Gibson County, Tennessee.

Children of Geraldine Browning and John White are:
        471   i.   Thomas Edward[15] White, born April 18, 1947.
        472   ii. John Lovelace White, born March 05, 1946.
    +   473   iii. Kenneth David White, born December 24, 1957 in Gibson County, Tennessee.

363. William Robert[14] **Cooke** (Eleanor Louise[13] Browning, Ida[12] Thomas, Eliza Ann[11] Hess, James A.W.[10], Margaret[9] Daveiss, Joseph[8] Davis, James[7], Nathaniel[6] Davis (2), Robert[5] Davis (1), Elizabeth[4] Hughes, Nicketti[3] Powhatan, Cleopatra[2], Chief[1] Powhatan) was born January 11, 1932. He married **Peggy Carter**.

Children of William Cooke and Peggy Carter are:
    474   i.   Jay[15] Cooke.
    475   ii. Suzanne Cooke.
    476   iii. Janna Cooke.
    477   iv. Jim Cooke.

364. Charles Browning[14] **Cooke** (Eleanor Louise[13] Browning, Ida[12] Thomas, Eliza Ann[11] Hess, James A.W.[10], Margaret[9] Daveiss, Joseph[8] Davis, James[7], Nathaniel[6] Davis (2), Robert[5] Davis (1), Elizabeth[4] Hughes, Nicketti[3] Powhatan, Cleopatra[2], Chief[1] Powhatan) was born April 07, 1933.

Children of Charles Browning Cooke are:
    478   i.   Lisa[15] Cooke. She married Pierre Balnquart.
    479   ii. Christy Cooke.

366. Kimbrough Lafayette[14] **Dunlap, Jr.** (Kimbrough Lafayette[13], Warner Ebenezer[12], Susan[11] Hess, James A.W.[10], Margaret[9] Daveiss, Joseph[8] Davis, James[7], Nathaniel[6] Davis (2), Robert[5] Davis (1), Elizabeth[4] Hughes, Nicketti[3] Powhatan, Cleopatra[2], Chief[1] Powhatan) was born May 28, 1941 in Nashville, Tennessee. He married **Patricia Carter** September 1959. She was born May 21, 1941.

Kimbrough Lafayette Dunlap, Jr. graduated from U.T. Knoxville in the 60's. Was in the insurance business with Prudential in Montgomery, Alabama until joining his father as a partner in the Kimbrough L. Dunlap Insurance and Real Estate Business in Humboldt in 1968. He continues operation of this business started by his father, Kimbrough, Sr.

As a youth, he was serious about Scouting. Once when his Scout Master, "Gibby" Gibson asked him to come to his Hardware Store and demonstrate the folding of the American flag, he used the flag from his father's World War II ship, a freighter, plying the North Atlantic. He found out that day just how big a ship's flag is. One end started at a store on the West side of 14th Avenue, crossed the street - through "Gibby's" front door, through the store and out the back, through the alley ending somewhere near Central Avenue. Kimbrough says, "Gibby never asked me to demonstrate flag folding again, but he did help me in many ways to become an Eagle Scout."

Children of Kimbrough Dunlap and Patricia Carter are:
  + 480   i.   Kimbrough Lafayette[15] Dunlap III, born November 07, 1962.
  + 481   ii. Susan Dunlap, born September 21, 1964.
  + 482   iii. Sally Dunlap, born January 01, 1970.
    483   iv. Thomas Judson Dunlap, born September 13, 1973.

367. Dr. Warner Benjamin[14] **Dunlap** (Kimbrough Lafayette[13], Warner Ebenezer[12], Susan[11] Hess, James A.W.[10], Margaret[9] Daveiss, Joseph[8] Davis, James[7], Nathaniel[6] Davis (2), Robert[5] Davis (1), Elizabeth[4] Hughes, Nicketti[3] Powhatan, Cleopatra[2], Chief[1] Powhatan) was born July 01, 1943 in Nashville, Tennessee. He married **Jane Brewer Fowler** June 15, 1968 in Columbia, Tennessee, daughter of James Fowler and Anna Brewer. She was born October 15, 1943 in Columbia, Tennessee.

Dr. Warner Benjamin Dunlap attended Humboldt's first Kindergarden run by Mrs. Lanier and her sister. Graduated from Humboldt High School in 1961. Attended U.T., Knoxville...then earned his degree in Medicine from U.T. Med. School in Memphis, June of 1968. Later that month, Warner and Jane Fowler married. He completed his Internship, and Residency in Pediatrics at City of Memphis Hospital. He was commissioned a 2nd Lt. in the Navy and served at Camp LeJune, N.C. where daughter Mary was born. After discharge he practiced in Newport, Arkansas, where Warner, Jr. was born, then about 1979 moved his family to Humboldt, Tennessee where he practices Pediatrics at this time.

Children of Warner Dunlap and Jane Fowler are:
- 484   i.   Dr. Mary Fowler[15] Dunlap, born January 13, 1972 in Camp LeJeune, North Carolina. She married Dr. Dillon Wells.
- 485   ii.   Warner Benjamin Dunlap, Jr., born November 17, 1975 in Newport, Arkansas. He married Hannah Wilkinson July 17, 1999 in Nashville, Tennessee.

368. Hulon Otis[14] Warlick (Hulon Otis[13], Willie Mai Chester[12] Dunlap, Willietta[11] Hess, James A.W.[10], Margaret[9] Daveiss, Joseph[8] Davis, James[7], Nathaniel[6] Davis (2), Robert[5] Davis (1), Elizabeth[4] Hughes, Nicketti[3] Powhatan, Cleopatra[2], Chief[1] Powhatan) was born August 14, 1931 in Memphis, Tennessee. He married **Sandra Eleanor Hall** November 05, 1960 in Idlewild Presbyterian Church, Memphis, Tennessee. She was born in Memphis, Tennessee.

Children of Hulon Warlick and Sandra Hall are:
- 486   i.   Hulon, IV. Hulon Otis[15] Warlick, born March 30, 1962 in Memphis, Tennessee.
- 487   ii.   Frank Hall Warlick, born April 15, 1963 in Memphis, Tennessee. He married Ellen Camille Gillespie March 13, 1999 in Memphis, Tennessee.
- + 488   iii.   David Martin Warlick, born October 23, 1967 in Memphis, Tennessee.
- 489   iv.   Daniel Johnson Warlick, born April 05, 1974 in Memphis, Tennessee.

369. Katherine Webb[14] Warlick (Hulon Otis[13], Willie Mai Chester[12] Dunlap, Willietta[11] Hess, James A.W.[10], Margaret[9] Daveiss, Joseph[8] Davis, James[7], Nathaniel[6] Davis (2), Robert[5] Davis (1), Elizabeth[4] Hughes, Nicketti[3] Powhatan, Cleopatra[2], Chief[1] Powhatan) was born August 05, 1934. She married **Walter Ray Martin** December 28, 1954 in St. Michaels Episcopal Church, Arlington, Virginia. He was born in Danville, Virginia.

Notes for Katherine Webb Warlick:
A Real Estate agent who enjoys playing bridge.

Notes for Walter Ray Martin:
In 1961 was a Captain in the United States Air Force, stationed in Orlando, Florida. This information from Hulon Otis Warlick to Lillian Gardiner in January of 1961.
Retired as Col. from the United States Airforce and is currently [2002] a Financial Planner in Tucson, Arizona. He loves the game of tennis and is ranked 6th in the state.

Children of Katherine Warlick and Walter Martin are:

+ 490   i. Laura Rhyss[15] Martin, born April 07, 1956 in Sacramento, California.
+ 491   ii. Susan Katherine Martin, born July 09, 1958 in Orlando, Florida.

370. Frances Goulder[14] Warlick (Hulon Otis[13], Willie Mai Chester[12] Dunlap, Willietta[11] Hess, James A.W.[10], Margaret[9] Daveiss, Joseph[8] Davis, James[7], Nathaniel[6] Davis (2), Robert[5] Davis (1), Elizabeth[4] Hughes, Nicketti[3] Powhatan, Cleopatra[2], Chief[1] Powhatan) was born November 26, 1938 in Memphis, Tennessee. She married **James Leake** September 23, 1961 in Dallas, Texas. He was born August 13, 1933 in Marshall, Texas.

Notes for Frances Goulder Warlick:
Frances and Jim divorced in 1980.

Children of Frances Warlick and James Leake are:

+ 492   i. Kathiann[15] Leake, born August 28, 1962 in Dallas, Texas.
  493   ii. Jane Elizabeth Leake, born March 29, 1966 in Beaumont, Texas. She married Michael Cain Benton November 14, 1992 in LaJolla, California; born June 06, 1966 in Jacksonville, Florida.

372. Winfred F.[14] Jones, Jr. (Mildred[13] Warlick, Willie Mai Chester[12] Dunlap, Willietta[11] Hess, James A.W.[10], Margaret[9] Daveiss, Joseph[8] Davis, James[7], Nathaniel[6] Davis (2), Robert[5] Davis (1), Elizabeth[4] Hughes, Nicketti[3] Powhatan, Cleopatra[2], Chief[1] Powhatan) was born April 18, 1936 in Humboldt, Gibson County, Tennessee. He married **(1) Mary Julia Murray** July 15, 1958 in Carroll, County, Tennessee. She was born April 30, 1936. He married **(2) Cathey Mitchell** December 11, 1978.

Notes for Winfred F. Jones, Jr.:
Ted and Judy divorced in June of 1978.

Children of Winfred Jones and Mary Murray are:

  494   i. Ted Murray[15] Jones, born January 05, 1960 in Fort Eustis, Virginia.

Notes for Ted Murray Jones:
Ted married Sandy Stella December 23, 1982. They later divorced. There were no children.

+ 495   ii. Robert Clayton Jones, born December 27, 1965 in Humboldt, Gibson County, Tennessee.
+ 496 iii. Julie Virginia Jones, born January 07, 1968 in Humboldt, Gibson County, Tennessee.

373. Rena[14] Jones (Mildred[13] Warlick, Willie Mai Chester[12] Dunlap, Willietta[11] Hess, James A.W.[10], Margaret[9] Daveiss, Joseph[8] Davis, James[7], Nathaniel[6] Davis (2), Robert[5] Davis (1), Elizabeth[4] Hughes, Nicketti[3] Powhatan, Cleopatra[2], Chief[1] Powhatan) was born December 31, 1937 in Humboldt, Gibson county, Tennessee. She married **William Marvin Johnson** August 22, 1959 in Humboldt, Tennessee, son of Ammon Johnson and Mary Hill. He was born June 12, 1936 in Sparta, White County, Tennessee.

Rena attended Randolph—Macon Woman's College in Lynchburg, Virginia 2 years, and graduated from the University of Tennessee in 1959. After marriage to William M. Johnson, "Bill," in August of 1959, the couple lived in Southern Pines, North Carolina and Humboldt, Tennessee, finally settling in Sparta, Tennessee which was Bill's hometown.

She has been involved in local school and community activities as well as University of Tennessee Woman's organizations. Both are active members of the First United Methodist Church in Sparta.

"Bill" is a 1958 graduate of the University of Tennessee, Knoxville and was co-captain of the 1957 football team. He was selected to several All American teams.

After settling in Sparta, Tennessee in March of 1961, Bill started the Sparta First Federated Savings and Loan Association, then affiliated with the First National Bank in 1963, becoming President in 1969. He retired from banking in 1993 and became associated with Meridian Corporation. Meridian was then sold to Martin- Marietta in January of 2000 and he remains with them as a consultant.

Bill was a trustee of Martin Methodist College in Pulaski, Tennessee several years and served on the University of Tennessee Board of Trustees 25 years.

He is married to the former Rena Jones of Humboldt, Tennessee. They have three children and eleven grandchildren.

Children of Rena Jones and William Johnson are:
+ 497   i.   Cynthea[15] Johnson, born December 06, 1961 in Sparta, White County, Tennessee.
+ 498   ii. Cathryn Johnson, born November 03, 1964 in Sparta, White County, Tennessee.
+ 499   iii. Carolyn Johnson, born December 11, 1967 in Sparta, White County, Tennessee.

374.   Kitty Ann[14] Clark (Monie[13] Warlick, Willie Mai Chester[12] Dunlap, Willietta[11] Hess, James A.W.[10], Margaret[9] Daveiss, Joseph[8] Davis, James[7], Nathaniel[6] Davis (2), Robert[5] Davis (1), Elizabeth[4] Hughes, Nicketti[3] Powhatan, Cleopatra[2], Chief[1] Powhatan) was born December 22, 1940. She married **Michael Geoffrey Donovan** August 01, 1969 in Melbourne, Florida. He was born in Melbourne, Florida.

Notes for Michael Geoffrey Donovan:
   Died from cancer.

Children of Kitty Clark and Michael Donovan are:
+ 500   i.   Kelly[15] Donovan, born October 08, 1972 in Melbourne, Florida.
  501   ii. Cayce Donovan, born January 25, 1975.

375.   Riley[14] Clark, Jr. (Monie[13] Warlick, Willie Mai Chester[12] Dunlap, Willietta[11] Hess, James A.W.[10], Margaret[9] Daveiss, Joseph[8] Davis, James[7], Nathaniel[6] Davis (2), Robert[5] Davis (1), Elizabeth[4] Hughes, Nicketti[3] Powhatan, Cleopatra[2], Chief[1] Powhatan) was born August 05, 1943 in Humboldt, Gibson County, Tennessee, and died 1986 in Charlotte, North Carolina. He married **Carole Shaver** August 15, 1964 in Charlotte, North Carolina. She was born June 12, 1945 in Charlotte, North Carolina.

Notes for Riley Clark, Jr.:
   Died from complications of "Agent Orange." He was a Sergeant in the Air Force and served in Viet Nam during 1964 to 1968.

Child of Riley Clark and Carole Shaver is:

>   502   i.   Lee Anna[15] Clark, born June 02, 1972. She married Cameron Forest Robinson April 24, 1999 in Pauley's Island, South Carolina; died March 17, 2000 in Troutman, Lake Norman, North Carolina.

Notes for Cameron Forest Robinson:
>   Died in drowning accident about a year after they married, March 17, 2000.

376. Charles Warlick[14] Clark (Monie[13] Warlick, Willie Mai Chester[12] Dunlap, Willietta[11] Hess, James A.W.[10], Margaret[9] Daveiss, Joseph[8] Davis, James[7], Nathaniel[6] Davis (2), Robert[5] Davis (1), Elizabeth[4] Hughes, Nicketti[3] Powhatan, Cleopatra[2], Chief[1] Powhatan) was born July 29, 1952 in Humboldt, Gibson county, Tennessee. He married **Karen Hamilton** June 1974, daughter of Jack Hamilton and Sybil Nowell. She was born December 03, 1953.

Child of Charles Clark and Karen Hamilton is:

>   503   i.   Charles Hamilton[15] Clark, born August 06, 1979.

378. John Mann[14] Johnson (Alsay[13], John Orgain[12], Katherine Nelson[11] Hess, James A.W.[10], Margaret[9] Daveiss, Joseph[8] Davis, James[7], Nathaniel[6] Davis (2), Robert[5] Davis (1), Elizabeth[4] Hughes, Nicketti[3] Powhatan, Cleopatra[2], Chief[1] Powhatan) was born April 26, 1957 in Orleans, France. He married **Lori Ann Sewell** July 22, 1989.

Notes for John Mann Johnson:
>   Attorney.

Children of John Johnson and Lori Sewell are:

>   504   i.   Anna Claiborne[15] Johnson, born July 07, 1991.
>   505   ii.   John Lucien Johnson, born December 24, 1992.

379. Julia Claiborne[14] Johnson (Alsay[13], John Orgain[12], Katherine Nelson[11] Hess, James A.W.[10], Margaret[9] Daveiss, Joseph[8] Davis, James[7], Nathaniel[6] Davis (2), Robert[5] Davis (1), Elizabeth[4] Hughes, Nicketti[3] Powhatan, Cleopatra[2], Chief[1] Powhatan) was born May 12, 1959 in Heidelberg, Germany. She married **Chris Marcil** April 1991.

Notes for Julia Claiborne Johnson:
>   Occupation: Writer.

Children of Julia Johnson and Chris Marcil are:

>   506   i.   William Amade'e[15] Marcil, born March 04, 1997.
>   507   ii.   Mary Davis Marcil, born June 10, 1999.

380. Jane Clementine[14] Knowles (Lillian Jeanette[13] Lannom, Marian Lucinda[12] Campbell, Jane Hamilton[11] Hess, James A.W.[10], Margaret[9] Daveiss, Joseph[8] Davis, James[7], Nathaniel[6] Davis (2), Robert[5] Davis (1), Elizabeth[4] Hughes, Nicketti[3] Powhatan, Cleopatra[2], Chief[1] Powhatan) was born October 20, 1933 in Jackson, Madison County, Tennessee. She married **(1) Jack Law** 1952 in Corinth, Mississippi. She married **(2) Thomas Lynn McCollough** 1965 in Atlanta, Georgia. He was born February 04, 1941.

Jane and Jack Law divorced in 1958 in Jackson, Tennessee.

A gifted musician and vocalist, she played piano for the First Presbyterian Sunday School Activities in Jackson, then after moving to Atlanta, sang in the choir of her church there.

She now resides with husband, Tom McCollough, in Jacksonville, Florida where she is active with Animal Rescue and the Humane Society.

Thomas Lynn McCollough retired after 15 years as Vice President of Sales with the Beech Trading Company in Jacksonville, Florida.

Child of Jane Knowles and Jack Law is:

+ 508   i. Walter Harris[15] Law, born January 04, 1953 in Jackson, Tennessee.

381. Marian Lucinda Campbell[14] Knowles (Lillian Jeanette[13] Lannom, Marian Lucinda[12] Campbell, Jane Hamilton[11] Hess, James A.W.[10], Margaret[9] Daveiss, Joseph[8] Davis, James[7], Nathaniel[6] Davis (2), Robert[5] Davis (1), Elizabeth[4] Hughes, Nicketti[3] Powhatan, Cleopatra[2], Chief[1] Powhatan) was born July 27, 1936 in Jackson, Madison County, Tennessee. She married **Jere Baxter Albright** August 24, 1958 in Jackson, Tennessee, son of Charles Albright and Mettie White. He was born February 18, 1933 in Humboldt, Gibson County, Tennessee.

Marian Lucinda Campbell Knowles graduated from Jackson High School, Jackson, Madison County, Tennessee in 1954. Attended Southwestern College [now Rhodes College] in Memphis Tennessee, graduated from Methodist Hospital School of Nursing in Memphis, practiced mainly in the Surgical Theatre until retirement in 1999.

After marriage to Jere Albright, they lived in Knoxville, Nashville and Memphis, Tennessee finally settling in Humboldt. Member of First Presbyterian Church of Humboldt where she teaches Sunday School, is past President of the Women of the Church Organization, and serves on various committees.

Member of Clement-Scott Chapter Daughters of the American Revolution—held office of Historian several years. Member of Colonial Dames of America.

Marian is enjoying her two grandchildren and rediscovering her love if art. She is currently taking lessons in watercolor.

Jere Baxter Albright graduated from Humboldt High School, Humboldt, Tennessee. Attended Union University Jackson, Tennessee, and University of Tennessee. Served in the United States Army, 1954-1956 spending most of his military time in Newfoundland. After discharge, completed under-graduate studies at Memphis State University in Memphis Tennessee. Graduated from U.T. Knoxville School of Law in 1961, and began practice in Humboldt. Was appointed Assistant United States Attorney for the Western District of Tennessee and served in that capacity in Memphis from 1964 until 1966, after which he returned to practice in Humboldt.

Member of First Presbyterian Church Humboldt, Tennessee where he teaches Sunday School and serves as Elder. Past President of Humboldt Rotary Club, past President of Humboldt Chamber of

Commerce, member of the board of Helping Hand, Attorney for the Humboldt Board of Public Utilities since 1974.

Jere holds a Private Pilot License and has been flying 45 years. He is Chairman of the Humboldt Municipal Airport Committee.

Children of Marian Knowles and Jere Albright are:

509   i.   Lucinda Gay[15] Albright, born August 23, 1959 in Knoxville,Tennessee.

Lucinda Gay Albright graduated from Old Hickory Academy [now University School of Jackson] in Jackson, Tennessee, and from the University of Tennessee, Martin.

At the time of this writing, Cindy is living and working in Cordova, Tennessee. She is an active member of Independent Presbyterian Church in Memphis, where she teaches Sunday School to the Elementary Classes, and is a Wedding Coordinator for the church.

510   ii.   Jere Baxter Albright, Jr., born September 04, 1960 in Knoxville,Tennessee. He married Bonnie Jean McCormac May 23, 1998 in Humboldt, Tennessee; born June 19, 1959 in Pinehurst, North Carolina.

Jere Baxter Albright, Jr. graduated from Old Hickory Academy [now University School of Jackson], Jackson, Tennessee, 1978. Attended U.T. Martin, graduated from U.T. Knoxville 1985 with a B.S. Degree in Mechanical Engineering. Jay is a Design Engineering Manager with Coleman Powermate, Inc. in Kearney, Nebraska where he and his wife, Bonnie, reside.

Bonnie Jean McCormac graduated from Pinecrest Senior High, and from Sand Hills Community College, Southern Pines, North Carolina with an Associate Degree in Architectual Engineering.

+ 511   iii.   Marian Davies Albright, born October 22, 1965.

382. Lillian Alice[14] Knowles (Lillian Jeanette[13] Lannom, Marian Lucinda[12] Campbell, Jane Hamilton[11] Hess, James A.W.[10], Margaret[9] Daveiss, Joseph[8] Davis, James[7], Nathaniel[6] Davis (2), Robert[5] Davis (1), Elizabeth[4] Hughes, Nicketti[3] Powhatan, Cleopatra[2], Chief[1] Powhatan) was born December 21, 1941 in Jackson, Tennessee. She married **Clifford Donald Cleveland** September 11, 1965 in Gainesville, Georgia. He was born March 01, 1939 in Atlanta, Georgia.

Lillian Alice Knowles graduated from Georgia State University, Atlanta, Georgia. Currently working with Karafotias Realty and is a lifetime member of DeKalb Board of Realtors Million Dollar Club. Alice enjoys her pets, walking, reading, tennis, traveling, and taking classes of most any kind. Presently she and husband, Cliff, are taking classes at one of Atlanta's Art Centers - she in jewelry making and Cliff in drawing. They are both very active in the Presbyterian Church where she holds the office of Elder.

Clifford Donald Cleveland graduated from Georgia Institute of Technology in Atlanta, Georgia. Cliff retired from the Sealed Air Corporation [a specialty packaging firm] in 1999 and is enjoying golf, working in the yard—especially his rose garden, reading and drawing. He and Alice recently renovated a vintage Atlanta home for which Cliff acted as architect and general "dogsbody." He beautifully refinished most of the woodwork in their home.

Children of Lillian Knowles and Clifford Cleveland are:

+ 512   i.   Lillian Claire[15] Cleveland, born December 22, 1969 in Atlanta, DeKalb County, Georgia.
+ 513   ii.   Clifford Wyatt Cleveland, born November 23, 1975 in Atlanta, Georgia.

386. Robert Lydon[14] Kuhns (Jane Hess[13] Long, Gabrilla Hess[12] Campbell, Jane Hamilton[11] Hess, James A.W.[10], Margaret[9] Daveiss, Joseph[8] Davis, James[7], Nathaniel[6] Davis (2), Robert[5] Davis (1), Elizabeth[4] Hughes, Nicketti[3] Powhatan, Cleopatra[2], Chief[1] Powhatan) was born September 24, 1936. He married **Astrida**. She was born November 11, 1937.

Children of Robert Kuhns and Astrida are:

+ 514   i.   Vicki A.[15] Kuhns, born August 01, 1964.
   515   ii.   Kristine D. Kuhns, born August 18, 1966. She married Kenneth W. Kern June 17, 1995; born April 28, 1969.

392. Jean[14] Hoeglund (Grace Campbell[13] Long, Gabrilla Hess[12] Campbell, Jane Hamilton[11] Hess, James A.W.[10], Margaret[9] Daveiss, Joseph[8] Davis, James[7], Nathaniel[6] Davis (2), Robert[5] Davis (1), Elizabeth[4] Hughes, Nicketti[3] Powhatan, Cleopatra[2], Chief[1] Powhatan) was born October 15, 1939 in Kitchican, Alaska. She married **Willis Edward Meiss** July 06, 1963 in Pueblo, Colorado. He was born April 15, 1935.

Jean was born in Ketchikan, Alaska because there was no hospital in the town of Metlakahtla, Alaska where her parents lived at the time. She and her husband Willy both became school teachers like her parents. Children of Jean Hoeglund and Willis Meiss are:

+ 516   i.   William Allen[15] Meiss, born July 08, 1966 in South Bend, Indiana.
+ 517   ii.   John Arthur Meiss, born April 25, 1968 in South Bend, Indiana.
   518   iii.   James Michael Meiss, born January 27, 1971 in South Bend, Indiana.

393. Anne[14] Hoeglund (Grace Campbell[13] Long, Gabrilla Hess[12] Campbell, Jane Hamilton[11] Hess, James A.W.[10], Margaret[9] Daveiss, Joseph[8] Davis, James[7], Nathaniel[6] Davis (2), Robert[5] Davis (1), Elizabeth[4] Hughes, Nicketti[3] Powhatan, Cleopatra[2], Chief[1] Powhatan) was born May 11, 1941 in Emporia, Kansas. She married **(1) Don Carey** July 04, 1964 in Pueblo, Colorado. She married **(2) Hugh Hannon** February 14, 1992 in Carmel, California.

Children of Anne Hoeglund and Don Carey are:

+ 519   i.   Stephen Donald[15] Carey, born July 18, 1968 in Boulder, Colorado.
   520   ii.   Suzanne Grace Carey, born July 07, 1972 in Boulder, Colorado.

394. Gabrilla[14] Hoeglund (Grace Campbell[13] Long, Gabrilla Hess[12] Campbell, Jane Hamilton[11] Hess, James A.W.[10], Margaret[9] Daveiss, Joseph[8] Davis, James[7], Nathaniel[6] Davis (2), Robert[5] Davis (1), Elizabeth[4] Hughes, Nicketti[3] Powhatan, Cleopatra[2], Chief[1] Powhatan) was born July 30, 1944 in Humboldt, Gibson County, Tennessee. She married **(1) Dave Ellsworth** August 04, 1968 in Pueblo, Colorado. She married **(2) Peter Lissaman** June 21, 1980 in Boulder, Colorado.

Notes for Gabrilla Hoeglund:
Gay Lee was born in Humboldt, Tennessee in the home of Grace's widowed mother.

Child of Gabrilla Hoeglund and Dave Ellsworth is:
    521   i.   Katherine Ann[15] Ellsworth, born March 03, 1974 in Boulder, Colorado. She married Kamal Sen; born in India.

395. Karen Sue[14] Hoeglund (Grace Campbell[13] Long, Gabrilla Hess[12] Campbell, Jane Hamilton[11] Hess, James A.W.[10], Margaret[9] Daveiss, Joseph[8] Davis, James[7], Nathaniel[6] Davis (2), Robert[5] Davis (1), Elizabeth[4] Hughes, Nicketti[3] Powhatan, Cleopatra[2], Chief[1] Powhatan) was born September 07, 1950 in Yakima, Washington. She married **Michael O'Shea** April 03, 1971 in Boulder, Colorado.

Notes for Karen Sue Hoeglund:
Karen and Michael divorced in 1991.

Children of Karen Hoeglund and Michael O'Shea are:
    522   i.   Michael Casey[15] O'Shea, born November 09, 1971 in Boulder, Colorado.
    523   ii.   Colin Patrick Francis O'Shea, born March 13, 1975 in Walnut Creek, California.

402. Levi RossCampbell (Levi Ross[13], Levi Ross[12], Jane Hamilton[11] Hess, James A.W.[10], Margaret[9] Daveiss, Joseph[8] Davis, James[7], Nathaniel[6] Davis (2), Robert[5] Davis (1), Elizabeth[4] Hughes, Nicketti[3] Powhatan, Cleopatra[2], Chief[1] Powhatan) was born February 09, 1968. He married **Sara Leigh Fish** November 28, 1996 in Memphis, Tennessee.

Children of Levi Campbell and Sara Fish are:
    524   i.   Mary Erin[15] Campbell, born March 24, 1999 in Singapore.
    525   ii.   Annika Leigh Campbell, born October 27, 2000 in Singapore.
    526   iii. Charity Esther Campbell, born January 18, 2002.

403. Dr. Dorothy Kathleen[14] Campbell (Levi Ross[13], Levi Ross[12], Jane Hamilton[11] Hess, James A.W.[10], Margaret[9] Daveiss, Joseph[8] Davis, James[7], Nathaniel[6] Davis (2), Robert[5] Davis (1), Elizabeth[4] Hughes, Nicketti[3] Powhatan, Cleopatra[2], Chief[1] Powhatan) was born January 15, 1971 in Memphis, Tennessee. She married **Dr. David T. Kizer** February 28, 1998 in Memphis, Tennessee.

Children of Dorothy Campbell and David Kizer are:
    527   i.   Carolyn Adeline[15] Kizer, born December 07, 1999 in Memphis Shelby County, Tennessee.
    528   ii.   David Thomas Kizer,Jr., born May 14, 2002.

404. Elmer Leroy[14] Hunt (Jane Bright[13] Johnson, Lillian Jeanette[12] Campbell, Jane Hamilton[11] Hess, James A.W.[10], Margaret[9] Daveiss, Joseph[8] Davis, James[7], Nathaniel[6] Davis (2), Robert[5] Davis (1), Elizabeth[4] Hughes, Nicketti[3] Powhatan, Cleopatra[2], Chief[1] Powhatan) was born August 10, 1933. He married **Jennie Davis**.

Notes for Elmer Leroy Hunt:

Graduated from Columbia Military Academy as Valedictorian in 1951. Earned a B.A. Degree [cum laude] from Vanderbilt University, 1955; J.D. [with distinction], 1960 from the University of Mississippi, and continued studies in the field of Law at the University of California, Berkeley, and at Yale.

Roy served his country in the United States Navy as Ensign 1955 to 1956, LTJG from 1956 to 1958, then served as Lt. in the Naval Reserve.from 1958 until 1968.

A national and international traveler and lecturer, Roy speaks on a variety of subjects, many dealing with Historic Preservation and legalities associated with such. He was a Fulbright Lecturer in International Law at the Graduate Law School, Seoul National University, Seoul, Korea in 1967, and spoke on Problems of International Trade at Escuela Libre de Derecho in Mexico City in the summers of 1971 and 1974. He is an active supporter of the Fine Arts and holds membership in several Councils, as well as memberships in National and State Preservation Societies.

From 1965 to 1982 Roy held the positions of Associate Dean, Acting Dean and Interim Dean at the University of Florida College of Law. He is a published author of books and articles dealing with Legal matters, and with Historic Preservation.

At present, Roy holds the title - Distinguished Service Professor of Law, Emeritus - University of Florida College of Law in Gainesville. He is Special Advisor for International Affairs, Historic Preservation, and Cultural Resources; Office of International Affairs, the Capitol, Tallahasse, Florida.

Child of Elmer Hunt and Jennie Davis is:
+ 529   i.   Jennifer Johnson[15] Hunt, born September 01, 1957; died March 11, 2002 in Oxford, Mississippi.

408. Juliet Campbell[14] Graves (Marian Lucille[13] Johnson, Lillian Jeanette[12] Campbell, Jane Hamilton[11] Hess, James A.W.[10], Margaret[9] Daveiss, Joseph[8] Davis, James[7], Nathaniel[6] Davis (2), Robert[5] Davis (1), Elizabeth[4] Hughes, Nicketti[3] Powhatan, Cleopatra[2], Chief[1] Powhatan) was born July 18, 1948 in Union City, Tennessee. She married **(1) Norman Dale Irwin**. She married **(2) Paul David Worthen**. He was born November 15, 1947 in Regensburg, Germany. She married **(3) Mike Malloy**. He was born February 22, 1956 in New Orleans, Louisiana.

[Julie married first Norman Dale Irwin. They had a son, Norman Michael Irwin. After Julie and Dale divorced, she married Paul David Worthen who adopted Norman. She and "Dave" had two children of their own, Robert and Lisa. Later, after she and Dave divorced, Julie married Mike Malloy.]

After graduation from Brainerd High School in Chattanooga, Tennessee, Julie received her Nursing Degree from Cleveland Community College in Cleveland, Tennessee. She is presently working as a Home Health Care Registered Nurse. At this time she lives in Chattanooga with husband, Mike Malloy, who is a restaurant manager. Mike has two daughters by a previous marriage, Mollie and Caroline.

Mike Malloy is a restaurateur. At the time of this writing manages Picadilly Restaurant in Chattanooga, Tennessee.

Children of Juliet Graves and Paul Worthen are:
530   i.   Robert[15] Worthen, born October 02, 1980 in Chattanooga, Tennessee.

Notes for Robert Worthen:

Robert has lived all his life in Chattanooga, Tennessee. Worked for Fed.Ex. while in college. In September of 2001, he joined the United States Army and in February of 2002 graduated from Boot

Camp at Ft. Benning, Georgia. He is at present in Paratrooper training and upon completion will be assigned duty in Italy.

 531 ii. Lisa Michelle Worthen, born November 21, 1981 in Chattanooga, Tennessee.

Notes for Lisa Michelle Worthen:

Graduated Valedictorian from her high school in Chattanooga where she was a leader in many of the school's activities. She was a Company Commander in the Rangers, the elite of the R.O.T.C., and in her Senior year was President of the Student Body. At this writing, 2002, Lisa is a student at the University of Tennessee, Chattanooga campus.

Child of Juliet Graves and Norman Irwin is:

 + 532 i. Major Norman Michael Irwin[15] Worthen, born August 17, 1966 in Chattanooga, Tennessee.

409. Corrinne Campbell[14] Currie (Dorothy Nesbitt[13] Campbell, Zachariah Joseph[12], Jane Hamilton[11] Hess, James A.W.[10], Margaret[9] Daveiss, Joseph[8] Davis, James[7], Nathaniel[6] Davis (2), Robert[5] Davis (1), Elizabeth[4] Hughes, Nicketti[3] Powhatan, Cleopatra[2], Chief[1] Powhatan) was born January 14, 1936 in Humboldt, Gibson County, Tennessee. She married **James Hunter Lane** in Covington, Tipton County, Tennessee. He was born in Memphis, Tennessee.

Children of Corrinne Currie and James Lane are:

 533 i. Dorothy Currie[15] Lane, born October 02, 1958 in Memphis Shelby County, Tennessee. She married John T. McClure; born January 02, 1962.

 534 ii. James Hunter Lane, Jr., born September 13, 1960 in Memphis Shelby County, Tennessee. He married Linda Battes; born November 02, 1964.

 + 535 iii. William Martin Lane, born February 06, 1964 in Memphis Shelby County, Tennessee.

410. Richard Mann[14] Currie, Jr. (Dorothy Nesbitt[13] Campbell, Zachariah Joseph[12], Jane Hamilton[11] Hess, James A.W.[10], Margaret[9] Daveiss, Joseph[8] Davis, James[7], Nathaniel[6] Davis (2), Robert[5] Davis (1), Elizabeth[4] Hughes, Nicketti[3] Powhatan, Cleopatra[2], Chief[1] Powhatan) was born April 09, 1943 in Cape Giradeau, Missouri. He married **Sarah Evelyn Price**. She was born June 26, 1945.
Children of Richard Currie and Sarah Price are:

 536 i. Richard Mann[15] Currie III, born March 10, 1980.

 537 ii. Elizabeth McWhorter Currie, born April 29, 1982.

412. Austin Campbell[14] Lewis (Juliet Miriam[13] Campbell, Zachariah Joseph[12], Jane Hamilton[11] Hess, James A.W.[10], Margaret[9] Daveiss, Joseph[8] Davis, James[7], Nathaniel[6] Davis (2), Robert[5] Davis (1), Elizabeth[4] Hughes, Nicketti[3] Powhatan, Cleopatra[2], Chief[1] Powhatan) was born January 19, 1943 in Humboldt, Gibson County, Tennessee. He married **Patricia Ann Parrish** February 14, 1976. She was born January 07, 1944 in San Francisco, California.

Children of Austin Lewis and Patricia Parrish are:

 538 i. Elizabeth Robertson[15] Lewis, born March 13, 1981 in Jackson, Madison County, Tennessee.

 539 ii. Juliet Mills Lewis, born February 11, 1985 in Jackson, Madison County, Tennessee.

413. Susan[14] **Lewis** (Juliet Miriam[13] Campbell, Zachariah Joseph[12], Jane Hamilton[11] Hess, James A.W.[10], Margaret[9] Daveiss, Joseph[8] Davis, James[7], Nathaniel[6] Davis (2), Robert[5] Davis (1), Elizabeth[4] Hughes, Nicketti[3] Powhatan, Cleopatra[2], Chief[1] Powhatan) was born April 15, 1947 in Humboldt, Gibson County, Tennessee, and died May 20, 2001 in Humboldt, Gibson County, Tennessee. She married **(1) Thomas Alfred Atkins** July 03, 1970.   She married **(2) Donald Richard Schoenemann** June 27, 1980. He was born March 30, 1932 in Brooklyn, King County, New York.

Susan and Thomas Atkins divorced.

Child of Susan Lewis and Thomas Atkins is:
+ 540   i.   Lewis Wright[15] Atkins, born January 23, 1974 in Jackson, Madison County, Tennessee.

414. Bailey Edison[14] **Lewis** (Juliet Miriam[13] Campbell, Zachariah Joseph[12], Jane Hamilton[11] Hess, James A.W.[10], Margaret[9] Daveiss, Joseph[8] Davis, James[7], Nathaniel[6] Davis (2), Robert[5] Davis (1), Elizabeth[4] Hughes, Nicketti[3] Powhatan, Cleopatra[2], Chief[1] Powhatan) was born June 29, 1953 in Humboldt, Gibson County, Tennessee. He married **Sharon Ann Ford** February 12, 1988. She was born October 23, 1950 in McComb, Pike County, Mississippi.

Bailey Edison Lewis is a Federal bank examiner.

Children of Bailey Lewis and Sharon Ford are:
541   i.   Bailey Edison[15] Lewis,Jr., born April 25, 1989 in Houston, Harris County, Texas.
542   ii.   Margaret Campbell Lewis, born April 05, 1992 in Framingham, Middlesex County, Massachusetts.

416. William Max[14] **Roy** (Janice[13] Campbell, Zachariah Joseph[12], Jane Hamilton[11] Hess, James A.W.[10], Margaret[9] Daveiss, Joseph[8] Davis, James[7], Nathaniel[6] Davis (2), Robert[5] Davis (1), Elizabeth[4] Hughes, Nicketti[3] Powhatan, Cleopatra[2], Chief[1] Powhatan) was born September 10, 1943, and died July 29, 1993 in Memphis Shelby County, Tennessee. He married **Mimi Mitchell** December 27, 1969.

Children of William Roy and Mimi Mitchell are:
543   i.   Stephen Campbell[15] Roy, born October 19, 1967; Adopted child.
544   ii.   Jon Brockman Roy, born October 02, 1972; Adopted child.

417. Linda Joyce[14] **Roy** (Janice[13] Campbell, Zachariah Joseph[12], Jane Hamilton[11] Hess, James A.W.[10], Margaret[9] Daveiss, Joseph[8] Davis, James[7], Nathaniel[6] Davis (2), Robert[5] Davis (1), Elizabeth[4] Hughes, Nicketti[3] Powhatan, Cleopatra[2], Chief[1] Powhatan) was born December 23, 1946 in Memphis Shelby County, Tennessee. She married **Charles Harrison Reed** May 19, 1973. He was born July 20, 1947 in Birmingham, Jefferson County, Alabama.

Children of Linda Roy and Charles Reed are:
545   i.   Sara Corrinne[15] Reed, born February 27, 1978 in Memphis Shelby County, Tennessee.
546   ii.   Elizabeth Ann Reed, born April 14, 1981 in Lubbock, Lubbock County, Texas.

419. James Elbert[14] Campbell III (James Elbert[13], James Elbert[12], Jane Hamilton[11] Hess, James A.W.[10], Margaret[9] Daveiss, Joseph[8] Davis, James[7], Nathaniel[6] Davis (2), Robert[5] Davis (1), Elizabeth[4] Hughes, Nicketti[3] Powhatan, Cleopatra[2], Chief[1] Powhatan) was born February 20, 1950 in Humboldt, Gibson County, Tennessee. He married **Mona Faye Ratcliff** November 11, 1973 in Newport, Tennessee. She was born 1951.

Children of James Campbell and Mona Ratcliff are:
        547 i.   James Elbert[15] Campbell IV, born 1980.
        548 ii. Tiffany Ratcliff Campbell, born 1982.

420. Charles Wray[14] Campbell (James Elbert[13], James Elbert[12], Jane Hamilton[11] Hess, James A.W.[10], Margaret[9] Daveiss, Joseph[8] Davis, James[7], Nathaniel[6] Davis (2), Robert[5] Davis (1), Elizabeth[4] Hughes, Nicketti[3] Powhatan, Cleopatra[2], Chief[1] Powhatan) was born January 08, 1952 in Humboldt, Gibson County, Tennessee. He married **Deborah Lynn Metcalf**. She was born 1957.

Children of Charles Campbell and Deborah Metcalf are:
        549 i.   Charles Wray[15] Campbell, Jr., born 1981.
        550 ii. Nick Courtland Campbell, born 1983.

421. John Lytle[14] Campbell (James Elbert[13], James Elbert[12], Jane Hamilton[11] Hess, James A.W.[10], Margaret[9] Daveiss, Joseph[8] Davis, James[7], Nathaniel[6] Davis (2), Robert[5] Davis (1), Elizabeth[4] Hughes, Nicketti[3] Powhatan, Cleopatra[2], Chief[1] Powhatan) was born April 01, 1957 in Humboldt, Gibson County, Tennessee. He married **Mary Jane Truett** June 24, 1978 in Humboldt, Gibson County, Tennessee. She was born 1957.

Children of John Campbell and Mary Truett are:
        551 i.   John Russell[15] Campbell, born 1982.
        552 ii.   Matthew Sullivan Campbell, born 1987.
        553 iii. Amy Truett Campbell, born 1991.

422. Joseph Cannon[14] Campbell (Jack Cannon[13], James Elbert[12], Jane Hamilton[11] Hess, James A.W.[10], Margaret[9] Daveiss, Joseph[8] Davis, James[7], Nathaniel[6] Davis (2), Robert[5] Davis (1), Elizabeth[4] Hughes, Nicketti[3] Powhatan, Cleopatra[2], Chief[1] Powhatan) was born 1954. He married **Patricia Ann Ballard** June 12, 1976. She was born 1954.

Notes for Joseph Cannon Campbell:
    Lumber broker in Birmingham, Alabama.
Children of Joseph Campbell and Patricia Ballard are:
        554 i.   Jeffrey Cannon[15] Campbell, born 1984.

Notes for Jeffrey Cannon Campbell:
    Jeffery is the adopted son of Joseph and Patricia Campbell.

        555 ii. Jesse Andrew Campbell, born 1988.

423. Faye Lynn[14] Campbell (Jack Cannon[13], James Elbert[12], Jane Hamilton[11] Hess, James A.W.[10], Margaret[9] Daveiss, Joseph[8] Davis, James[7], Nathaniel[6] Davis (2), Robert[5] Davis (1), Elizabeth[4] Hughes, Nicketti[3] Powhatan, Cleopatra[2], Chief[1] Powhatan) was born June 27, 1953 in Tupelo, Mississippi. She married **Arnold Mark Strength** July 28, 1979 in Birmingham, Alabama, son of Delphin Strength and Ellen Kleinschmidt. He was born February 08, 1953 in Ithaca, New York.

Children of Faye Campbell and Arnold Strength are:
- 556   i.   Adam Mark[15] Strength, born November 26, 1983 in Jackson, Madison County, Tennessee.
- 557   ii.   Joseph Benjamin Strength, born August 10, 1987 in Nashville, Tennessee.
- 558   iii.   David Christopher Strength, born February 17, 1992 in Nashville, Tennessee.

424. Kathy Rae[14] Campbell (Jack Cannon[13], James Elbert[12], Jane Hamilton[11] Hess, James A.W.[10], Margaret[9] Daveiss, Joseph[8] Davis, James[7], Nathaniel[6] Davis (2), Robert[5] Davis (1), Elizabeth[4] Hughes, Nicketti[3] Powhatan, Cleopatra[2], Chief[1] Powhatan) was born 1958. She married **Robert Wayne McGuffie** June 28, 1980. He was born August 23, 1952.

Children of Kathy Campbell and Robert McGuffie are:
- 559   i.   Cory Brenton[15] McGuffie, born 1984.
- 560   ii.   Matthew Reid McGuffie, born December 17, 1993.
- 561   iii.   John Garrett McGuffie, born June 16, 1996.

425. Robert Hess[14] Campbell, Jr. (Robert Hess[13], James Elbert[12], Jane Hamilton[11] Hess, James A.W.[10], Margaret[9] Daveiss, Joseph[8] Davis, James[7], Nathaniel[6] Davis (2), Robert[5] Davis (1), Elizabeth[4] Hughes, Nicketti[3] Powhatan, Cleopatra[2], Chief[1] Powhatan) was born 1957. He married **Nancy Lynvel Heard**. She was born 1957.

Notes for Robert Hess Campbell, Jr.:
A Doctor in Huntsville, Alabama. Was M.D. in the United States Army.

Children of Robert Campbell and Nancy Heard are:
- 562   i.   Sydney Claire[15] Campbell, born 1986.
- 563   ii.   Robert Hess Campbell III, born 1988.
- 564   iii.   George Patrick Campbell, born 1992.

426. William Thomas[14] Campbell (Robert Hess[13], James Elbert[12], Jane Hamilton[11] Hess, James A.W.[10], Margaret[9] Daveiss, Joseph[8] Davis, James[7], Nathaniel[6] Davis (2), Robert[5] Davis (1), Elizabeth[4] Hughes, Nicketti[3] Powhatan, Cleopatra[2], Chief[1] Powhatan) was born 1959. He married **(1) Sherry Renee Wright**. She was born 1959. He married **(2) Lisa Darby** 1996. She was born December 26, 1969.

Child of William Campbell and Sherry Wright is:
- 565   i.   William Thomas[15] Campbell, Jr., born 1990.

427. Mark Sanders[14] Campbell (Robert Hess[13], James Elbert[12], Jane Hamilton[11] Hess, James A.W.[10], Margaret[9] Daveiss, Joseph[8] Davis, James[7], Nathaniel[6] Davis (2), Robert[5] Davis (1), Elizabeth[4] Hughes, Nicketti[3] Powhatan, Cleopatra[2], Chief[1] Powhatan) was born 1964. He married **Robin Marie Weeks** August 1989. She was born 1962.

Children of Mark Campbell and Robin Weeks are:

    566   i.   Taarna Marie[15] Campbell, born 1990.
    567   ii.   Alexander Barnett Campbell, born 1991.

430. Rose Lee[14] Allen (William Nimrod[13], Charles Grube[12], Nimrod Bryant[11], Rose C.[10] Davis, John[9], Joseph[8], James[7], Nathaniel[6] Davis (2), Robert[5] Davis (1), Elizabeth[4] Hughes, Nicketti[3] Powhatan, Cleopatra[2], Chief[1] Powhatan) was born December 08, 1945 in Eureka Springs, Arkansas. She married **Wayne Royce Oliver** June 27, 1970. He was born July 08, 1945 in Graves County, Kentucky.

Child of Rose Allen and Wayne Oliver is:

+ 568   i.   Susan Aretae[15] Oliver, born September 25, 1971.

Generation No. 15

436. Virginia[15] Brooks (Virginia[14] Walton, Virginia[13] Feild, Henry Allison[12], Katherine Malvina[11] Hess, William Randolph[10], Margaret[9] Daveiss, Joseph[8] Davis, James[7], Nathaniel[6] Davis (2), Robert[5] Davis (1), Elizabeth[4] Hughes, Nicketti[3] Powhatan, Cleopatra[2], Chief[1] Powhatan) She married **Allen Martin**.

Child of Virginia Brooks and Allen Martin is:

    569   i.   Ann[16] Martin. She married (1) Aldrich. She married (2) Chris Putnam.

457. James Clifton[15] Cox (Mary Elizabeth[14] Tribble, Clifton Eugene[13], Estelle Rebecca[12] Bennett, Kate[11] Price, Maria L.[10] Hess, Margaret[9] Daveiss, Joseph[8] Davis, James[7], Nathaniel[6] Davis (2), Robert[5] Davis (1), Elizabeth[4] Hughes, Nicketti[3] Powhatan, Cleopatra[2], Chief[1] Powhatan) was born August 27, 1957 in Fort Lauderdale, Florida. He married **Jill Taylor** October 12, 1985 in Vidalia, Georgia. She was born June 22, 1962 in Vidalia, Georgia.

Notes for James Clifton Cox:
    Studied at Pine Crest Prep. School in Fort Lauderdale, Rolle, in Switerland, Stetson University, the Sorbonne in Paris, France, graduating Stetson, Summa Cum Laude in 1979, receiving the Algernon Sydney Sullivan Award. He received a Law Degree from Vanderbilt University in Nashville, Tennessee in 1982 and returned to Fort Lauderdale to practice.
    After marriage to Jill Taylor they moved to Gainesville, Florida where he earned his Masters Degree in Tax Law at the University of Florida. He and friend Douglas Reynolds formed the new firm of Cox and Reynolds. In 2000 Clifton and his family moved to Tallahassee, where he accepted a position in the office of the Attorney General of Florida, where he practices Tax Law exclusively.

Children of James Cox and Jill Taylor are:
      570   i.   Charles Clifton[16] Cox, born June 20, 1991.
      571   ii. Katherine Emily Cox, born January 08, 1996.
      572   iii. Taylor Julia Cox, born October 21, 1999.

458. Jeffrey Curtis[15] Cox (Mary Elizabeth[14] Tribble, Clifton Eugene[13], Estelle Rebecca[12] Bennett, Kate[11] Price, Maria L.[10] Hess, Margaret[9] Daveiss, Joseph[8] Davis, James[7], Nathaniel[6] Davis (2), Robert[5] Davis (1), Elizabeth[4] Hughes, Nicketti[3] Powhatan, Cleopatra[2], Chief[1] Powhatan) was born June 23, 1966 in Fort Lauderdale, Florida. He married **Diana Lynn Edwards** March 24, 1989 in Fort Lauderdale, Florida. She was born April 12, 1965 in Miami, Florida.

Notes for Jeffrey Curtis Cox:
    From an early age, Jeff was an exceptional student and one who excelled in extra curricular activities such as Wrestling and Drama. He received many awards during his student years. Graduating Pine Crest Prep. School, he entered the University of Florida where he was a Justice on the Student Honor Court, active in the College Republican Organization. While at the University, he spent a summer in England at Oxford, Christ Church College. After receiving his Bachelor's Degree in 1988, he returned to Fort Lauderdale where he was associated with Macy's for the next ten years.
    Jeff and Diane were married in the Coral Ridge Presbyterian Church where both are active members. She is a soprano soloist, and writes for "The Communicator," the monthly church magazine. She is an accomplished actress, having starred in "Oklahoma," "The Music Man," "Oliver," "The King and I," and other productions.
    Jeff continues dramatic interests, having recently portrayed Peter Marshall in "A Man Called Peter." He is a popular speaker, currently serves as Committeeman for the Broward County Republican Party and teaches American History. Diane teaches English and Creative Writing.

Child of Jeffrey Cox and Diana Edwards is:
      573   i.   Savannah Leigh[16] Cox, born November 2002.

473. Kenneth David[15] White (Geraldine[14] Browning, Benjamin Hess[13], Ida[12] Thomas, Eliza Ann[11] Hess, James A.W.[10], Margaret[9] Daveiss, Joseph[8] Davis, James[7], Nathaniel[6] Davis (2), Robert[5] Davis (1), Elizabeth[4] Hughes, Nicketti[3] Powhatan, Cleopatra[2], Chief[1] Powhatan) was born December 24, 1957 in Gibson County, Tennessee. He married **Joetta Turbeville** May 25, 1996 in Weakley County, Tennessee. She was born March 31, 1965 in Weakely County, Tennessee.

Notes for Kenneth David White:
    Educator. Had been assistant Principal of Dyer School, promoted this year [2002] to Principal at Rutherford Tennessee.

Child of Kenneth White and Joetta Turbeville is:
      574   i.   Kendra Jo[16] White, born September 29, 2000.

480. Kimbrough Lafayette[15] Dunlap III (Kimbrough Lafayette[14] Dunlap, Jr., Kimbrough Lafayette[13], Warner Ebenezer[12], Susan[11] Hess, James A.W.[10], Margaret[9] Daveiss, Joseph[8] Davis, James[7],

Nathaniel[6] Davis (2), Robert[5] Davis (1), Elizabeth[4] Hughes, Nicketti[3] Powhatan, Cleopatra[2], Chief[1] Powhatan) was born November 07, 1962. He married **Paula Hood**.

Child of Kimbrough Dunlap III and Paula Hood is:
> 575   i.   Kimbrough Lafayette Dunlap[16] IV., born August 04, 1991 in Nashville, Davidson County, Tennessee.

481. Susan[15] Dunlap (Kimbrough Lafayette[14], Kimbrough Lafayette[13], Warner Ebenezer[12], Susan[11] Hess, James A.W.[10], Margaret[9] Daveiss, Joseph[8] Davis, James[7], Nathaniel[6] Davis (2), Robert[5] Davis (1), Elizabeth[4] Hughes, Nicketti[3] Powhatan, Cleopatra[2], Chief[1] Powhatan) was born September 21, 1964. She married **Dennis Wilson**.

Children of Susan Dunlap and Dennis Wilson are:
> 576   i.   Sarah Anna[16] Wilson, born July 1995.
> 577   ii.   Keeton Wilson, born June 1997.

482. Sally[15] Dunlap (Kimbrough Lafayette[14], Kimbrough Lafayette[13], Warner Ebenezer[12], Susan[11] Hess, James A.W.[10], Margaret[9] Daveiss, Joseph[8] Davis, James[7], Nathaniel[6] Davis (2), Robert[5] Davis (1), Elizabeth[4] Hughes, Nicketti[3] Powhatan, Cleopatra[2], Chief[1] Powhatan) was born January 01, 1970. She married **Robert Hendrick**.

Children of Sally Dunlap and Robert Hendrick are:
> 578   i.   Zoe[16] Hendrick, born October 27, 1999.
> 579   ii.   Kate Hendrick, born October 27, 1999.

488. David Martin[15] Warlick (Hulon Otis[14], Hulon Otis[13], Willie Mai Chester[12] Dunlap, Willietta[11] Hess, James A.W.[10], Margaret[9] Daveiss, Joseph[8] Davis, James[7], Nathaniel[6] Davis (2), Robert[5] Davis (1), Elizabeth[4] Hughes, Nicketti[3] Powhatan, Cleopatra[2], Chief[1] Powhatan) was born October 23, 1967 in Memphis, Tennessee. He married **Timmi Evelyn Graves** November 21, 1992 in Clarksdale, Mississippi.

Children of David Warlick and Timmi Graves are:
> 580   i.   Robert Joshua[16] Warlick, born April 25, 1995 in Memphis, Tennessee.
> 581   ii.   Cassie Graves Warlick, born January 09, 1999 in Memphis, Tennessee.

490. Laura Rhyss[15] Martin (Katherine Webb[14] Warlick, Hulon Otis[13], Willie Mai Chester[12] Dunlap, Willietta[11] Hess, James A.W.[10], Margaret[9] Daveiss, Joseph[8] Davis, James[7], Nathaniel[6] Davis (2), Robert[5] Davis (1), Elizabeth[4] Hughes, Nicketti[3] Powhatan, Cleopatra[2], Chief[1] Powhatan) was born April 07, 1956 in Sacramento, California. She married **Carey Robert Leviss**. He was born February 26, 1952.

Children of Laura Martin and Carey Leviss are:
> 582   i.   Rachael Savannah[16] Leviss, born September 12, 1994 in Tucson, Arizona; Adopted child.
> 583   ii.   Sarah Renee Leviss, born August 27, 2000 in Tucson, Arizona; Adopted child.

491. Susan Katherine[15] **Martin** (Katherine Webb[14] Warlick, Hulon Otis[13], Willie Mai Chester[12] Dunlap, Willietta[11] Hess, James A.W.[10], Margaret[9] Daveiss, Joseph[8] Davis, James[7], Nathaniel[6] Davis (2), Robert[5] Davis (1), Elizabeth[4] Hughes, Nicketti[3] Powhatan, Cleopatra[2], Chief[1] Powhatan) was born July 09, 1958 in Orlando, Florida. She married **Paul David Couture**. He was born February 12, 1952, and died July 21, 1989.

Notes for Paul David Couture:
    Died in an automobile accident.

Children of Susan Martin and Paul Couture are:
    584   i.   Katharine Era[16] Couture, born March 24, 1980 in Tucson, Arizona.
    585   ii.   David Ray Couture, born August 16, 1982 in Tucson, Arizona.

492. Kathiann[15] **Leake** (Frances Goulder[14] Warlick, Hulon Otis[13], Willie Mai Chester[12] Dunlap, Willietta[11] Hess, James A.W.[10], Margaret[9] Daveiss, Joseph[8] Davis, James[7], Nathaniel[6] Davis (2), Robert[5] Davis (1), Elizabeth[4] Hughes, Nicketti[3] Powhatan, Cleopatra[2], Chief[1] Powhatan) was born August 28, 1962 in Dallas, Texas. She married **Peter DeCleva** May 07, 1994. He was born February 05, 1964 in Dallas, Texas.

Children of Kathiann Leake and Peter DeCleva are:
    586   i.   Jane[16] DeCleva, born April 1993 in Dallas, Texas.
    587   ii.   Frances DeCleva, born October 1999 in Dallas, Texas.

495. Robert Clayton[15] **Jones** (Winfred F[14], Mildred[13] Warlick, Willie Mai Chester[12] Dunlap, Willietta[11] Hess, James A.W.[10], Margaret[9] Daveiss, Joseph[8] Davis, James[7], Nathaniel[6] Davis (2), Robert[5] Davis (1), Elizabeth[4] Hughes, Nicketti[3] Powhatan, Cleopatra[2], Chief[1] Powhatan) was born December 27, 1965 in Humboldt, Gibson County, Tennessee. He married **Shelby Sudduth French** November 01, 1997 in Humboldt, Tennessee.

Children of Robert Jones and Shelby French are:
    588   i.   Clayton Fort[16] Jones, born March 27, 1998 in Gibson County, Tennessee.
    589   ii.   Oliver Mason Jones, born May 29, 2000 in Gibson County, Tennessee.

496. Julie Virginia[15] **Jones** (Winfred F[14], Mildred[13] Warlick, Willie Mai Chester[12] Dunlap, Willietta[11] Hess, James A.W.[10], Margaret[9] Daveiss, Joseph[8] Davis, James[7], Nathaniel[6] Davis (2), Robert[5] Davis (1), Elizabeth[4] Hughes, Nicketti[3] Powhatan, Cleopatra[2], Chief[1] Powhatan) was born January 07, 1968 in Humboldt, Gibson County, Tennessee. She married **Bradley Scott Tunnell** January 06, 1990 in Lambuth Univ. Jackson, Madison County, Tennessee.

Children of Julie Jones and Bradley Tunnell are:
    590   i.   Mary Julia[16] Tunnell, born April 10, 1991 in Chapel Hill, North Carolina.
    591   ii.   Scott Christian Tunnell, born January 13, 1993 in Atlanta, Georgia.
    592   iii. Millie Grace Tunnell, born March 08, 1995 in Atlanta, Georgia.
    593   iv.   Josie Jones Tunnell, born December 02, 1998 in Nashville Tennessee.
    594   v.   Bailey Virginia Tunnell, born December 20, 2001.

497. Cynthea[15] **Johnson** (Rena[14] Jones, Mildred[13] Warlick, Willie Mai Chester[12] Dunlap, Willietta[11] Hess, James A.W.[10], Margaret[9] Daveiss, Joseph[8] Davis, James[7], Nathaniel[6] Davis (2), Robert[5] Davis (1), Elizabeth[4] Hughes, Nicketti[3] Powhatan, Cleopatra[2], Chief[1] Powhatan) was born December 06, 1961 in Sparta, White County, Tennessee. She married **George Phillip Amason** May 30, 1987 in Sparta, Tennessee, son of Cornelius Amason and Alma Peterman.

Cynthea attended Southwestern [now Rhodes College] in Memphis, Tennessee 2 years, and graduated from the University of Tennessee, Knoxville. She and her husband, Philip Amason, live in Athens, Georgia, and are campus staff with Campus Crusade for Christ.

"Phil" is a graduate of the University of Georgia. He and his wife, Cynthea Johnson Amason, are staff with Campus Crusade for Christ, in Athens, Georgia.

Children of Cynthea Johnson and George Amason are:
    595   i.   Phillip Johnson[16] Amason, born August 08, 1989 in Lee County, Alabama.
    596   ii.   Mary Hill Amason, born June 04, 1992 in Lee County, Alabama.
    597   iii.   Stephen Marshall Amason, born May 10, 1996 in Clarke County, Georgia.
    598   iv.   Saralee Meredith Amason, born May 10, 1996 in Clarke County, Georgia.

498. Cathryn[15] **Johnson** (Rena[14] Jones, Mildred[13] Warlick, Willie Mai Chester[12] Dunlap, Willietta[11] Hess, James A.W.[10], Margaret[9] Daveiss, Joseph[8] Davis, James[7], Nathaniel[6] Davis (2), Robert[5] Davis (1), Elizabeth[4] Hughes, Nicketti[3] Powhatan, Cleopatra[2], Chief[1] Powhatan) was born November 03, 1964 in Sparta, White County, Tennessee. She married **William Vaughn Rolfe** May 19, 1990 in Sparta, Tennessee, son of Charles Rolfe and Margaret Oliver. He was born July 07, 1963 in Nashville, Tennessee.

Cathryn graduated from the University of Tennessee, Knoxville and the University of Tennessee Law School. She currently works as an attorney for Christian Music artist, Mark Schultz. She and her husband "Billy" live in Brentwood, Tennessee and are active in the First Presbyterian Church of Nashville, Tennessee.

William Vaughn Rolfe is a graduate of Vanderbilt University in Nashville, Tennessee. "Billy" is currently a sales representative for Johnson and Johnson Orthopedic Implants.

Children of Cathryn Johnson and William Rolfe are:
    599   i.   Rena Clayton[16] Rolfe, born December 08, 1994 in Nashville Tennessee.
    600   ii.   Austin Oliver Rolfe, born April 25, 1996 in Nashville Tennessee.

499. Carolyn[15] **Johnson** (Rena[14] Jones, Mildred[13] Warlick, Willie Mai Chester[12] Dunlap, Willietta[11] Hess, James A.W.[10], Margaret[9] Daveiss, Joseph[8] Davis, James[7], Nathaniel[6] Davis (2), Robert[5] Davis (1), Elizabeth[4] Hughes, Nicketti[3] Powhatan, Cleopatra[2], Chief[1] Powhatan) was born December 11, 1967 in Sparta, White County, Tennessee. She married **John Thomas Bronson** August 26, 1989 in Sparta, Tennessee, son of Thomas Bronson and Sara McKeithan. He was born December 29, 1966 in Brooksville, Florida.

Carolyn Johnson is a graduate of the University of Tennessee, Knoxville. Carolyn is active in the life of Faith Evangelical Presbyterian Church in Brooksville, Florida. She and her husband, "Tom" have 5 children.

"Tom" graduated from the University of Tennessee, Knoxville and is at this writing engaged in Real Estate Management in Brooksville, Florida.

Children of Carolyn Johnson and John Bronson are:
- 601   i.   William Thomas[16] Bronson, born June 19, 1992.
- 602   ii.   Robert Hill Bronson, born March 13, 1994.
- 603   iii.   John McAllister Bronson, born February 21, 1996.
- 604   iv.   Alice Rachel Bronson, born June 19, 1998.
- 605   v.   David Hale Bronson, born Aug. 13, 2000.

500. Kelly[15] Donovan (Kitty Ann[14] Clark, Monie[13] Warlick, Willie Mai Chester[12] Dunlap, Willietta[11] Hess, James A.W.[10], Margaret[9] Daveiss, Joseph[8] Davis, James[7], Nathaniel[6] Davis (2), Robert[5] Davis (1), Elizabeth[4] Hughes, Nicketti[3] Powhatan, Cleopatra[2], Chief[1] Powhatan) was born October 08, 1972 in Melbourne, Florida. She married **Joseph Daniel Wells** November 06, 1994 in Melbourne, Florida.

Child of Kelly Donovan and Joseph Wells is:
- 606   i.   Erin Riley[16] Wells, born September 29, 1999.

508. Walter Harris[15] Law (Jane Clementine[14] Knowles, Lillian Jeanette[13] Lannom, Marian Lucinda[12] Campbell, Jane Hamilton[11] Hess, James A.W.[10], Margaret[9] Daveiss, Joseph[8] Davis, James[7], Nathaniel[6] Davis (2), Robert[5] Davis (1), Elizabeth[4] Hughes, Nicketti[3] Powhatan, Cleopatra[2], Chief[1] Powhatan) was born January 04, 1953 in Jackson, Tennessee. He married **Sue Jaynes**.

Children of Walter Law and Sue Jaynes are:
- \+ 607   i.   Sharon Marie[16] Law.
- 608   ii.   Richard Dale Law.
- 609   iii.   Heather Renee Law, born February 25, 1982. She married Brandon Miller in Beech Bluff, Tennessee.

511. Marian Davies[15] Albright (Marian Lucinda Campbell[14] Knowles, Lillian Jeanette[13] Lannom, Marian Lucinda[12] Campbell, Jane Hamilton[11] Hess, James A.W.[10], Margaret[9] Daveiss, Joseph[8] Davis, James[7], Nathaniel[6] Davis (2), Robert[5] Davis (1), Elizabeth[4] Hughes, Nicketti[3] Powhatan, Cleopatra[2], Chief[1] Powhatan) was born October 22, 1965. She married **Jeffrey Dean Harbin** June 18, 1988, son of Roger Harbin and Sandra Brasfield. He was born May 09, 1966 in Humboldt, Gibson County, Tennessee.

Marian Davies Albright attended Methodist Hospital School of Nursing in Memphis, Tennessee. Graduated from Middle Tennessee State University in Murfreesboro, Tennessee as a Registered Nurse, in 1987.

Jeffrey "Jeff" Dean Harbin graduated from Humboldt High School, attended Middle Tennessee State University, graduated from University of Tennessee, Martin in the field of Agri-business, in 1991. Along with his wife, Marian, started a company, H&H Trucking operating out of Humboldt, Tennessee.

Children of Marian Albright and Jeffrey Harbin are:

    610   i.   William Jeffrey[16] Harbin, born February 19, 1990.

    611   ii.   Robert Clayton Harbin, born June 04, 1992.

512. Lillian Claire[15] Cleveland (Lillian Alice[14] Knowles, Lillian Jeanette[13] Lannom, Marian Lucinda[12] Campbell, Jane Hamilton[11] Hess, James A.W.[10], Margaret[9] Daveiss, Joseph[8] Davis, James[7], Nathaniel[6] Davis (2), Robert[5] Davis (1), Elizabeth[4] Hughes, Nicketti[3] Powhatan, Cleopatra[2], Chief[1] Powhatan) was born December 22, 1969 in Atlanta, DeKalb County, Georgia. She married **Robert Theodore Ratcliff, Jr.** October 01, 1994 in Atlanta, Georgia. He was born June 11, 1971 in Rapides Parrish, Alexandria, Louisiana.

Lillian Claire Cleveland is a graduate of Rhodes College in Memphis, Tennessee, Claire is at present a very busy homemaker: wife, mother, and Charitable Volunteer.

Robert "Rob" Theodore Ratcliff, Jr. is a graduate of Rhodes College in Memphis, Tennessee. Is presently in business with his father in the Ratcliff Construction Company in Alexandria, Louisiana.

Children of Lillian Cleveland and Robert Ratcliff are:

    612   i.   Robert Theodore[16] Ratcliff III, born August 22, 1998 in Alexandria, Lousiana.

    613   ii.   Nicholas Wyatt Ratcliff, born August 15, 2001.

513. Clifford Wyatt[15] Cleveland (Lillian Alice[14] Knowles, Lillian Jeanette[13] Lannom, Marian Lucinda[12] Campbell, Jane Hamilton[11] Hess, James A.W.[10], Margaret[9] Daveiss, Joseph[8] Davis, James[7], Nathaniel[6] Davis (2), Robert[5] Davis (1), Elizabeth[4] Hughes, Nicketti[3] Powhatan, Cleopatra[2], Chief[1] Powhatan) was born November 23, 1975 in Atlanta, Georgia. He married **Emily Watkins** March 04, 2000 in Watkinsville, Georgia. She was born December 12, 1976 in Memphis, Tennessee.

Notes for Clifford Wyatt Cleveland:

Graduated from the University of Georgia School of Veterinary Medicine in May of 2002. He is currently practicing with the Due West Animal Hospital Clinic in Marietta, Georgia. His wife Emily gave birth to a son, Samuel Wyatt, August 1, 2002.

Notes for Emily Watkins:

Graduated suma cum laude from the University of Georgia in May of 1999, and began a teaching career in Special Education in Loganville, Georgia. She is now a busy housewife and new mother making a home for the family in Marietta, Georgia.

Child of Clifford Cleveland and Emily Watkins is:

    614   i.   Samuel Wyatt[16] Cleveland, born August 01, 2002.

514. Vicki A.[15] Kuhns (Robert Lydon[14], Jane Hess[13] Long, Gabrilla Hess[12] Campbell, Jane Hamilton[11] Hess, James A.W.[10], Margaret[9] Daveiss, Joseph[8] Davis, James[7], Nathaniel[6] Davis (2), Robert[5] Davis (1),

Elizabeth[4] Hughes, Nicketti[3] Powhatan, Cleopatra[2], Chief[1] Powhatan) was born August 01, 1964. She married **James D. Keys** June 25, 1988. He was born November 03, 1965.

Children of Vicki Kuhns and James Keys are:
- 615   i.   Robert E.[16] Keys, born March 21, 1990.
- 616   ii. Kristen E. Keys, born February 10, 1992.
- 617   iii. Andrew J. Keys, born April 19, 1994.
- 618   iv. Timothy W. Keys, born September 21, 1997.

516. William Allen[15] Meiss (Jean[14] Hoeglund, Grace Campbell[13] Long, Gabrilla Hess[12] Campbell, Jane Hamilton[11] Hess, James A.W.[10], Margaret[9] Daveiss, Joseph[8] Davis, James[7], Nathaniel[6] Davis (2), Robert[5] Davis (1), Elizabeth[4] Hughes, Nicketti[3] Powhatan, Cleopatra[2], Chief[1] Powhatan) was born July 08, 1966 in South Bend, Indiana. He married **Christy**.

Child of William Meiss and Christy is:
- 619   i.   Cassidy[16] Meiss.

517. John Arthur[15] Meiss (Jean[14] Hoeglund, Grace Campbell[13] Long, Gabrilla Hess[12] Campbell, Jane Hamilton[11] Hess, James A.W.[10], Margaret[9] Daveiss, Joseph[8] Davis, James[7], Nathaniel[6] Davis (2), Robert[5] Davis (1), Elizabeth[4] Hughes, Nicketti[3] Powhatan, Cleopatra[2], Chief[1] Powhatan) was born April 25, 1968 in South Bend, Indiana. He married **Kim**.

Child of John Meiss and Kim is:
- 620   i.   Josie[16] Meiss.

519. Stephen Donald[15] Carey (Anne[14] Hoeglund, Grace Campbell[13] Long, Gabrilla Hess[12] Campbell, Jane Hamilton[11] Hess, James A.W.[10], Margaret[9] Daveiss, Joseph[8] Davis, James[7], Nathaniel[6] Davis (2), Robert[5] Davis (1), Elizabeth[4] Hughes, Nicketti[3] Powhatan, Cleopatra[2], Chief[1] Powhatan) was born July 18, 1968 in Boulder, Colorado. He married **(1) Jamie**. He married **(2) Sacha**.

Stephen and Jamie divorced.

Children of Stephen Carey and Jamie are:
- 621   i.   Katie[16] Carey, born January 20, 1989 in Texas.
- 622   ii. Connor Carey, born March 15, 1991.

529. Jennifer Johnson[15] Hunt (Elmer Leroy[14], Jane Bright[13] Johnson, Lillian Jeanette[12] Campbell, Jane Hamilton[11] Hess, James A.W.[10], Margaret[9] Daveiss, Joseph[8] Davis, James[7], Nathaniel[6] Davis (2), Robert[5] Davis (1), Elizabeth[4] Hughes, Nicketti[3] Powhatan, Cleopatra[2], Chief[1] Powhatan) was born September 01, 1957, and died March 11, 2002 in Oxford, Mississippi. She married **Cary McGonagill**. He was born July 25, 1958.

Children of Jennifer Hunt and Cary McGonagill are:
  623 i. Jennie[16] McGonagill, born August 04, 1980.
+ 624 ii. Hunter McGonagill, born January 10, 1983.
  625 iii. Sara Jane Lillian McGonagill, born May 20, 1991.

532. Major Norman Michael Irwin[15] Worthen (Juliet Campbell[14] Graves, Marian Lucille[13] Johnson, Lillian Jeanette[12] Campbell, Jane Hamilton[11] Hess, James A.W.[10], Margaret[9] Daveiss, Joseph[8] Davis, James[7], Nathaniel[6] Davis (2), Robert[5] Davis (1), Elizabeth[4] Hughes, Nicketti[3] Powhatan, Cleopatra[2], Chief[1] Powhatan) was born August 17, 1966 in Chattanooga, Tennessee. He married **Sherry Gillis**. She was born January 23, 1969 in Tuscaloosa, Alabama.

Notes for Major Norman Michael Irwin Worthen:
Although Norm is on friendly relations with his natural father, he was adopted by Julie's second husband, Dave Worthen.

Norm graduated as Valedictorian from Soddy-Daisey High School, received an appointment to the United States Air Force Academy in 1984 from which he graduated in 1988. He is a B-52 pilot with the rank of Major, and is making a career of the service.

In 1991, while stationed at Barksdale A.F.B. in Shreveport, Louisianna, he flew missions in the Persian Gulf War. Also while in Shreveport, he married Sherry Gillis and they now have one child, Diana Michelle, and are expecting another in 2002.

At present, he and his family are at Offurt A.F.B. in Omaha, Nebraska where Norm is preparing to enter "Staff and Command School" at Maxwell A.F.B., Montgomery, Alabama as he works toward promotion to Lt. Col. They will move in July or August of this year, 2002.

Child of Norman Worthen and Sherry Gillis is:
  626 i. Diana Michelle[16] Worthen, born November 13, 1996 in Shreveport, Louisiana.

535. William Martin[15] Lane (Corrinne Campbell[14] Currie, Dorothy Nesbitt[13] Campbell, Zachariah Joseph[12], Jane Hamilton[11] Hess, James A.W.[10], Margaret[9] Daveiss, Joseph[8] Davis, James[7], Nathaniel[6] Davis (2), Robert[5] Davis (1), Elizabeth[4] Hughes, Nicketti[3] Powhatan, Cleopatra[2], Chief[1] Powhatan) was born February 06, 1964 in Memphis Shelby County, Tennessee. He married **Susan Stevens**. She was born June 16, 1962.

Child of William Lane and Susan Stevens is:
  627 i. Anna Currie[16] Lane, born May 02, 1993.

540. Lewis Wright[15] Atkins (Susan[14] Lewis, Juliet Miriam[13] Campbell, Zachariah Joseph[12], Jane Hamilton[11] Hess, James A.W.[10], Margaret[9] Daveiss, Joseph[8] Davis, James[7], Nathaniel[6] Davis (2), Robert[5] Davis (1), Elizabeth[4] Hughes, Nicketti[3] Powhatan, Cleopatra[2], Chief[1] Powhatan) was born January 23, 1974 in Jackson, Madison County, Tennessee. He married **Ginger Martin** November 07, 1997. She was born May 20, 1977 in Murfreesboro, Tennessee.

Children of Lewis Atkins and Ginger Martin are:
  628 i. Tyler Jacob[16] Atkins, born July 12, 1998 in Jackson, Madison County, Tennessee.

629 ii. Carrie Moriah Atkins, born October 27, 1999 in Jackson, Madison County, Tennessee.

630 iii. Lanna Grace Susan Atkins, born May 08, 2001 in Jackson, Madison County, Tennessee.

568. Susan Aretae[15] Oliver (Rose Lee[14] Allen, William Nimrod[13], Charles Grube[12], Nimrod Bryant[11], Rose C.[10] Davis, John[9], Joseph[8], James[7], Nathaniel[6] Davis (2), Robert[5] Davis (1), Elizabeth[4] Hughes, Nicketti[3] Powhatan, Cleopatra[2], Chief[1] Powhatan) was born September 25, 1971. She married **Robert D. Rushing** June 24, 1995. He was born June 26, 1972.

Child of Susan Oliver and Robert Rushing is:

631 i. Rose Caroline[16] Rushing, born August 04, 1998.

Generation No. 16

607. Sharon Marie[16] Law (Walter Harris[15], Jane Clementine[14] Knowles, Lillian Jeanette[13] Lannom, Marian Lucinda[12] Campbell, Jane Hamilton[11] Hess, James A.W.[10], Margaret[9] Daveiss, Joseph[8] Davis, James[7], Nathaniel[6] Davis (2), Robert[5] Davis (1), Elizabeth[4] Hughes, Nicketti[3] Powhatan, Cleopatra[2], Chief[1] Powhatan) She married **Mark Bray**.
Child of Sharon Law and Mark Bray is:

632 i. Dalton Tyler[17] Bray, born July 21, 1995.

624. Hunter[16] McGonagill (Jennifer Johnson[15] Hunt, Elmer Leroy[14], Jane Bright[13] Johnson, Lillian Jeanette[12] Campbell, Jane Hamilton[11] Hess, James A.W.[10], Margaret[9] Daveiss, Joseph[8] Davis, James[7], Nathaniel[6] Davis (2), Robert[5] Davis (1), Elizabeth[4] Hughes, Nicketti[3] Powhatan, Cleopatra[2], Chief[1] Powhatan) was born January 10, 1983. He married **Paige Melanie Hodge**.

Child of Hunter McGonagill and Paige Hodge is:

633 i. Ethan Jerimiah[17] McGonagill, born 2000 in Oxford Mississippi.

Family Reunion 1999
Presbyterian Church, Humboldt, Tennessee

Bibliography

"Virginia Notes"
> by Thomas Nimo, Petersburg, VA Library

"Floyd Biographical Genealogies"
> - of the Virginia-Kentucky Floyd Families by N.J. Floyd, Baltimore, 1912

"The Cabells and Their Kin"
> by Alexander Brown

"Maryland Historical Society Documents"
> Jamestown Records, 1630 to 1641

"Genesis of the United States"
> by Alexander Brown

"Pocahontas and Her World"
> by Philip L. Barbour

"History of Virginia"
> by William Strachey

"History of Virginia"
> by Robert Beverly, London 1722, 2nd Edition

"History of Southwestern Virginia"
> by B.F. Kegley

"A History of Rockbridge County, Virginia"
> by Oren Morton

"Captain John Smith's America"
> edited by John Lankford

"Historic Families of Kentucky"
> by Thomas Marshall Green

"Annals of Augusta County, Virginia"
> —from 1726 to 1871, by Joseph A. Waddell

"Draper Manuscript"
   -5B67 - [Mr. Draper, at a very advanced age, traveled the country visiting the survivors of Indian encounters, or members of families who could tell eye witness accounts of Indians, early settlers and their conflicts].

"History of Virginia"
   by William Stith, republished 1865

"History of Kentucky"
   by Lewis Collins

"The Wilderness Road"
   by Kincaid

"Kegley's Virginia Frontier"
   by B.F. Kegley

"True Travels and Works of Captain John Smith"
   edited by Arber, Edinburgh 1910

"Yesterday When It Is Past"
   by Rose Chambers Goode McCullough

"Narratives of Early Virginia"
   1606 to 1625, edited by Tyler

"Historical Rarities"
   - article in "Climbing Your Family Tree" by Hugh Watson, Sunday, July 27, 1958

"Historical Jamestown Narratives, Eyewitness Accounts of the Virginia Colony the First Decade"
   by William Strachey

"Old Churches and Families of Virginia"
   by Meade

"Colonial Virginia"
   by William Brodus Cridlin

"Irish Burks of Colonial Virginia and New River"
   by Patricia G. Johnson

"The Conquest of Virginia, The Forest Primeval"
    by C.W. Sams

"Historical Recollections of Virginia"
    by Henry Howe, Charleston, South Carolina, 1845

"History of Augusta County, Virginia"
    by Peyton

"Journal of the House of Burgesses of Virginia"
    1773 to 1776

"Memoirs of Letitia Preston Floyd"
    [Library] University of North Carolina, Southern Collection 1790, p. 24, 25

Index of Individuals

Family Reunion
At the home of Lillian & Walter Knowles
Sunday, July 3, 1955
Jackson, Tennessee

1. Walter Law
2. Alice Smith
3. Julie Graves
4. Bailey Lewis
5. Susan Lewis
6. Lynda Roy
7. Judy Roy
8. Rick Currie
9. Austin Lewis
10. Billy Roy
11. Charles Campbell
12. Lloyd Riley
13. Jimmy Campbell
14. Campbell Long
15. Jimmy C. Long
16. Beverly Ann Long
17. Barbara Long
18. Karen Sue Hoeglund
19. Brenda Kay Long
20. John Hoeglund
21. Ann Hoeglund
22. Alice Knowles
23. Jane K. Law
24. Kathleen S. Campbell
25. Zach Campbell
26. Corinne B. Campbell
27. Lytle Belle C. Campbell
28. Joseph Cannon Campbell
29. Elbert Campbell
30. Gay C. long
31. Lillian C. Johnson
32. Russell Graves
33. Gay Lee Hoeglund
34. Juliet C. Lewis
35. Dot C. Currie
36. Laurence Gardiner
37. Walter Knowles
38. Lillian L. Knowles
39. Grace L. Hoeglund
40. Frances L. Aldrich
41. Marian J. Graves
42. Elizabeth C. Riley
43. Helen S. Long
44. Joan Campbell
45. Jack Campbell
46. Mary Frances W. Campbell
47. Sandra Williams
48. Lillian J. Gardiner
49. Lena Hill
50. Rosetta Peoples Campbell
51. Hattie Howard
52. Charles Lewis
53. Dick Currie
54. Louise M. Long
55. Jean Hoeglund
56. Walter Warmath
57. Robert Long
58. Roy Aldrich
59. Sweet Long
60. Jane Smith
61. Hassell Smith
62. Ross Campbell, Jr.
63. Charles Lewis, Jr.
64. Bobby Campbell
65. James E. Campbell
66. John Long
67. Campbell Long
68. Betty C. Long
69. Robert Long, Jr.
70. Janice C. Roy
71. Shirley Aldrich

Printed in the USA
CPSIA information can be obtained
at www.ICGtesting.com
JSHW060054150824
68134JS00032B/2733